Cat Lo

a memoir of invincible youth

Virgil Erwin

Virgil Erwin

7 NOV 2009

Charts of Vietnam created by Scott Collins.
Photographic interior layout by Darryl Glass, Solution 111 Design, San Diego.

First published by Dog Ear Publishing
4010 W. 86th Street, Ste H
Indianapolis, IN 46268
                          www.dogearpublishing.net

ISBN: 978-159858-985-6

This book is printed on acid-free paper.

Printed in the United States of America

Memory

If any one faculty of our nature may be called more wonderful than the rest, I do think it is memory. There seems something more speakingly incomprehensible in the powers, the failures, the inequalities of memory, than in any other of our intelligences.

The memory is sometimes so retentive, so serviceable, so obedient; at others, so bewildered and so weak; and at others again, so tyrannic, so beyond control! We are, to be sure, a miracle in every way, but our powers of recollecting and of forgetting do seem peculiarly past finding out.

—Jane Austen (1775 – 1817) Mansfield Park

Cat Lo was drawn from memory and with monumental help from old men remembering, or trying to remember, what they did or what they said. There was help from a quartermaster's logbook and from the US Naval Archives, but logs and archives do not convey emotion, do not speak of laughter or tears. There was an audio tape of an ambush. It's not comfortable to listen to.

As Jane Austen wrote, memory is so tyrannic. Every Swift Boat Sailor I talked to struggles to recount events, and yet each possesses indelible capsules of time, as if they were only an hour old.

This memoir is as honest as I can make it, and written with deep respect for the South Vietnamese people and for the men who fought for them. Please forgive me, for undoubtedly there are errors.

—Virg Erwin
January 28, 2009

For my sons, Christopher and Bret

CONTENTS

FOREWORD
By Weymouth D. Symmes

I first became aware of the literary skills of Virg Erwin when I was doing the research for my book *This is Latch: The Story of Rear Admiral Roy F. Hoffmann*. The key chapter in *This is Latch* concerns Admiral Hoffmann's leadership of Task Force 115, which included the Swift boats of Vietnam. And within that key chapter was perhaps the key event, the fierce firefight on April 12, 1969, on the Duong Keo River during the Vietnam War, which resulted in the destruction of PCF 43. Virg Erwin was there that day and to assist my understanding, he sent me what is now Chapter 18 of the book you are about to read, "The Death of a Swift Boat."

"The Death of a Swift Boat" recalled that day in vivid detail, with penetrating analysis and heartfelt sorrow at the deaths, most particularly that of Lieutenant Don Droz. It was a stirring account of what it was like to be a sailor at war in that time and place. And so it is with the rest of *Cat Lo*, a book that will grip the reader and challenge long-held beliefs about wars and the men who fight them.

Cat Lo begins with "Pinky Stub," as Virg and another Swift Boat skipper deliver a check from the Admiral Roy F. Hoffmann Foundation, created to support wounded warriors from the Afghanistan and Iraq Wars. You will be drawn into Virg's narrative as he relates the pathos, and yes, the nobility of war. Delivery of the check to a wounded marine recently returned from Iraq secures that continuum connecting warriors of all wars, one to another. From that moment, this fine book delineates the intense feelings and universal experiences of the warrior.

There are laugh out loud moments in *Cat Lo* as the men deal with sea snakes, root out a Swift Boat that has grounded far into a rice field, and a drunken excursion that sends a commandeered Jeep off on a voyage to the Philippines. There is the burden of command, where young men make life or death decisions in a flash of time; the burdens we carry from the expectations of our fathers, the men we serve with, and those who command us; and the love and sorrow felt for Vietnamese civilians, whose only hope is that the nightmare of their lives will end in peace.

Swift Boat operations were once an obscure part of the Vietnam War, fought in remote swamps far from the attention of the press. Now much has been written about Swift Boats; within the pages of this book will be found the true story of the honor, bravery, sacrifice and horror of serving on those sometimes-coffins that were the Swift Boats of Vietnam.

Appropriately, Virg Erwin's compelling memoir doesn't end with his departure from Vietnam. He tells of the difficulty of coming home, his denial for many years of the scourge of PTSD, and how he finally completed his journey back with the comradeship of men he had served with so many years ago.

I served on Swift Boats at the same time and in many of the same rivers as Virg Erwin. He has written an outstanding book of our service, and of the consequences of war for the warrior. I am grateful for this book, and I think Don Droz would nod his head in appreciation as well.

Chapter One

Pinky Stub

A man comes back into my life without invitation, without warning, without the merest hint I would ever hear his voice again.

"This is Roy Hoffmann," he says over the phone. I feel shock, the kind of shock that takes away your breath, makes you stop everything you are doing and focus attention only on the immediate.

"Yes sir?" I respond, as if I'm still under his power to command. My body stiffens as if I am still on a Swift Boat in 1969, on a river, answering his call, ready for orders.

"I have a favor to ask," he says. "I've created a foundation for wounded veterans." His deep gravelly voice ignites memory cells that race through my brain too fast to stop. His radio call sign was "Latch" when I last heard his voice, thirty-six years ago on a river in Vietnam. "Could you deliver a check to a wounded marine at Camp Pendleton?"

I'm caught off guard. I need time to think and pause before answering. My brief silence must sound like rejection.

"You wouldn't be going alone," Hoffmann says, perhaps understanding my hesitation. "Chuck Rabel will be there. He's a Swift Boat skipper too. He has the check."

"It would be an honor," I finally respond. I'm embarrassed my words come out as if something is caught in my throat.

"Who was that?" my wife asks as I hang up the phone. Jacqueline looks at my eyes, her forehead scrunched with wrinkles. I must look startled. Maybe she thinks I've just received bad news.

"Someone I knew a long time ago. An admiral. He's retired now."

"What did he want?"

"Just a favor," I say and walk into the backyard to be alone for a minute. I'm not sure I can do this, not sure what I'll see. But it's clear, after all these years, Admiral Hoffmann has not lost compassion for those who go into harm's way—and come home less than whole.

It's a warm Saturday afternoon in San Diego as Chuck and I sit with a young sergeant convalescing from war. I watch the marine grip a glass of water with two gnarled hands. The marine sees my concern and laughs.

"My nickname is Pinky Stub—for missing fingers," he says, and then he laughs again. His laugh helps me relax, but his missing fingers are minor wounds compared to horrific scars on his face, his arms, and his legs.

"Do you want to talk about it?" I ask, almost in a whisper. Maybe he'll think I'm invading privileged ground. It's a question no one has ever bothered to ask me.

"We were in Fallujah," Pinky Stub says, "looking for insurgents. It was hard to know who were civilians, who were bad guys."

"You were going house to house?"

"Yeah, clearing them, one at a time. I took the point, in front my squad, something I never do, but this time I did. I spotted the IED too late. I remember a white flash."

Pinky Stub begins to describe a violent ambush and reflections of Vietnam rush to the surface with a staggering flood of emotion. His words are like a concussion bleeding my ears—I smell the smoke of cordite mixed with the sound of machine guns and urgent yelling. Visions tucked safely away in a dark-musty closet leap into my face like dirty gray moths, awakened by light.

My visions are a jumbled kaleidoscope—distorted images, bizarre, broken pieces of shattered glass; nothing fitting together in any cohesive manner. Slowly, they take shape as I piece them together: a marine dying in my arms, a young girl's burned skin, my friend Bruce vaporized into a cloud while defusing a mine. I fight an involuntary muscle quivering my chin, a prelude to tears.

"How do you feel? Are you okay now?" I ask. I try to concentrate on his answers, not on memories. It would not do for me to lose composure in front of this brave marine.

"I'm okay—pain's not bad. But I'm worried they're going to give me a medical discharge. I can't pass the physical."

"What will you do then?"

"Don't know. I've always dreamed of a career in the marines. Made sergeant in three years. I keep hoping they'll change their mind, let me stay. But if they don't, I'll understand."

I am in awe of the character of this young man so fresh from the battlefield. I want to hold him in my arms, to console him as if he were my son.

His absence of self-pity stands out with enormous clarity, like the man without limbs in a Vietnam hospital ward.

"This is for you," Chuck Rabel says, handing him an envelope, "from the Admiral Hoffmann Foundation. Thank you for your service." Chuck is taken with this man, impressed with the exceptional maturity of a twenty-one-year-old marine. "I have an electronics firm. Join us; you could start tomorrow. I'll coach you, show you the ropes."

"Thank you," Pinky Stub says with an air of dignity, but he's not ready to give up his quest to remain in the marines. Pinky Stub, with his distorted flesh, conveys neither recrimination nor regret for his wounds, only strength of conviction to move on, to remain focused on his future. Things I deal with today are so superficial, so trivial—so insignificant to what he now confronts.

"I wanted a military career too," I say to Pinky Stub, "in the navy. I was full of ambition and pride like you." But I don't tell him I felt lost when that dream died. I needed to start over—but I wasn't wounded, at least not on the outside. "Your experience and your leadership skills are more valuable than a degree from Harvard."

"Doubt that," Pinky Stub says with a laugh.

"You are a marine, a leader—you are elite! Never forget that."

It is one thing to be moved by patriotic images on TV; it is altogether different to sit with Pinky Stub, face to face, while he smiles and ignores his disfigured body as if it's just another challenge in life.

I compare this marine of today with how Swift Boat sailors felt returning from their tour. I think how Vietnam veterans might have healed more quickly or died more proudly if our society had given some acknowledgement for their burden, some respect for their sacrifice.

Like this marine, Swift Boat sailors, who fulfilled their commitment in Vietnam, did not talk of bravery, did not beat their chests of medals or bring attention to their wounds. But unlike this marine, they were pariahs when they returned home. Swift Boat sailors became subdued, while holding within their hearts the memory of names that would someday be engraved on a wall.

My youngest son, Bret, is a marine; home from Iraq.

"Hey Dad," Bret says, "I found something in the garage you might want—a box."

He's found my "going-home" box, long since forgotten. I used it to ship my gear home from Vietnam.

I'm startled by this treasure of memorabilia from 1969: letters from Dad, pictures of men trying to escape from waist-deep mud on a canal in

Vietnam, a logbook from my Swift Boat, PCF 67, and an audio tape of radio conversations—sounds of men fighting to stay alive on the Duong Keo River.

The dust-covered box is an unexpected catalyst, like the phone call from Admiral Hoffmann and meeting Pinky Stub. I discover I left Vietnam with something else, something unnoticed, hidden too deep to see. The Vietnam War implanted a seed and it germinated, grew and replicated over the years, slowly threading its way through the ganglia of my soul until it permeated my total being, taking hold of my sub-conscious and pouring out now, thirty-six years later, with tears I don't understand.

This seed is survivor's guilt and there is no refuge. It is imbued so deep it cannot be expunged. After hiding for three decades, I have taken the courage to remember the past, to let my feelings out—even though no one asked.

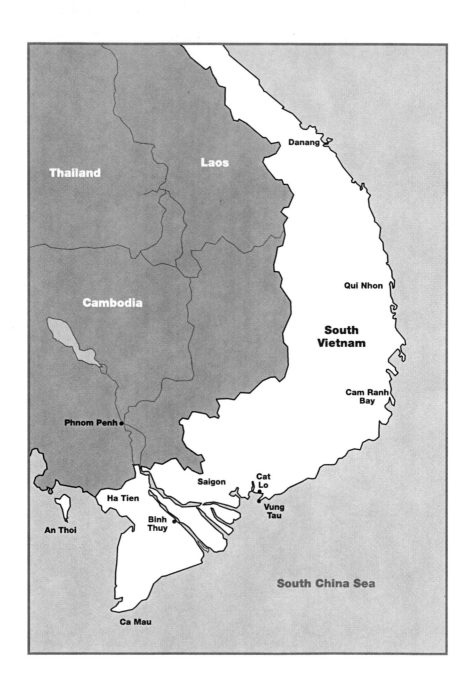

Chapter Two

October 1968 – Arriving in Cat Lo, Vietnam

I'll be twenty-five next month and feel brash cockiness as I leave for Vietnam. I'm impatient to know what lies ahead.

"Going to Nam?" someone asks at the airport.

"Yeah, I am," I answer. I can't help smiling; I will soon have command of a Swift Boat.

This gunboat, with nearly one thousand horsepower, is like a gazelle—fast, elegant and graceful. Her twin-fifty-caliber machine guns are like the gazelle's ringed horns. Swift Boat is just the right name for the speed and power she wields.

I've grown up fast these past two years at sea, standing watch on the bridge of a destroyer. My tarnished insignia gives an illusion of experience, enhanced by soaking the silver lieutenant bars in saltwater, dulling the shine to make me look older. I glow in a sense of triumph, being selected to command a Swift Boat, which is not the same as having command of a destroyer, but it is the trust I've been given that stands out.

Going to war is wearisome. My eagerness fades to fatigue during a flight from San Diego to Tacoma, and now I'm somewhere over the Pacific on a military charter that departed hours ago. This flight to Vietnam is sobering. I try to sleep, but my brain won't shut down. Time is a blur.

There are four other officers from Swift Boat School aboard this packed Boeing 707. I see two of the officers: Mike Hudson squirming in his seat, trying to get comfortable; Doug Armstrong, reading a book. I'm not the only one who can't sleep.

We land in Cam Ranh Bay. I feel like a zombie, half awake, following someone's directions to pick up my bag and climb on a bus. It's midnight and the heat is like a steam bath in the dark, my khakis like ruddy-wet rags. I'm sitting in the back of a gray colored school bus that's taking the five of us to our squadron headquarters. The interior lights of this bus are blinding me, making it impossible to see anything outside. Hot-wet air swirls through open windows covered with chicken wire—wire to prevent the Viet Cong from tossing in hand grenades.

"This is crazy; why are the lights on?" I say, but no one responds. The VC can see us, but we can't see them. No one has a gun, not even the driver. We're vulnerable, a bright illuminated target without guns. Adrenalin is pumping through my body—any second we can be hit by a rocket-propelled grenade. I didn't think I'd be scared, but I am. We pull into a compound and we're shown where to sleep. I still don't have a gun.

I wake to bright shafts of sun through my window in the officer's quarters. I see a blue pastel sky and a white sand beach with palm trees, wooden lounge chairs, umbrellas and a beautiful emerald cove. Men are casually walking to the mess hall in starched khakis or pressed dungarees. No one has guns and no one acts like they need them. The scene before me is like a movie set for *South Pacific*. I have a sudden feeling this war is a hoax, sensationalized by the military looking for purpose and the press looking for readers. This is paradise and I'm embarrassed by how scared I was last night. How can I write to Dad and be honest that I, too, have experienced war? How can I make him proud of me if I am sunbathing on a beach?

I feel anxious, wondering when I will get command of my boat.

"They lost my seabag!" Mike Hudson yells. "All I got is what I'm wearing."

"Never trust the Air Force with your luggage," Doug Armstrong says. Doug is as big as a fullback. He looks calm and confident compared to Mike, whose beanstalk body seems to move like a rusty tin man.

A yeoman comes into the officer's quarters. "There's a briefing at 0900 in the operations office," he says.

A lieutenant stands at the head of the operation's room. A map of Vietnam stretches from ceiling to floor. The map is cluttered with military graffiti—arrows, scribbles and circles.

"Attention on deck," the lieutenant says and the five of us "Newbies" snap to a standing position. I stifle a yawn. The lieutenant introduces Captain Hoffmann, commander of the Coastal Surveillance Force. All of the surveillance centers, all five coastal divisions and all eighty-four Swift Boats belong to this man.

Captain Hoffmann looks like a mean, hardened drill sergeant. His cobalt eyes and deep resonant voice is a perfect match for a five-seven frame that must have been honed on a whetstone. I doubt this man has ever told a funny joke. He stands like a coiled viper, poised, ready to strike at anything that moves.

"What's the first rule of engagement?" Captain Hoffmann barks at Bob Elder. Bob is a big as Doug.

"Never fire unless fired upon," Bob answers without hesitation. How in hell did he know that?

"And number two?" he asks Doug.

"I don't know, sir, but I'll find out."

"Damn right you will—or you won't skipper any of *my* boats. Understood?"

"Yes sir."

Captain Hoffman glares at each of us in turn, then spins around and leaves the room. I hear a collective exhale of air. The lieutenant smiles, recognizing the impact his boss has just made. It's clear to me—I would never want to incur the wrath of this man.

The lieutenant begins a short briefing on Operation Market Time and coastal activity.

"For the past month," the lieutenant says, "there've been fourteen hostile-fire incidents. Two men killed, both on Swift Boats out of Cat Lo."

Well, there is a whiff of war, at least in Cat Lo, and it's hostile—something to write Dad about.

"Where's Cat Lo?" I ask.

"Three Corps, south of here," the lieutenant says.

Our names are called and we're told our assignments.

"Armstrong, Erwin, Coastal Division 13, the Black Cats."

"Where's that?" I ask.

"Cat Lo."

Bob Elder and Jim Harwood are assigned to An Thoi, a base at the southern tip of Vietnam. Mike Hudson gets to stay here in Cam Ranh Bay.

"Work on your tan," I say to Mike as Doug Armstrong and I gather our gear and head back to the airstrip.

Our flight is aboard an Army Caribou. We strap into canvas seats in the cavernous tunnel, facing wooden pallets covered by a tarp. The whole fuselage shakes as twin-radial engines make a fluttering sound. I fear we're overloaded.

As we fly south to Cat Lo, I stare out the window, looking down at white surf dividing a turquoise sea from verdant fields, and canopied forests and brown-silt rivers draining mist-shrouded mountains. This postcard picture looks too pristine for war.

I wonder if we can be shot down. I want to ask one of the crew if there is a risk of SAM missiles, but I don't.

We land in Vung Tau, an in-country R&R center, which implies to me it must be as safe as Cam Ranh Bay. A sailor picks us up in a Ford Bronco for the five-mile trip to Cat Lo. The sailor doesn't have a gun. I'm glad it's not dark.

The road is crowded—bicycles with wicker baskets and motor scooters overloaded with bulging burlap bundles or passengers or both. As we approach the base, I see a ten-foot wall on the left with concertina wire along the top and guards with machine guns standing under covered watchtowers. On the right is a row of small houses shaded by thick groves of banana, teak and nippa palms. Children are playing on wooden porches, mongrel dogs lying underneath, and chickens and pigs roaming the yards. It looks peaceful, almost serene. A sign in front of one house advertises a massage.

Inside the compound, Doug and I find the small operation's shack, Coastal Division 13. The duty yeoman tells us where to bunk. The officer's quarters are in faded green Quonset huts with chicken wire over the windows. I meet Lieutenant Ked Fairbank. He's wearing a striped red and blue towel, and I assume he's fresh from a shower. I doubt his towel is Navy issue, but it goes well with his red curly hair and flaming mustache.

"Welcome to the Black Cats. What's your call sign?" Ked asks.

"I don't know."

"When on patrol, everyone goes by personal radio call signs," Ked says. "I'm 'Harvard Yard.'" He says it as if a tongue depressor is in his mouth. I think Ked went to some exclusive finishing school in Boston. "You and Doug will get your call sign soon enough."

Ked points to empty bunks, each with a locker, a small cardboard table and chair. He welcomes me aboard and begins giving advice on where to find the chow hall and where to shower. I pass by the shower and the water is dirt brown.

"Keep your mouth shut when you shower," Ked says, "it's straight from the canal."

Ked introduces me to Lieutenant Jim Barrett, the Operations Officer. Jim's call sign is "High 'n Dry", but he doesn't say how he got that tag. Jim tells me he's had over six months of patrols before turning over his boat, PCF 23, to take on administrative duties. I can't imagine anyone giving up command of a Swift Boat to do paperwork.

"I heard about PCF 96," I say reverently, "in the headquarters briefing, about the firefight, losing Radioman Pachel, and about PCF 98, the mortar explosion." Jim doesn't reply. Maybe it's not something anyone talks about, especially with a Newbie.

We walk over to the Operations shack and Jim shows me a wall-mounted chart of our area. There are small colored pins designating various points of interest and lines dividing the coast into patrol areas.

"Your job," Jim says, "will be to patrol the coast—prevent trawlers, junks and sampans from smuggling supplies from Hanoi to support the Viet Cong." Jim gives me a mimeographed page with *official* call signs, air support scramble codes, a folder with radio frequencies and a waterproof chart of Vietnam. The chart has a hole in it and it's smeared with a red stain. I must look alarmed.

"Ketchup," Jim grins. "French fries."

Jim begins a "Do-Not" lecture on the Rules Of Engagement. I remember Captain Hoffmann grilling us on the importance of ROEs.

"Rule number one," Jim says, "do not fire unless fired upon, even if you think it's the enemy. Rule number two, do not fire in support of another unit without proper authorization. 'Sepia' is the call sign for your operational command. And most important, rule number three, do not go into the fucking rivers. Any questions?"

"When do I get my boat?"

Jim points to lined Plexiglas nailed to the wall. It has boat numbers written in grease pencil, columns for dates, patrol assignments, maintenance and comments. Jim scribbles my name, "Erwin" next to PCF 67. I like the last letter in this acronym, Patrol Craft *Fast*.

"I'm assigning you to Lieutenant 'Duck' McFarland, skipper of the sixty-seven. As soon as he qualifies you as Officer-in-Charge, you'll take command. Duck's been here for eleven months. We try to get the skipper and crew off the boats the last month of their tour."

"Why?"

"They get nervous, start acting weird. Don't worry about that now, pay attention to what Duck says; it could save your life *and* your crew. Duck is a good boat driver, knows the ropes, but without his OK, you won't get his boat—someone else will."

"When do I start?"

"He's on patrol. I'll call him—tell him to pick you up at the pier at nineteen hundred. Get over to the armory, get a flak jacket, helmet, check out a sidearm and be on time."

I like Jim's crisp-clear direction. I've just arrived this morning and going on patrol tonight. Things are moving fast. I'm in a war zone and feel defenseless. I'm eager to get a gun. I pick up my gear, grab a sandwich and explore the base.

The base compound is built on black dirt and walled on three sides, open at the rear where it slopes down to a canal, the source for our brown water showers. Jim Barrett said this is the rainy season. Trucks have left deep ruts in the mud. Close to the water, perforated steel mats have been laid to prevent trucks and jeeps from slipping into the canal and becoming amphibious vehicles.

Flat rusting barges are moored to the bank to create a makeshift pier. Six gray Swift Boats are nested alongside. I see crews taking on fuel and ammo, as if preening for combat. Boxes of green cans are stacked on the deck: C-Rats. I've tasted C-Rats. I'd rather starve.

A few men are kneeling next to soiled oily rags spread out on decks, cleaning scattered parts of disassembled machine guns. The crew's dress code is "tropical-relaxed": boots, shorts, no shirt, no hat. They look tired, dirty and in my eyes, elite.

I sit on my helmet and wait for my ride, a new .38 pistol holstered to my waist. I feel like a cowboy. I notice some sailors staring and suppose it's my flak jacket. It's brand new, not sweat soaked, ragged, and stained with diesel like theirs. They must know I'm still cherry.

A Swift Boat pulls to the pier, numbers six-seven stenciled on her bow. God, she is beautiful, a lady without weakness of structure. Fifty-feet long with sleek nautical lines, she's built for speed and purpose, a balance of power to go fast into harm's way. She stands out from the rest with her guns uncovered. I half run, half stumble across the stern of three boats, ready to leap aboard.

A lieutenant in khakis is at the aft helm using engine throttles to hold her alongside the pier. I see the boat's bow wave, as if she's still moving, and realize the skipper is fighting a strong current. His crew, dressed in dungarees, tries to look preoccupied, but I sense that same curious stare.

"Request permission to come aboard," I say as I salute.

"Jesus!" the lieutenant says. "Get aboard and don't salute again." Without another word, he pushes the throttles and we're underway. It's not exactly a welcome. I notice the steering wheel jerk back and forth and he lets go. I know from training, someone in the pilothouse now has the helm, steering us through this brown water canal.

Lieutenant Duck McFarland introduces himself and then me to his crew. They will soon be my crew. Duck says saluting is unhealthy.

"It's like target designation, if a sniper is watching," he says. "The VC love to shoot officers."

"Sorry," I say. I feel I've not made a good first impression with the crew.

"Never say sorry, say *Xin Loi*," Duck says. "It also means 'Tough Shit.' We're going to the Rung Sat tonight," Duck continues. "Not a nice place; only bad guys, especially at night. The Long Tao River is the shipping channel to Saigon. Goes right up the middle of the Rung Sat."

"Are we patrolling that river?" I'm confused about what we're doing.

"No, just the coastline. We don't go into the rivers without orders." He gives a short laugh, as if there's something more he's not telling me. Duck is a full lieutenant, maybe two years older than me, but he talks like some-one much older, his voice deep without emotion and he's short on words. He looks tired and his khakis are frayed, small bits of thread dangling at each seam—"Irish Pennants" as we say in the navy.

Duck tells me to pretty much stay out of the way for this first patrol. "It's just orientation," he says. I think orientation would be nice if we could go someplace less hostile—and in daylight.

Duck stands in the pilothouse on the port side, studying charts, occa-sionally talking on the radio to Sepia, the call sign for our operational com-mand. The pilothouse is small and cramped, not much bigger than a closet. It's filled with radios and red lights mounted on the ceiling above the chart table.

Mike Carr sits at the helm in the center of the pilothouse behind a panel of engine instruments. There's a large compass in front of the center window. Carr holds throttles with his left hand and frequently peers at the Decca radar and fathometer on his right.

There's only room for me on the starboard side next to the radar. It's gotten darker and the radar casts an orange-yellow glow on the ceiling. The panel of instruments is backlit in red.

Above and behind Carr is Taylor, a tough looking gunner's mate, standing in the gun tub. I can only see Taylor's feet and legs, but he has a solid build. He is griping twin-fifty-caliber machine guns mounted in a tur-ret that rotates above the pilothouse.

On the stern of the boat is Suggs, an engineman, manning the mortar. It's a dangerous weapon if a round gets stuck inside—and then explodes. A fifty-caliber machine gun is mounted on top of the mortar. The last two crewmen are stationed aft of the main cabin, pointing M-16 machine guns to each side.

"The VC shoot B-40 rockets," Duck says. "The rockets penetrate the hull, the pilothouse or cabin, then explode inside. When we're near the Rung Sat, being inside is not a good idea."

I stand on the six-inch gunnels *outside* the pilothouse door, hanging onto the railing with a death-grip. It would be embarrassing to fall over-board, but better than splattered on cabin walls.

We're at full throttle, making twenty-five knots, our wake leaving a foamy trail across the smooth wide bay. The evening is warm and black as ink with no moon. After two months of training, thirty hours of flying and two days in-country, I am finally in Vietnam, on a Swift Boat and on patrol.

"Check your guns," Duck says.

"Check guns," Carr repeats over a phone to Taylor and Suggs.

I see the chart of the Rung Sat in dim red light. It looks like a maze of canals and mangrove swamps. I'm startled by the sudden intense beam of our searchlight as it illuminates a forest of trees fifty yards dead ahead. Is this the Rung Sat, so soon, so close? I misjudged the scale of the chart—I thought the enemy would be farther away. I'm both scared and excited. More scared.

We're slowing to a stop.

"What are we doing?" I ask Duck.

"Be quiet; I'm busy."

My anxiety is building, wondering if the VC can hear our rumbling engines. To the Viet Cong, these engines must sound like two Harley-Davidson motorcycles—not quite the stealth we should have.

The narrow beam of light scans the edge of a swamp. Gigantic tangled roots anchored beneath the water hold a jungle of trees on their shoulders. We creep closer and the light captures an empty sampan, a small wooden boat, tied to a branch.

"Hit it!" Duck says. The burst of fire from Taylor's twin-fifty machine guns is immediate. The sampan disintegrates from a sawmill of bullets and tracers, geysers erupting from the water. It's over in seconds, only wooden debris left floating. The searchlight continues its nervous hunt, exposing thick ferns, bamboo and palms as we coast along the perimeter of the Viet Cong's lair.

"VC sampan," Duck says.

"How do you know?" I ask.

"This is VC country, Charlie's backyard—only Viet Cong come here. They store weapons and explosives—stage attacks on cargo ships headed upriver to Saigon. Their goal is to sink a ship in the Long Tao Channel—block this supply route."

"You ever see the VC?"

"No. They shoot from bunkers or from behind trees. It's always an ambush."

The searchlight blinks off and we sit motionless. Now the engines are off too. No sounds except for my own heart. My night vision is shot from the searchlight. I wonder what we are doing, what to listen for. I can smell the swamp, sweet like gardenias and mango. We drift for what seems like an eternity, hiding in the dark, waiting for the VC.

Warm rays of morning sun wake me. I must have dozed off, sitting on an engine hatch, my back propped against the cabin. I've stayed outside the cabin all night. I was just dreaming of bacon, eggs and coffee.

"As soon as our relief arrives," Duck says, "we'll head for Cat Lo."

My first patrol. Not bad, I think.

We pull into Cat Lo to refuel and rearm. I walk to the officer's quarters for a shower and meet Wade Sanders. He looks like a California surfer with his shorts, shower-shoes, blond hair and dark tan.

"What boat do you have?" I ask.

"The ninety-eight," Wade says. I remember the briefing in Cam Ranh Bay. Wade has lost a crewman from a mortar accident. I'm unsure what to say.

"What's your call sign?"

"Wallaby 54," Wade says, but he doesn't say what that means. Wade acts cocky, as if he's the big man on campus, and he's full of stories. He already has a war trophy, proudly displaying a captured AK-47.

I'm envious. I'm glad I've arrived before this hostile war has ended.

Chapter Three

Storm

I've completed two indoctrination patrols. Duck and I go through a checklist of equipment. I sign for each one and assume command of Patrol Craft Fast 67. Duck shakes hands with each of his crew, wishes me luck and heads for the Quonset hut to pack his gear into a plywood box, his going-home box. He's made his last patrol. I'm sure he feels strong emotion for his men, but he doesn't look back.

We cast off our dock lines and get underway. It's my first patrol as Officer-in-Charge of PCF 67. I finally have my own command. Mike Carr sits at the helm, driving us through a brown water canal toward the clean salty ocean. The wind is picking up and I smell a whiff of ozone.

"Could get a little wet," Carr says, pointing toward dark rain clouds building into towering columns on the horizon.

Carr is the quartermaster, my leading petty officer. He plans the watch rotation, keeps our nautical charts up to date, and is in command should something happen to me. I don't dwell on that. We're nearing the end of the southwest monsoon, the wet season. Short heavy downpours come each day—black dirt on the base turns to muck.

"Wipe your boots," I've heard Carr say before letting anyone step aboard. Carr is fair skinned, thin like me, and has a bright, engaging smile.

"This patrol's a piece of cake," Carr says. "First sector north of the harbor. Some take hours to get to and hours to get home."

"Lucky assignment," I say.

"Well sir, most new skippers get this one."

"Why?"

Carr laughs. "So they don't get lost."

I can tell Carr likes to drive the boat. When we set General Quarters, he jumps into the pilothouse, grabs the wheel and dons his helmet and earphones. After each crewman reports in, he says to me, "All stations, manned and ready." He always grins at me when he says that. I'm not sure why.

Dan Taylor is a gunner's mate. He mans the twin fifty-caliber guns when we're at GQ. He's tall and tan. He has the build of a middleweight boxer with a stone-chiseled face. Taylor is stoic, as if thinking about something serious, and he's always serious when schooling the crew on machine-gun maintenance. I haven't heard him talk about himself, where he's from or whether he's got a girl. But he does comment on the Viet Cong.

"They're cowards," Taylor says, "assassins in black pajamas." Taylor talks as if he has a personal passion to rid the world of cancerous villains.

Jim Hoffman is the opposite of Taylor. He has a small wiry build, short curly hair and he's fidgety—always busy doing something or chatting about news from home.

"Hoffman," I ask as we cruise through the canal, "any chance your father is a captain in the navy?"

"No sir. I spell my name the right way, just one 'n.' "

Hoffman is a radarman. He seems engrossed when tinkering with the Decca radar, tuning the display to perfection or checking the PRC 25, one of our radios. Hoffman affectionately calls it his "Prick 25."

"Our best radio," Hoffman boasts, "clear as bell, but short on range. We use the Prick to talk to other Swift Boats."

"And this one?" I ask, pointing to a gray box with lots of dials and switches.

"HF," Hoffman says, shaking his head. "High frequency. That's for talking to Sepia. Always has static—takes a magician to operate."

"And you're the magician," I say, giving him a pat on his shoulder and hoping he is.

Hoffman always seems to have a cigarette hanging from the corner of his mouth and a pack rolled up in the sleeve of his tee shirt. He uses an empty C-Rats can, "Beans with Vienna Sausage" for an ashtray.

Our designated cook is Ron Suggs, an odd fit for an engineman, but he loves to eat and he's fat. He looks tired all the time and struggles to squeeze through the engine-room hatch. Suggs sweet-talks two massive V-12 diesels, his pride and joy. "My babies," he says. But he curses the one-cylinder Onan generator.

"Craps out all the time," Suggs says. "Onan powers our refrigerator, freezer and hotplate. When the Onan is kaput, we lose our frozen steaks—no way to cook 'em."

"And then he servers C-Rats," Hoffman says. "Taste like fish bait, all except the beans with Vienna sausage."

"Which we're now out of," Moison says, laughing and pointing at Hoffman.

Moison is a boatswain's mate. He has brown curly hair, a dough-boy face and a dimpled grin that reminds me of someone who's just raided the cookie jar and can't keep it a secret. I wonder what he's hiding, like maybe a case of beer smuggled aboard in an empty ammo box. He reminds me of me.

"Hey Moison," I say, "know what the three most dangerous men in the navy are?"

"No sir."

"A yeoman with your pay record, an ensign with an idea, and a boatswain's mate with a pencil."

"Oh, I never heard *that* one sir." I guess he has.

Boatswains are experts at handling boats, anchors and lines. Each crewman has a special tool for their unique talent. Carr has parallel rules and dividers for navigation and Taylor has a head-spacing tool for the fifty-caliber firing pins. Hoffman pockets a miniature screwdriver for the radar and probably a hammer for the HF. Suggs has either a crescent wrench or a spatula.

Moison has a marlinspike, a thin dagger like piece of steel, sheathed at his waist. I watched him use it to splice an eye, looping the line and weaving it back into itself—a talent of patience. I've seen him use his mar-linspike to untie some knot that Carr has screwed up. Carr is a quartermaster. Quartermasters are not known for tying knots.

Jim Barrett assigned my first patrol to a benign sector, guarding the Vung Tau R&R beach just beyond Cap Saint Jacques. But the beach is deserted, no one to protect.

The beach is deserted for good reason: we're suddenly caught in the middle of a punishing gale, screaming with hysterical wind, brutal waves seeming to come from every direction and torrential rain, stinging like pellets from a BB gun—all heaving our boat as if we have no right to be in its way. The violent sea has all of us gripping handholds or being slammed against bulkheads. Taylor squeezes into the small pilothouse.

"Gotta get closer to the beach," Taylor says. "Can't see any sampans this far from the beach." I doubt the Viet Cong are dumb enough to be out in this storm, but Taylor's been in Vietnam longer than me.

"Carr," I say, "get us closer to the beach."

"Aye-aye, sir," Carr says as he turns the wheel. Carr is trying to take each wave at an angle to lessen the blow as I cling to the chart table, staring at monster waves smashing our windshield.

Carr twists the range dial on our Decca radar. "Three miles to the beach," he says before I think to ask. He always seems to be a step ahead of me; he gives me a sense of confidence that the boat is under control.

Taylor leaves the pilothouse to cover the guns with tarps while the rest of us dog down hatches. It's ninety-degrees and there's no air circulation. I'm soaked in sweat from stagnant, humid air. There aren't any fans and the boat has a nautical perfume, a mixture of lube oil, diesel fumes and navy paint. I think about how long it will take to open a hatch if I need to vomit.

Sheets of green water are smashing into the pilothouse with a force beyond reason. I'm suddenly shoved against the port hatch.

"Excuse me, sir," Moison says, thrown off balance as he enters the pilothouse. I watch him install aluminum braces in the windows. "Lost our center window in June," he says and then laughs. "Carr took the full brunt—right in his face."

"Saltwater wiped out the radar," Carr says, "and it wasn't that funny."

A huge green growler smashes into our bow, knocking us off course.

"Mind your helm," I say to Carr as I step down into the main cabin behind the pilothouse. On the port side is a bunk with storage underneath and another bunk above it, suspended from the ceiling with chains. Along the starboard side is a counter with radios and a small galley. The galley is nothing more than a sink and a hot plate with a freezer and refrigerator underneath.

Hoffman is sitting on a pedestal chair next to the crackling HF radio, scribbling in a notebook as some sailor at Sepia talks in a slow, monotonous drone, sending us a coded message in four-letter groups.

"Hate this damn radio," Hoffman says. "Can't get a clear signal."

"Let me know as soon as you have that message decoded. Might be some intel on VC activity."

"Sepia," Hoffman says into his microphone, "say again your last."

Ron Suggs is sitting on the lower bunk. His green tee shirt has dark stains of sweat. His bulky legs are spread and one hand is holding a rib of the hull, trying to keep from being tossed onto the deck.

"Onan generator crapped out again," Suggs says. "Can't work on it in these rough seas."

I don't reply and I don't care. The Onan is for cooking. Food is the last thing on my mind.

The HF radio has gone quiet. Hoffman has his code book open, deciphering four-letter groups into words. It's a laborious task while he fights heavy rolling. I cling to an overhead railing as he deciphers the message.

"I'll read it to you," Hoffman growls. "Says here, strong tropical depression is expected, coming in from the southeast."

"You're kidding," I say. "*That* was the message?"

"Except for barometric pressure, that's all it said."

Sepia is located on the highest hill above the R&R beach. From our patrol area, I can see their white air-conditioned building with a dozen antennas on the roof.

"Can't believe Sepia just sent that message," I say to Hoffman. "Haven't they looked out their window? And why'd they send it in code?" Hoffman just shakes his head. I think about responding with my own message, but I'm too seasick to compose sarcasm.

I step back up into the pilothouse and think about opening a hatch.

"Tired?" I ask Carr. "Ready for a break?"

"Yeah, it's tough holding a course. Can't see shit."

The windshield wipers are useless, but in one brief second, as the bow rises up a steep-curling wave, I see something black dead ahead, surrounded by white foam.

"Starboard," I yell, "starboard, turn starboard, quick!" Carr spins the helm to the right, but my alarm is too late. We hit the reef with our port screw. Vibration from our propeller shakes the whole boat like an overloaded washing machine gone mad. Carr hits the kill switch for the port engine. I hear Suggs grumble some seaman-like obscenity as he struggles out of the bunk and heads aft to the engine room.

"Propeller shaft probably leaking," he says. Taylor holds the heavy engine hatch open as Suggs lowers his broad girth down between two, burning-hot diesels, each one almost the size of a Volkswagen.

"Moison," I call, "come up here and relieve Carr."

We continue to patrol on the starboard engine. I draft a message to Sepia that we're under reduced power. I draft another message to Cat Lo Maintenance, telling them we'll need to be pulled out of the water tomorrow to replace our screw. Hoffman codes each message into four-letter groups and sends them off, emulating a monotonous Sepia drawl.

"No leaks," Suggs reports as he heads back to the bunk.

This is not good. My first patrol and I hit a reef. I wonder how much trouble I'm in, but we were lucky. If I hadn't seen that reef, it would have punched a hole through our hull. We would have sunk in minutes.

At noon I grip lifelines, staggering to the fantail to suck in fresh air. Gusting wind carries diesel exhaust into my face, a catalyst I didn't need. My stomach erupts. I heave a fire-hose stream of bile that shoots from my mouth. I turn to see Taylor looking at me from the aft cabin hatch. An officer barfing over the side does not instill confidence.

"This patrol is a waste of time," he yells into the blasting wind. "We're not going to find any VC in this storm."

I feel embarrassed that he sees me puke and his comment sounds like a reproach, as if it's my fault there aren't any VC for Taylor to shoot. I stagger past Taylor without responding. I need to check our position. God help me if we hit something else.

"You volunteer?" I ask Moison as I check the radar.

"Yes sir. All of us requested Swift Boats."

"Well, that's one thing we have in common. Why'd you volunteer?"

"I like fast boats. Best duty in the navy. And you, sir?"

"Just figured it was the right thing to do—stop the communist."

"Roger that."

For my crew, Vietnam may just be a search for adventure, or like Taylor, a desire for a gunfight with the Viet Cong. I sense their eagerness for excitement. But no matter our reasons, I think we feel invincible, that we'll all come home as long as we keep our heads down. I wonder if my dad is proud I volunteered.

Moison throttles back the starboard engine as we slide down the trough of a wave.

"Bosuns," he says, "are the best at driving boats."

"Well, just try not to hit another reef."

Our twenty-four hours are up and we're relieved by Lieutenant Matt D'Amico aboard PCF 37. I wish him luck over the Prick 25 as we crawl back to Cat Lo. We slip past fishermen shacks that hang over the edge of the canal next to the base, their boats lining the muddy bank, tied securely. The fishermen are safe in their homes, too smart to be out in this storm.

We should have a day off, but instead help sailors from Cat Lo Maintenance as they attach cables from a crane and hoist our boat above water. It takes four hours to replace our screw and straighten the rudder.

I feel relief Jim Barrett doesn't say anything about hitting the reef, but he tells me to alert my crew for a new patrol assignment.

"You depart tonight," Jim says. "Pack a toothbrush and enough toothpaste for eight days."

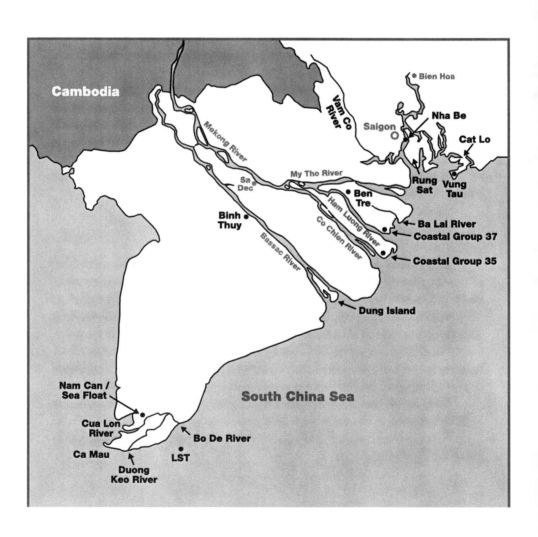

Chapter Four

Rule Number Three

It is 0100, "O' dark early" as PCF 67 pulls away from the Cat Lo Pier. The rank fecal aroma of the canal mixes with our exhaust as we pass fishermen shacks—their boats still tied up. Lieutenant Ked Fairbank and his crew have the watch. Together with my crew, there are twelve of us aboard.

"Have you done this before?" I ask Ked.

"Yeah. At twenty-five knots, it'll take us six hours to reach our mother ship, the *Litchfield County*."

"What's it like? What'll we do?"

"*Litchfield's* an LST, a Landing Ship Tank, anchored off the southern tip of Vietnam. She'll be our temporary base for refueling, rearming and sleep. It's not bad. *Litchfield's* got air conditioning, clean showers, hot meals and movies. We'll rotate patrols aboard your boat for the next eight days. You and your crew will have the first patrol, so you'd better get some sleep."

Ked arrived in Vietnam months before me. His cool professional demeanor gives me confidence that he knows where all the rocks and reefs are. There are only four bunks, two in the main cabin and two in the crew's quarters below the pilothouse. I crawl into the lower bunk in the cabin. The remaining three bunks are divvied up among my crew by seniority, which means two of my crew are sleeping on the floor or on top of an engine hatch.

We pull alongside the *Litchfield* at 0700. Ked and his crew climb a cargo net to board the LST and to get some sleep. Moison and Hoffman manhandle a fuel hose passed down from sailors leaning out over the railing. Suggs tops off the tanks and we get underway again. The storm from the past two days has taken away every semblance of breeze, leaving us to bake under a burning tropical sun. Clean blue ocean swells roll in from the southeast.

Jim Hoffman is sitting at the helm, following a parallel course to the coastline and keeping an eye on the fathometer.

"We're two miles off the beach," Hoffman says, "and it's only twenty feet deep."

I peer over the side. The water is incredibly clear, sunlight reflecting off a white sand bottom. It is ninety degrees. I wish the pilothouse had a fan. It would be nice to jump over the side to cool off. Moison is perched in the gun tub above the pilothouse, scanning a dense tree-lined beach with binoculars.

"See anything?" I ask.

"Nothing," Moison replies with a yawn. Moison is stripped down to shorts and boots; his flak jacket and helmet stacked on the pilothouse roof. Suggs is off watch, sleeping on top of the ready-service locker, obviously not concerned that it's full of high explosive mortar rounds. I hear idle chatter from Taylor and Carr, sitting in the main cabin.

It's almost noon, already five long hours of boredom. There's nothing to do in this sultry heat, not a sampan or junk in sight.

"I heard fisherman avoid this area," I say to Hoffman.

"Good reason. This is the Ca Mau. So many Viet Cong hidden in that jungle—everyone jokes it's their R&R center." Hoffman lights a cigarette and then asks, "Think we'll see any trawlers?"

"I don't know." I think about stories I heard in training, steel-hulled trawlers from Hai Phong, loaded with ammunition for the Viet Cong, trying to sneak into the rivers. I heard stories of dramatic gun fights between trawlers and Swift Boats. But I think it would be remarkable if we do encounter an enemy trawler. First, they need to remain undetected. P2V Neptune's are flying surveillance. They have radar and they don't miss a thing. And then the trawlers need to get past destroyers and coast guard cutters.

"Not one has made it all the way to the beach," Hoffman says. "If they make it this far, we'll nail 'em. Think Hanoi has given up trying?"

"Maybe." But privately I wonder what it would be like. It'll be a gun battle for sure. I just hope our guns are bigger.

There are only two blips on our radar. One is the LST where Ked and his crew are sleeping in air-conditioned rooms, watching a movie or eating ice cream. The other blip is PCF 25, Doug Armstrong's boat, patrolling the sector ten miles south of me. Doug's radio call sign is "Big Daddy." He recently earned it by helping to deliver a baby while searching a sampan near Cat Lo.

We cruise up and down the empty coastline, back and forth, back and forth. Carr and Taylor corner me in the pilothouse.

"Mister Erwin," Taylor says, "we aren't accomplishing anything patrolling the coast. We haven't seen a single sampan. Word has it from other crews, we won't see any. If you want to do more, maybe push the rules a little, we're behind you."

Being addressed as "Mister Erwin" isn't lost on me. While it's proper respect for a junior lieutenant, the formality is a reminder I'm a newbie here in Vietnam. Carr and Taylor are good sailors, good leaders, and know the feelings of the crew. I trust them. I trust all of them.

"What do you have in mind?" I ask.

"There's a large river at the southern end of our patrol area," Taylor says. "It's the Bo De. No one's been in there."

"No one's been in there for good reason; we're not allowed in the rivers. Our job is to patrol the coast." I notice Taylor's jaw muscles tighten, like he's holding back a comment. Carr looks away and Hoffman is sitting at the helm, pretending not to listen. I must sound like a wimp. I know this boredom is eating at my crew. They're young and eager. They want to get into the action; they think they're invincible. "Okay," I say, "let's take a look at the chart."

I'm stalling. I'm the new skipper—I'm in command—I need to act like it. I feel Taylor watching me as Carr and I study the chart. There's no depth indicated for the river, no villages marked, no roads, nothing to say that going into this river is a dumb idea—which it is. I look up and Taylor is staring straight into my eyes, as if trying to read my thoughts, waiting for me to say something.

"I don't know, rule number three—"

"Mister Erwin," Taylor interrupts, "we all volunteered to fight the Viet Cong. There's a lot men here in Vietnam risking their lives every day and we sit out here on the coast doing nothing." Taylor shifts his brawny frame, leaning toward me, crowding me. I think he's wondering if I have the courage to fight. I need to gain his respect and that of the crew.

"All right," I say without enthusiasm, "let's see what's in that river. Set General Quarters." Hoffman and Taylor bolt out of the pilothouse like school kids at recess, as if this is a playground, not a war zone. This is stupid, violating orders, but it's too late to take back my words.

Carr takes over the helm, his GQ station, and grabs earphones. With his microphone protruding from a breastplate, Carr looks like a telephone operator from the 1930s.

"We're goin' in!" I hear Taylor yell to the rest of the crew. Everyone starts putting on flak jackets, helmets, hooking in phones and checking their guns. I'm suddenly caught up in their excitement, ready to do something besides endure this idle monotony.

"Moison," Taylor says as he climbs into the gun tub, "load a willy-peet."

I watch Moison slip a white-phosphorous mortar round down into the barrel.

"If we get into a firefight," Carr says, "Moison will fire the mortar—mark the target. That phosphorous is nasty."

"That's not something they taught us in Coronado," I say.

"OJT, sir, on-the-job training."

"Big Daddy," I say, calling Doug over our Prick 25, "this is Preparation H." Ked decreed my radio call sign would be 'Preparation H' after hearing about my hemorrhoid surgery. I embellished the gruesome details. Big Daddy and I are both using the *Litchfield* for home base and the mouth of the Bo De is the dividing line between our patrol areas.

"This is Big Daddy," Doug responds. His slow growling voice sounds as if my call is interrupting a Sunday afternoon ball game on TV. I like Doug, but I still remember while we were training in Coronado he introduced me to oysters on the half-shell. I gagged and nearly puked.

"We're going to take a walk in the park," I say over the radio. "Can you stand by in case I need a band-aid? Message to follow." I think my improvised code is clever, but I use proper code to add the Bo De coordinates—the VC have radios too. I wait for Doug's response as he deciphers the coordinates in groups of four-letter code.

"Preparation H, this is Big Daddy. Understand your intention. Standing by to cover your ass with lots of band-aids." There's a pause and then, "Good luck, you dumb-ass sailor." He's right; I am a dumb-ass for going into this river.

"Pass the word," I say to Carr. "Do not fire unless fired upon." I wait for Carr to get a reply from each man over their phones.

"All stations manned and ready," Carr says. He grins. "Everyone acknowledged." I'm not sure why Carr is grinning.

Taylor is manning the twin-fifties. I hear him cock each barrel and see his boots and hairy legs at the bottom of the gun tub. Moison is on the aft fifty and mortar, wearing his oversized helmet to make room for his earphones. Hoffman and Suggs stand outside the rear of the main cabin with their M-16s. I stand at the chart table next to the open pilothouse hatch, looking through a thin Plexiglas window and feeling like I need to pee.

Taylor yells down into the pilothouse, bypassing the phone, "Skipper, request permission to test-fire." It's the first time he's called me "Skipper." I hope it's a sign of confidence.

"Permission granted," I reply. Carr relays the message to Moison on the fantail. First Taylor and then each crewman fires a short burst from their gun. It's prudent to make sure our weapons are ready, but I hate announcing our arrival with the sound of our guns. On the other hand, the VC most likely keep some kind of coast watch. If they're there, they'll see us coming.

"Okay, here we go," I say, and then scribble in the log: "15 October, 1215—Entering Bo De." The aqua-clear water of the ocean changes to light chocolate brown as we slip into the river. Large clumps of green plants float in the current and a dense canopy of trees and thick foliage obscures the riverbank. Our fathometer jumps from only ten feet at the mouth to fifty feet just inside the river. I'm surprised and relieved the river is deep.

"Stay close to the center," I tell Carr. "Could be shallow near the banks. Don't want to get stuck on the bottom."

"Or bend a screw," he says.

Actually, that's not my biggest worry.

We're cruising at a cautious ten knots, everyone alert for any movement. There's no sign of life, no sampans, no villages. I look for a hint of smoke from someone's fire, but there's nothing, just giant trees climbing straight up, lining the bank as if this were a jungle fjord. Sharp leafy ferns stretch out, the current tugging at branches too close to the water. They're like fingers, capturing debris floating downriver.

I wonder how far we should go, how long to trust our luck. Ominous shadows from tangled leaves seem to cast a foreboding spell on the silty river. It's too quiet.

It's been thirty minutes; five miles up this river. Still nothing. The knot in my stomach begins to relax.

"Carr, increase speed to—" My voice is blotted out from the sound of machine guns coming from trees on the right. A metallic clink-clink rings like a bell in the pilothouse. Taylor's twin-fifty-machine guns respond with a deafening cacophony—a pulsing concussion of air. I drop to my knees in a cowering reflex. Carr instinctively jams throttles to their stops, accelerating our speed. I hear Moison, Hoffman and Suggs firing from the fantail.

The sound of ear-splitting machine guns overwhelm my thinking. It takes a second to recognize I am acting like a coward, crouched low, trying to crawl under a flimsy chart table. I look up to see Carr still in the helmsman's seat, pushing on throttles as if they could go farther. He's exposed and vulnerable. I can't believe he's not hiding on the deck with me. I jump up and look to the right past Carr. Through the starboard hatch I see muzzle fire coming from the base of trees, pulsing tongues of blood-orange flame.

Everything is happening too fast. I'm frozen by rhythmic, booming reverberations. Hot empty brass is raining down behind me from Taylor's guns, filling the bottom of the gun tub at an incredible rate, like he's hit the jackpot on a slot machine in Vegas.

An enormous explosion on the riverbank spews billowing phosphorous into the trees. Subconsciously, I know Moison fired his mortar—he marked the target. A white cloud of smoke is pierced by red tracers from Taylor's guns. Brilliant crimson light streaks into the forest, branches splintering and dropping into the river. It seems an impossible onslaught no one can survive.

"Turn starboard, *starboard*!" I yell to Carr as if he's twenty feet away. I help him spin the wheel to the right. It's a quick decision with little thought. I want to get the hell out of this river! Turning around is my only strategy; turning right keeps Taylor's guns on target.

For brief seconds in our turn, we are headed straight toward the riverbank—it's getting closer! Shit, why did I say starboard? Dozens of geysers erupt on the water in front of me. I see more muzzle flashes from bushes—blistering flames that sizzle through air. Taylor must see them too. Brown water boils into white froth as Taylor walks his tracers into the bunker. It's an unrelenting assault.

Our bow seems to take forever to come around. I will it to go faster. Without thinking or looking, I grab the Prick 25 microphone.

"Big Daddy, taking fire, taking fire; we're headed out!" It's as if I'm a little boy calling my father, pleading for help. I have no idea if Doug hears me or if he responds—sound from the fifties obliterating everything but fear.

The hull is banked hard over, leaning into our turn as we race past the bunker. I feel its closeness through the open hatch—but I don't look—afraid I'll be shot in the face. I'd rather take a hit in my shoulder. Our guns are firing without pause. I feel their power, an intense crackling thunder; a bellowing roar—it racks my body. In a sudden thought, I sense the sound is a shield protecting me. I don't want the sound to stop.

I see the ocean. God, I want to get out of this river! I push the throttles, but they won't go farther.

We've stopped firing, but I didn't say, "Cease fire." I never would have said, "Cease fire."

Bright sunlight sparkles off ocean waves. Beautiful clean ocean waves. I squint as we leave the dark shadows. I step out of the pilothouse and look up at Taylor's guns, smoke streaming off searing hot barrels. I look back at Moison on the fantail, still pointing his fifty-caliber at trees. Suggs is crouched low, cradling his M-16. Hoffman gives me a thumbs-up. Everyone's okay.

PCF 25 is waiting outside the river mouth and we tie alongside. I'm still shaking from adrenalin. I think we all are, except maybe Taylor. He has his emotions in check and begins inspecting our boat, looking for damage. He takes a K-bar knife from his hip scabbard and pries a bullet out of the combing from the pilothouse door.

"Souvenir," Taylor says, smiling as he hands it to me, as if this is a prize for passing some test of manhood. I spot a couple of bullet holes in the main cabin, sunlight streaming in. Suggs and Hoffman kneel on the fantail helping Moison scoop spent shell casings, tossing them over the side.

"Got some holes next to our fuel tank," Taylor says while leaning over the starboard side. I need something to do to hide my shaking hands and climb down into the lazarette, a sealed compartment behind the engine room.

"Can't see any leaks," I say, but I'm sure there must be. I'm shaking so much I linger for a minute.

Doug is looking at me as I climb out of the hatch. "How was it?" he asks.

My ears are still ringing. I don't know what to say. It's my first time to be shot at. I'm thinking about how I had initially reacted. I wonder if Carr has told the crew that I dropped to my knees when the firing started.

"Thick foliage," I say. "River's deep."

"See the VC?"

"No, just muzzle flashes. Didn't even see the bunkers."

"You going to report this?"

We just entered a river without authorization, breaking rule of engagement number three. I could be in serious trouble, but at least no one is hurt.

"Yeah. The LST monitors our radio traffic; we can't keep it a secret. We'll need the fuel tank plugged by Cat Lo Maintenance. How would I explain that?"

"Should've thought of that before going into the Bo De."

Our two crews exchange questions and answers that flow too fast for me to follow. Here is something to talk about besides boring patrols. As we both get underway to continue our patrols, I notice Taylor rubbing bright red splotches on his legs.

"What happened?" I ask.

"No big deal—hot brass," Taylor says.

"Maybe wear long pants next time." The burns on his legs remind me of our firing range practice in Coronado. I shoot left handed. Hot shells ejecting from the M-16 went down my shirt collar, searing my chest. Fifty-caliber brass is a lot hotter.

At 1900 we close on the mouth of the Bo De. Taylor tilts the 81mm mortar at forty-five degrees. Moison drops a round down the barrel and it fires instantly with a loud deep-throated thump. The mortar round arcs through the air and explodes in the forest. We shoot one after another, twenty-six rounds. Carr logs our expended mortars as "H&I," harassment and interdiction. I'm pissed off at being shot at and want to disturb Charlie's sleep as much as possible.

It's midnight as I sit at the chart table and write my report. Moison is driving, his face bathed in yellowish glow from the radar. Hoffman is sitting up in the gun tub, everyone else asleep. I'm proud of my crew, the way they reacted today. But I wonder what the point was, going into the Bo De. We were just a blind target waving our flag. I doubt I proved anything to my crew.

Hoffman codes my message and sends it out over our HF radio. It's addressed to Sepia and I copy my division commander, Lieutenant Knight, who I've never met. I wonder if I'm in trouble, violating orders.

I'm thankful I'm not staring at someone's dog tags, writing a letter to his parents.

Chapter Five

Reprimand

It's 0700 and the morning sun is already hot as Carr maneuvers our boat alongside the *Litchfield County*. Our first patrol off the Ca Mau is over. We clean the boat, refuel and rearm as Ked and his crew climb down the cargo net to come aboard. It's their turn.

"Keep a watch for leaking fuel," I say to Ked. I give him a brief description of our Bo De visit.

"Dumb-ass newbie," Ked says as I climb the cargo net.

I know he's right. I board the LST and find the officer's quarters. After a quick shower, I fall hard asleep in the cool air-conditioned room. I haven't slept for twenty-four hours. Someone is shaking my arm, telling me dinner is being served. I inhale a hot meal, skip the movie and sleep again.

We continue to rotate patrols with Ked and his crew; "hot-racking" it's called, taking their bunks on the LST before they cool. We're on twenty-four, off twenty-four. Time is becoming a blur. I decide not to push my luck with another venture into the Bo De. Our patrol has dropped back into mundane boredom.

Equipment failures are our only diversion and they are frequent.

"Port engine overheating," Suggs says. Without being asked, Moison crawls down into the engine room to help Suggs replace a broken water-pump impeller. Later, Carr gives Hoffman a hand replacing a voltage regulator that feeds the Decca radar. I'm impressed with my crew, how they work together as a team. They can fix anything, providing they have parts. Fortunately, they don't need a spare propeller.

Taylor is acting aggravated and impatient. "We know where they are," he says, "so why don't we go back in the Bo De and kick some ass."

I'm not feeling an urgent need to be shot at again. "Not without orders," I say. Taylor spins around and walks to the stern. I haven't heard Taylor say "Skipper" again.

We've been rotating patrols with Ked Fairbank's crew for five days, four of which have been logged as extreme tedium. We pull close to the beach twice a day and shoot H&I mortar rounds at random imaginary targets. There's no intelligent guidance to say where the VC are hiding. The intense heat is unending and there is little to challenge our minds with no sampans to inspect. My crew needs a boost in morale.

"Swim call," I announce. We're five miles from the beach in twenty feet of water and I hit the kill switch for our engines. Moison drops the anchor and Suggs puts one of our ugly car-tire fenders over the gunnels to act as a boarding ladder. Carr strips down to his skivvies and dives into the water from the pilothouse roof.

I watch with amusement as everyone pulls off their boots and uses the top of the pilothouse as a diving board, doing cannon balls and jackknife plunges, trying to launch the highest spray of water. Taylor sits in the gun tub with an M-16, designating himself as our lifeguard and shark watch.

I do a back flip off the bow and land in the water with a resounding splat on my stomach that hurts like hell. I dive down to the bottom and dig my fingers into the soft white sand, searching for shells. I only find a crumpled Coke can that someone threw over the side. The water is as clear as gin. Sunrays angle down from the surface, dancing and weaving like curtains, imitating an underwater aurora borealis.

I see a giant sea snake at least four feet long and as fat as a boa constrictor. Its undulating body is colored by bands of brown and yellow, and it turns toward me, moving with purpose. The snake has me locked in as its target. I'm petrified; I know sea-snake venom is as deadly as a cobra. I push off the sand bottom and dart for the surface, kicking my feet with adrenalin power. I look up toward the surface and see four feet churning the water next to the hull of our Swift Boat.

I join Carr and Moison, all three of us trying to get our feet into the car tire and climb out of the water—they've obviously seen the snake too. We're scrambling to gain a foothold and there's no attempt to take turns. Taylor fires a few rounds toward the snake, but he's laughing too hard to take accurate aim.

Now that we are all aboard and safe from certain death, I start to laugh too. It occurs to me that while we are a crew, bound to each other as if brothers, there is no chivalry, no gallant loyalty for each other when it comes to sea snakes.

We complete our patrol and return to the LST.

"Wish this damn 'T' had beer," I say to Carr. "I remember a class from college. We studied Maslow's 'Hierarchy of Need.' "

"Who's Maslow?" Carr asks, but I'm sure he's not interested.

"He proposed that while we don't really know it, our ultimate goal in life is gaining approval, recognition, esteem—something about self-actualization or some crap like that. But to get that esteem," I say to Carr, "we first need air to breathe and then shelter and food. And Maslow didn't mean C-Rats, but nourishing food, like lobster."

"Yeah, lobster."

"And after a good meal, Maslow said we need to be safe from danger."

"That'd be nice."

"Carr, I think beer belongs on that list—right after the part about air to breathe."

Carr gives me a laugh. "Maybe I can get Moison to work on the beer."

"Amazing how time flies," Ked says as our crews board PCF 67 for the return trip to Cat Lo. It's been eight days and I'm out of toothpaste.

"Can't wait for some I&I in Vung Tau," I say.

"You mean R&R," Ked says.

"No. I mean intercourse and intoxication." We both laugh. I tell Ked I've added I&I to Maslow's "Hierarchy of Need."

"I brought us down," Ked says. "You drive us back to Cat Lo."

It's rough going north, leaping over swells as we race home at twenty-five knots. The bow becomes airborne and the hull pounds with a thud as we drop back into the sea, the gnawing repetition burning my leg muscles into spent rubber. Carr and I are the only ones on watch—everyone else is horizontal and trying to sleep.

We pull into Cat Lo in time for breakfast. Jim Barrett walks down the pier to greet us. He quietly pulls me aside.

"We got a new division commander while you were down south," Jim says. "Lieutenant Commander Streuli has relieved Lieutenant Knight. Commander Streuli wants to talk to you."

I'm tired from the pounding eight-hour transit and I don't respond. My whole body is vibrating—trying to adjust to standing on something not jarring my teeth.

"Now," Jim says. "He'd like to see you *now.*" I finally understand his sense of urgency.

Commander Streuli is straight to the point. "Lieutenant Erwin, you've got about one hour to shower, get into clean khakis and meet me back here. You and I are flying to Cam Ranh Bay this morning. We have a meeting with Captain Hoffmann. Now get moving."

I keep my mouth closed as I take a brown water shower. Even though Commander Streuli hasn't given me details, I know our trip to Cam Ranh Bay is about the Bo De.

One of the sailors on duty drives us to the Vung Tau air strip.

"There's our bug smasher," Commander Streuli says, pointing to a twin-engine Beechcraft. "Captain Hoffmann's plane—sent to pick us up."

We're the only passengers. Under different circumstances, I would feel like a chauffeured VIP. The empty rattling vibration makes conversation difficult as we fly to Cam Ranh Bay. Each time I catch Commander Streuli's eye, there is a polite smile, but nothing more. This confirms it— I'm headed for a court-martial.

Just six months ago I was on a destroyer and had a collision at sea with a British nuclear submarine. It was a nasty affair, but no one was hurt. I was the newly qualified Officer-of-the-Deck—the collision happened on my watch. Fortunately, Margret Thatcher and President Johnson decided there would be no formal inquiry, a secret between friends. I was told the collision wasn't my fault and the incident would not be mentioned in my fitness report. But maybe it was.

In two years I lost two remote-controlled helicopters while maneuvering them near our destroyer. Both crashed into the sea, each worth a quarter of a million dollars. I was cleared—neither crash was my fault, but I bet *that* is mentioned in my fitness report.

Now, with my unauthorized river incident on the Bo De, I am being drummed out of the navy. The navy is fed up with my "no-fault incompetence." How will I explain this disgrace to my father? How will I live with the shame? Less than a month in Vietnam and I'm being sent home without honor.

Captain Hoffmann is sitting at his desk, reading a report. Lieutenant Commander Streuli and I stand at attention, waiting for Captain Hoffmann to acknowledge our presence. I could stand here forever if he would never look up. From the corner of my eye, I gaze at the view from Captain Hoffmann's window. It's the same idyllic cove with its white sand beach I awakened to just three weeks ago. I feel like a year has passed since then. I remember the beach had glittery mica in the sand: *Fool's Gold*. That now seems appropriate; I'm certainly a fool and there's no longer any gold to be had.

The chart of Vietnam on the wall behind Captain Hoffmann has familiar colored pins all denoting something important. I'm not surprised that one pin is stuck at the entrance to the Bo De River. It's red. I wonder how long it has been there. Captain Hoffmann's call sign is "Latch." It makes me think of the sound a jail door makes when it's slammed shut.

Captain Hoffmann gets up from his chair and looks squarely into my eyes. His short military haircut bristles, as if hair on the neck of an angry dog. His gravely voice is perfect for the tirade he delivers—but I don't understand what he's talking about.

"Mr. Erwin, your careless conduct, hitting a reef which was clearly marked on the chart, damaging your screw, and patrolling your sector on one engine, is unacceptable! Your lack of navigational awareness compromised your ability to perform your duties. What do you have to say for yourself?"

Shit, he's talking about my first patrol, ten days ago. How does he know about that? I bet Lieutenant Knight told him.

"Sir, I have no excuse. It was an error in judgment. I took my boat too close to the beach during foul weather. It won't happen again."

"You're damn right it won't! Erwin, wait outside."

As I sit in the hall, I hear Hoffmann's loud, rapid-fire voice berating Commander Streuli, but I can't make out what he's saying. I don't understand it. Capt. Hoffmann didn't mention the Bo De. He was talking about the time I hit a reef. Christ, one week in-country, green water smashing into our pilothouse, zero visibility. I was too seasick to plot a radar position and I hit a fucking reef during a storm. I was an idiot to allow us to be so close to the beach. But that is minor compared to willfully ignoring the rules of engagement. With Captain Hoffmann so irate over a bent screw, the Bo De will send him into "flail-state-twelve." He'll send me to the brig when he finds out. I am in very deep shit.

As Commander Streuli and I ride back to the airfield, I ask what is going to happen to me. I've come all this way for twenty seconds of wrath and an hour sitting in a purgatory hallway. I have no clue what is going on.

"Our division is messing up many screws," Streuli says, "due to the shallow waters we're operating in. You damaged your screw. The way the word came down to me, I was to bring you here and do some tall explaining as to why so many screws are being screwed up. After he got through with you, Hoffmann had you leave the room so he could chew me personally. I've just taken over command of this division. I saw my navy career going up in smoke, so I flat out told him if he wanted aggressive action by his boat skippers—he had to expect screw damage.

"Well, he calmed down and we had coffee. We had a laugh about Commander Charlie Horne chewing me out because I ordered the "brightwork" on the Swift Boat searchlights painted gray—so they wouldn't reflect moonlight on night patrols. I never heard another word about bent screws. You've been verbally reprimanded, nothing more."

"Thanks for sticking up for me with Captain Hoffmann."

"You're welcome. Are you married?"

"Engaged. She's French; met her on a cruise in the Med."

"What are your career plans?"

"I've always wanted to make the navy my life. Have I screwed that up?"

"Hell no." He laughs. "Just stay off the rocks. What do you want to do after Vietnam?"

"Department Head on a destroyer—weapons or operations. Anything but engineering. I don't want to be stuck in a hot engine room."

"You'll need destroyer school for that. You're in the reserves; you'll need to augment to the regular navy. We'll talk about this again," he says, and then turns away to look at the coastline.

I feel relaxed as we fly back to Cat Lo in the bug-smasher. I don't ask Commander Streuli whether the Bo De came up. Maybe Commander Streuli doesn't know—maybe Captain Hoffmann doesn't know either.

I'm impressed with Commander Streuli—he stood up for me. My trip to Cam Ranh Bay is instructive and the message is clear: Don't go aground. And if I do, don't mess up the screws. And if I do, don't report it.

I think I read in one of my navy manuals: "…and if your questionable conduct does not result in a court-martial, go directly to the bar and buy a round for the house." We return to Cat Lo and I head straight for the Officer's Club. I spot Lieutenant Hal Amerau and I join him.

Hal's call sign is "Kentucky Colonel" and he looks the part: tall, lean, straight shoulders, strong jaw, black hair and steely black eyes. Hal tells me that he just turned over his boat, PCF 96, to another officer and he's now the XO, the Executive Officer.

"Commander Streuli thinks Jim Barrett has too much on his plate as Ops Boss, so I'll take on some of the load as XO," Hal says.

"How did Barrett get the call sign High 'n Dry? He wouldn't tell me."

Hal laughs. "He doesn't like that call sign. Jim had PCF 23. He went aground off the mouth of the Bassac River. The tide went out and it was like his boat was sitting on an island. A 'Mike Boat' from an LST had to pull 'em off with help from the next high tide."

"Well, that explains a lot. Streuli said lots of boats are screwing up."

"How'd it go with Captain Hoffmann?"

"Cancel the firing squad," I say with a smile. "Next round's on me. Streuli covered my ass."

"I think Joe Streuli is going to be a great skipper," Hal says. "He's a Mustang—made chief just before he became an officer. He's got his shit together."

"The Bo De didn't come up," I say. I'm surprised as Hal gives me a dressing down.

"Your conduct as a skipper of a Swift Boat is questionable. You unnecessarily risked the lives of your crew." I realize Hal is talking to me like an XO—he just wants me to bring my crew home alive. Hal pauses, smiles and tells me he's made a few river explorations himself. "If I hadn't," he says, "my crew would have dumped me over the side."

"I know that feeling."

"You're not the first skipper to take your boat into the Bo De. DC Current and I were both patrolling off the Ca Mau in July. Skipper of the LST was Tony 'the Greek' Coulapides. He encouraged us to mix it up with the VC. We had intel there was a bunker just after the first turn in the Bo De."

"You went into the Bo De?"

"I went in first, DC following me. We took the bunker under fire. We were exiting the river at high speed through a huge rain squall. Thought I heard lightning. It was a recoilless rifle. The round exploded in the water and DC took a piece of shrapnel in his forehead. He was medivaced off the LST—spent six weeks in a Yokohama Army Hospital."

"How'd you explain that?"

"Weren't any questions. Think maybe Tony the Greek must have covered for us. But I'll tell you why the Bo De didn't come up," Hal says. "Your brief firefight was not significant. On October 4th, PCF 38 entered the Cua Lon River at the other end of the Bo De. Got into two firefights. Quartermaster David Clayton was wounded. Clayton was awarded the Navy Commendation for his actions under fire.

"And the day before your little stint, PCF 3 went up the Rach Giang Thran from Ha Tien. This penetration was way-the-hell-deep into VC country—bordering Cambodia. Mike Bernique, a dumb-ass lieutenant like you, was the skipper. He had intelligence about a tax collector—making fisherman and woodcutters pay money to the VC. Mike and his crew disrupted the tax operation—got into a huge firefight."

"Crew get hurt?"

"No, but the government of Cambodia claimed they killed Cambodian citizens. Mike was flown to Saigon to answer the accusations. Faced the possibility of a court-martial."

"Shit, I know the feeling."

"Mike told the Board of Inquiry, 'You can tell President Sihanouk he's a goddamn liar.' " Hal takes a sip of beer and laughs. "They gave Mike the goddamn Silver Star."

As I sit at the bar, feeling relieved my career is not yet on the rocks, I can't help wondering why my crew wanted to go into the Bo De. Or why I agreed. Or why other skippers and crews are also ignoring rule number three. All of us are voluntarily risking our lives—without orders. I know it's not for medals, especially those awarded posthumously. We can put in our year of Vietnam duty while remaining bored and relatively safe patrolling the coast. I wonder if I went into the Bo De to prove to my father I am as brave as he is.

Perhaps these numerous and unauthorized river incursions have been noticed by Captain Rex Rectanus, Admiral Zumwalt's senior navy strategists. Maybe he thinks Swift Boats can be more effective in the rivers than guarding the coast. Regardless of the impetus, Admiral Zumwalt and Captain Hoffmann have announced a new role for Swift Boats: Operation Sea Lords.

I sit in the Officer's Club listening to guys talk about the new operations.

"Just two days after your Bo De visit," Doug Armstrong says, "three Swift Boats followed a canal to a lake near the Ca Mau. They hit the Viet Cong's headquarters. They dubbed it 'VC Lake.' " I listen to Doug's animated description and visualize Swift Boats shooting up the Viet Cong's R&R haven as if it were a saloon in some cowboy western.

Ked Fairbank says, "A few days after that, four Swifts raced through the Cua Lon River. They were blasting away at VC bunkers like it was an arcade."

The stories keep flowing.

"Yesterday," Jim Barrett says, "there was a synchronized operation. Four Swifts headed up the Cua Lon and three Swifts entered the Bo De. Both groups got into firefights. Five sailors were wounded, but no one killed."

My brief firefight in the Bo De is hardly worth mentioning. But it's now clear: "Rule Number Three" has been scratched from the list. Operation Sea Lords is our new mission. What in the hell have we started?

Chapter Six

Duong Keo

"Is it true?" Taylor asks. "Scuttlebutt has it we're going to start river operations."

"Taylor, I don't have the full skinny," I say. "Best I know, there have been some river ops and there's probably going to be more."

"About time," Taylor says, standing with hands on his hips. "We know where they are; let's go kick some ass." Taylor smiles and then turns to walk toward a group of sailors drinking beer. They all seem to be waiting for Taylor to report any news.

I'm amazed how fast rumors fly among crews. One thing I sense, Taylor's morale has jumped a notch or two. The prospect of aggressive action has excited Taylor. He wants to do more, get into the fight. And not just to fight, but to win.

As I walk into the O' Club, heads spin around and there's a spontaneous laugh.

"We were just saying," Lieutenant Steve Hart says, "maybe your call sign should be 'Bent Screw.'" The boat skippers laugh again and I feel my face flush, but the conversation is quick to return to hot news: Operation Sea Lords.

Matt D'Amico says Sea Lords sound dramatic, as if he's thinking Horatio Hornblower himself will be leading us into battle. Their enthusiastic conversation is bubbling with anticipation, everyone expounding with an air of authority on what to expect, each officer offering an opinion, only to be interrupted by another, more extravagant upshot for Operation Sea Lords.

Lieutenant D.C. Current, call sign "Short Circuit", declares a grandiose theory.

"We'll soon be inserting marines and maybe SEALs into the rivers," he says. For the first time I notice a scar above his left eye, his souvenir from the Bo De. He never mentions it. I think his prediction is a little far-fetched. The only consensus is that patrolling the coast is useless.

I head back to the officer's quarters and start a letter to Mom and Dad. I have to be careful what I say—Mom worries. I wish I knew if Dad is proud I have command of a Swift Boat—that I volunteered for Vietnam. I feel I can't live up to his expectations. I know, even after all these years, he's embarrassed that I need these coke-bottle glasses.

I remember we were living in Pensacola when I was six years old. It was a summer day and I scanned the Florida sky, looking for my dad. I knew he was up there, his radial engine throbbing as he twisted and rolled inverted, teaching other pilots aerial combat.

Across the dirt road in front of our house, someone was burning a pyre of leaves twice my height. Billy Wood, my best friend, pulled a stick from the fire, waving hot embers in my face, teasing and chasing me. I was trying to escape, running across the dirt road to our house.

I woke up in a naval hospital. I remember seeing faint images as if looking through sterile fog; there was no smell, no taste, just confusion. I tried to turn my head, but stiff pain felt like a steel collar binding my neck. I heard Mom's soft voice, as if her words were caressing my cheek. My mouth was dry and she helped me sip water through a glass straw.

"Be careful," she said, "don't break it with your teeth. You were hit by a truck. Billy said to tell you he's sorry."

I heard Dad, too, his deep-throaty sound. I remember his shape leaning over me—dark, but reassuring.

"There was a man driving a pick-up," Dad said. "He brought you and your mother here. You're in a hospital. He's been waiting outside your room for the past three days."

I thought Dad was mad. I knew I was in trouble, running across the road without looking.

Hospital days were passing; it was hard to keep track. I remember feeling something on my bed, but I couldn't see it; I couldn't move my head. Dad lifted and held up a fire truck, a hook-n-ladder. It was bright shiny red. I'd never had a toy like this. It was the most beautiful toy in the world. Dad was smiling and I knew then he wasn't mad. Dad never says "I love you," but this gift was stronger than words.

A few weeks later, my mother held my chin and said, "Look at me." And then she said, "Your left eye is crossed." It scared me, the way she said that. More weeks went by and I started to walk. Dad took me to see an eye specialist in New Orleans. It was my first train ride and I loved it. I watched cars on the road. I pretended the cars were racing the train and I knew we were winning.

Coming back to Pensacola was less fun. Dad was a stone wall, not talking to me. I had a pair of thick glasses and a black patch over my left eye, like a pirate, but without bravado. From that day, I've felt a sense of rejection from my father, that my coke-bottle glasses cause him embarrassment in front of his aviator friends. I wonder if it's because I will never fly, never be a navy pilot like him.

I searched for ways to impress him. When I was ten years old, I joined a swim team. I practiced seven days a week, sometimes swimming with weights on my ankles. I developed strong muscles and lungs, and my hair was bleached from chlorine and sun. On race days I would launch from the starting-block and hold my breath for the first lap, kicking eight beats for every stroke of my arms as I followed a blurred-black line on the bottom of the pool. I won every race for two years and moved on to more serious competition.

Dad would stand next to the pool on these Saturday afternoons at the country club, drinking his Bloody Mary, accepting compliments on my race from other fathers. But he never said to me, "Well done," or "I'm proud of you." That didn't happen until two years ago—when I received my navy commission.

I'm tired and finish my letter to Mom and Dad about how nice Cat Lo is, especially the showers. I describe my first firefight, but I don't mention how scared I was, and I don't mention my reprimand from Captain Hoffmann. I overhear voices talking about rivers; it's hard to fall asleep.

The rush of excitement everyone feels about the possibility of new operations fade with more tedious patrols in turbulent seas. I wonder if Sea Lords is a flash-in-the-pan. I am once again assigned to patrol the R&R beach. I think Hal is keeping me on a short leash. Perhaps he only trusts I haven't forgotten where the reef is.

Monotony is pleasantly broken at 2000 when Jim Hoffman extinguishes an electrical fire in the Decca 202 radar. Without eyes for the night, we have an excuse to tie up at De Long Pier in the outer harbor of Vung Tau. The harbor provides a good lee from chaotic seas and protection from black reefs—reefs that are well marked on my chart.

We're underway again at 0500. I spot a destroyer at noon, *USS Isbell*, (DD 869) and we pull alongside to say "Hi." They give us a bucket of ice cream, which is our secret objective in the first place. After a thank you to the skipper, we get underway to continue protecting the deserted R&R beach.

"We know where they are," Taylor says, "and it ain't here."

At noon, Lieutenant Garlow on PCF 60 relieves our patrol and our boredom.

Hal Amerau invites me into the Ops shack and Jim Barrett briefs me on my next patrol. It's different.

"There's a river, the Duong Keo, south of the Bo De," Jim says while unfolding a chart on his desk. "Intel says there's a VC tax operation. There's an op planned and we need another boat. You'll rendezvous at the LST with the ninety-five boat."

I find Carr in the enlisted mess hall and fill him in.

"We're headed back down to the Ca Mau—Special Ops," I say. "Tell the crew we'll get underway tomorrow at 1100."

"River op?"

"Yeah."

"Lieutenant Fairbank coming?"

"He's already there, waiting for us. Carr, your tour is up in January. XO says he's got a job for you in Ops Planning when we get back. You'd be off patrols for four weeks before you head home—kind of an early Christmas present. You want to take it?"

"If you got someone to replace me, then you bet your sweet ass I do. I mean, yes sir." We both laugh. His eyes crinkle in the corners; his cheeks make dimples. Shit, he's so happy, I think he could almost wet his pants. He's a good kid. I'll miss him.

"Okay, I'll tell Hal. We got a transfer from PCF 51, Bob Gnau. He's a quartermaster. He'll take your spot when we get back from this Op. Now go brief the crew and get some rest."

I doubt Carr will rest any more than I will. I think about writing a letter to Chantal, just in case it's my last opportunity. I stare at her picture. She is so beautiful—her delicate face, her blonde hair, her legs. Wow, she's got great legs. I can hardly believe we'll be married in a year. I change my mind about writing. It seems too negative, too melodramatic.

It's 0800. I dress, grab breakfast, strap on my .38, and head down to the piers. Carr is in the pilothouse, bent over the chart table plotting a course. The small pilothouse is cramped; there's no room for me. Suggs is sitting at the helm, scanning engine instruments, and Hoffman is warming up the Decca radar.

I throw my bag into the main cabin and see Taylor and Moison stowing gear. I feel Taylor's anticipation, watching his meticulous attention to detail, securing anything not bolted down. His body seems to transmit a humming vibration, as if from a giant transformer.

"This is what it's all about," Taylor says. "Everything's squared away. We're ready to go."

It's November 20th and we're underway an hour earlier than planned. The wind is calm as we head south over a sea as smooth as glass. It's a luxury to lie on my stomach on top of the pilothouse and watch the shallow ocean bottom race by at twenty-five knots. We're ten miles off the Bassac River mouth and it's only ten feet deep. I think this is where Jim Barrett got his call sign High 'n' Dry.

Sometimes I spot a black stingray or a large sea snake, but I'm not looking for anything, just daydreaming about Chantal. I wonder what she's doing right now. Maybe the ski slopes in France have snow. She's a great skier. This Vietnam heat makes it hard to imagine snow.

We continue south and at 2100 we anchor in five feet of water at Hon Khoai Island off the Ca Mau. I can't sleep. I study the chart of the Duong Keo and think about our orders: "Explore the Duong Keo River; report tax operations and enemy action."

We're underway again at 0800. Suggs makes ham and cheese sandwiches as we approach the USS *Washoe County* (LST 1165) for fuel. Ked Fairbank is aboard PCF 95 waiting for us.

Sailors lower a fuel hose from the deck of the LST. As we top off our tanks, Ked gives me a briefing.

"I'll be OTC for this op," Ked says. "I might get busy, so you coordinate air cover." It's the first time I've been on an operation with another boat, so I guess it makes sense to have an Officer-in-Tactical-Command.

We need to reach the Duong Keo at high tide and pull away from the LST at noon. The wind has picked up and the seas are choppy as we head in.

"Set General Quarters," I tell Carr.

"I think they're already set," Carr says. I can tell he's not being flippant, just matter-of-fact and maybe a little tense. He doesn't give me a grin.

I review the scramble codes for air support and dial up the Forward Air Controller frequency. Ked said there'd be a spotter plane somewhere nearby.

"Bird Dog, this is Elbow Golf Six-seven," I say, using my official Cat Lo call sign. I doubt he'd respond to "Preparation H."

"This is Bird Dawg, go ahead," a voice says after my second call.

"Just checking in." I give coordinates printed on my chart.

"Roger," Bird Dog says. "Ya'll let me know if you need sumpthun."

I feel naked and vulnerable approaching this river. Bird Dog's slow, relaxed drawl is comforting. I wonder where he is. I scan the skies, looking for a little puddle-jumper airplane, but I can't see him.

We follow Ked's boat as I note in the log: "21 November—1315, entering Duong Keo." We hit bottom twice, trying to get past sandbars at the entrance to the river. I scribble another note: "Like the Bo De, shallow entrance, muddy water, deeper the farther we go."

This river is smaller than the Bo De, but there's still enough room to turn around, which is certainly on my mind. Thick jungle covers the bank like a theater's drop curtain, dark green ferns and bamboo bending out over the water. Taylor has his guns pointed to port, Moison's guns are to starboard and we're cruising at fifteen knots.

I scan a small clearing on the left bank. Rattling fire bursts from the right. The ninety-five boat returns fire and Carr jams throttles to their stops. Taylor swivels his guns, joining Moison as they hose down the trees, suppressing the fire almost as soon as it begins.

"Bird Dog, this is Six-seven," I say. "Scramble code three." (We're under fire, but we can escape.)

"Roger," Bird Dog says. "Got some help comin' yer way."

We follow the ninety-five boat and race farther upriver, evading the ambush. It's a pitiful ambush, over in a minute. I doubt there were more than a few VC. I know we'll have to turn around and come back through here again. I suspect the VC will be waiting.

"Carr, keep up with the ninety-five." I'm a little nervous. It feels safer being close to Ked's boat. I realize thick foliage along the bank is as much to our advantage as it is hiding the VC. They can't train their guns beyond point-blank range.

Another burst of automatic fire erupts from trees, again from the starboard side. I see Ked's boat speed up. Taylor and Moison unload a massive response and Carr hits the throttles, pushing our engines to escape.

The shooting stops. Now the only sound comes from our rumbling engines. I feel we're all part of a "Pavlov" experiment, as if being herded upriver by each short volley of gunfire, but I don't have any saliva to swallow.

"Any damage?" Ked asks over the radio.

"Taylor," I say, "you okay?"

"Yeah."

I stick my head out of the pilothouse and yell back to the fantail, "Moison, you guys okay?" Moison just nods his head without looking at me, not taking his eyes off the trees. I can see Suggs crouched low on the deck with his M-16. I can't see Hoffman; he's on the starboard side.

"No damage," I respond to Ked. I wish there were—some reason to get the hell out of this river.

"Where's that air cover?" Ked asks. He sounds pissed, like I'm not doing my job.

"Bird Dog, Six-seven, we could use some help," I call over the radio.

"Comin," Bird Dog responds. "It's comin."

We continue pushing through this bitter-chocolate river. I think it will be worse when we turn around. There's no other exit. I wish the air cover would hurry up.

"This is far enough," Ked says over the radio. "Let's get out of this river. Turn around, balls-to-the-walls."

Carr grins, spins the helm and floors the throttles. We're now leading the way, Ked following close behind.

"Bird Dog, this is Six-seven again," I say. "We're headed out." I give him the coordinates of the ambush site. "Can you offer cover?"

"Roger-dodger," Bird Dog says. His voice has a calming effect, but I'd sure like to know when his help is going to arrive.

We're racing downriver and I worry about what is waiting for us; worry because I'm in the lead boat and worry because we still don't have air cover.

"Carr, hug the left side," I say, "don't give 'em an angle to shoot."

"Skipper," Carr says, "Moison says look behind us."

I step out of the pilothouse and look back at Moison. An A-1 Skyraider is racing toward our stern, passing over the ninety-five boat. I see its graceful tan-colored wings spread like an albatross with a silver nose at the center of its propeller. In a split second it roars over the pilothouse just a hundred feet off the water. The plane is so low I duck out of reflex. The radial engine rattles my whole body. I watch him fly straight toward the ambush, following the river, his wings nearly touching the treetops. He suddenly pulls up into a steep banking climb. I can see the pilot's helmet through a sparkling-glass canopy.

Without warning, a gigantic eruption explodes in the middle of the river, a fireball shattering trees like matchsticks. A towering column of brown and white water shoots straight up like a massive "Old Faithful" from Yellowstone. I didn't even see the bomb drop.

I'm amazed at the precision of this pilot. He comes back around, making another pass, raking the left bank, smoke and fire spiting from wings like dragon breath. The sight is awesome—the intense sound of his guns chilling. The pilot wags his wings as he departs. I notice for the first time South Vietnamese Air Force markings. I'm surprised. I didn't know the South Vietnamese had their own planes.

"Six-seven, how's that?" Bird Dog asks. I wonder where he is, if can he see us.

"On the mark," I reply, "and thanks."

"Y'all take care now." I think that means he's leaving. I wish he wasn't. The Skyraider took a long time to get here. It occurs to me there aren't any airfields nearby.

We pass destruction left by the Vietnamese pilot. I wonder where he learned to fly; maybe Pensacola. He sure as hell earned his wings today. Taylor, Moison, Suggs and Hoffman all leave their mark, firing into the trees just in case someone is still waiting, peppering the bank until we exit the river. They've probably burned up their barrels.

It's 1610 as we pull alongside the "T." I watch Hoffman use a dustpan to scoop empty brass and toss them over the side while Suggs and Moison refuel. I notice Taylor's arm is bleeding. I think he's been grazed by a bullet.

"Just a scratch," Taylor says. He refuses any talk of a Purple Heart. Taylor looks macho as Carr ties white gauze around his arm. "Good run, skipper." It's the first time Taylor has said "skipper" since the Bo De.

Ked releases me to return to Cat Lo. I'm anxious to get back; I'm sure we all are, especially Carr. This is his last patrol.

We beat into the seas heading north, our bow relentlessly plunging into waves, sending white spray into the air. At our fast speed, even small seas feel rough. Our guns are covered, two men on watch, everyone else sound asleep. I rotate the watch with Carr, four on, four off.

It's 0500 as we pull into Cat Lo. My body feels like I've been inside a punching bag. We clean the boat and my crew takes a day off from the war.

I sit on my bunk in the Quonset hut while I draft my report. I try to fathom what we accomplished.

"How'd it go?" Matt D'Amico asks.

"Didn't see any tax operations. Doubt I'd recognize one if we did."

"Maybe it was just to show the flag—act like a target to draw out the VC."

"Seems odd to never see them. It's not like the movies."

I think about that Vietnamese pilot. I volunteered to defend the South Vietnamese, and here's this pilot defending me. I remember when I was in fourth grade living in Coronado, watching Skyraiders fly over the beach on final approach to the navy base. They are beautiful airplanes. I wish I could fly.

Chapter Seven

Vung Tau

I like Commander Streuli's policy, taking guys off patrol the last weeks before heading back to the "World." Men so close to going home, surviving eleven months of patrols, begin to calculate the probability their luck is running out. I've heard they start sleeping with guns. I'm sure Carr is relieved to be off patrols.

Bob Gnau reports aboard to relieve Carr. Bob is a quartermaster, like Carr. Gnau will now be my leading petty officer, the senior enlisted man aboard and second in command.

"You were on the fifty-one boat?" I ask Gnau.

"Yeah, Lieutenant Emory's boat. We had two quartermasters, me and Bud Kittle. They swapped me for a boatswain's mate. Can you believe that? For a boatswain's mate!"

Gnau is large boned, probably 190 pounds. He has blond hair and light skin. I figure he's going to get his share of sunburns. Gnau gives me the impression of competence, asking Carr questions about navigation, tide tables and charts.

"Checked the compass lately?" I hear him ask Carr.

"Hell," Carr says, "we haven't corrected the compass since I came aboard."

I wonder if we should, but I don't say anything. I leave the two quartermasters to chat about charts, compass variations, deviations and all that navigation stuff. As I walk to the O' Club bar, I laugh to myself, remembering the name of the Junior Officer's Club in Newport, Rhode Island. It was called "Datum." It's a navigation term for the last *known* position. After too much beer, it frequently was.

It's late afternoon and the O' Club is packed with thirsty customers. I see Steve Hart with a group of boat skippers.

"Hey, Bent Screw," he yells to me and then laughs. He's never going to let me forget about hitting the reef.

"Preparation H," I yell back. "It's Preparation H." I like Steve. He wears navy-issue glasses with thick black frames just like mine. Steve is always smiling or laughing about something. He seems happy; I'm not sure why.

"We're headed into Vung Tau," Steve says. "We got the Bronco. Wanta go?"

"Hell yes," I say without hesitation. I'm excited to see Vung Tau. I missed it the last time I had a chance, while being scolded by Captain Hoffmann. We all pile in: Ked Fairbank, Matt D'Amico, me, Doug Armstrong driving and Steve yelling, "Shotgun," as he takes the front seat.

Doug parks in front of a two-story hotel in Vung Tau, the Grand. It looks seductive, like a mansion in New Orleans with steps leading up to a wide shaded veranda surrounding three sides. It has louvered-shutter windows painted white. Inside are groups of bamboo-wicker chairs with river-brown cushions, coffee tables, a bar at one end, and lazy ceiling fans doing little to cool the air.

We're immediately greeted by four beautiful Vietnamese ladies wearing tight fitting dresses—they have inviting slits on each side to give a peek at their legs.

"Buy me Saigon Tea," one of the young ladies says, grabbing my arm. I'm drawn to her black almond eyes, easily her best feature, and to the intoxicating fragrance of small white petals of jasmine in her hair. She's five-foot, wearing a white silk dress embroidered with a dragon in soft pastel green. A notch at the collar of her dress exposes a tender, delicate throat and I watch it when she swallows her Saigon Tea. Her earrings are simple, tiny jade loops that she lets me see each time she tilts her head and sweeps back her black silky hair.

"Be careful," Doug says, "the tea costs more than a gin and tonic."

"Keep a tight lip," Steve says. "Never know."

"They're too beautiful to be VC," I say.

"They're just here to tease your imagination," Doug says. "They get a share of the bar's profit."

An hour of drinks with nothing to eat is beginning to soften my brain; my imagination is buying more Saigon Tea than I can afford. Ked leads us to a restaurant and we weave through a throng of soldiers, sailors and Vietnamese, all seeming to enjoy a quiet respite from the war.

I've never eaten with chopsticks and fumble at capturing shrimp coated in thick sweet and sour sauce that drips like honey down my chin. It's delicious. Eating the rice with chopsticks is impossible. I follow Doug's example, holding the bowl to my lips and shoveling it into my mouth like a conveyor belt. In San Diego, Doug ate oysters on the half shell the same way.

A lieutenant at the next table comes over.

"Bob Anders," he says, introducing himself. "Work at Sepia headquarters." Sepia is our nemesis, our operational command that we never see—we just know they exist from coded messages in four-letter groups. "Saw your Swift Boat badges," Anders says. He says he knows something about upcoming operations, something we don't know.

"Tell us," Steve Hart says.

"Can't say more," Bob says, looking around, "too many ears."

I hate people like that. I tell him his weather reports suck.

"Might help to look out your window once in a while," I say.

"Got room on our boat," Steve says, "if you want to know what it's like on patrol."

"Curfew's at ten," Doug announces, interrupting the exchange of retorts. "Load up unless you want to be Cinderella." I fall asleep on the way back to the base, too much alcohol and never enough sleep.

I have a hang-over. I suspect Hal has assigned another river incursion as punishment. It's into the Ba Lai River.

"PCF 27 will be going with you," Hal says. "You'll have two Army Huey's—you'll be OTC. Make radio contact with the pilots before you enter the river."

This is my first time to be Officer-in-Tactical-Command. I guess all that means is that if we screw up, I'm the one who will take the blame, and maybe take another trip to Cam Ranh Bay.

The skipper of PCF 27 joins me to study the chart as our boats sit tied to the Cat Lo Pier. The skipper is huge, towering over me like some massive line-backer as he stoops down to enter the pilothouse. We study the chart of the Ba Lai, a small river running parallel between the My Tho and Ham Luong.

"This is as far as we'll go," I say, pointing to a canal crossing the Ba Lai. "Links all three rivers—Ham Luong, Ba Lai and My Tho."

"Passes through Ben Tré," the line-backer says.

"Hal said it's a friendly village. They have a hospital. Don't fire in the direction of that village."

"Okay, when do we go?" His soft voice doesn't fit with his gargantuan size. He seems hesitant, like he doesn't realize he could smash a man to pieces with just a casual swing of his fist.

"Shove off in five minutes."

Carr is offering last minute advice to Bob Gnau as they sit in the main cabin. Gnau is still reorganizing the charts, a ritual all quartermasters go through, but I think this is the third time he has done it. I start to ask if he has checked our compass, but I don't.

We pull away from the pier with PCF 27 and Carr gives us a wave and grin. I'm sure he's glad he's not going.

The sea is rough and angry. Gnau tries to set a course to lessen the brutal pounding and PCF 27 follows in our wake. We enter the mouth of the Ba Lai at 1420. It's been two hours of torture.

A small island at the mouth of the river offers a lee, some protection from heavy seas. We idle our engines as Taylor and Gnau uncover our guns and stow the canvas.

"I'll man the aft fifty," Gnau says. "Hoffman will drive." He tells Moison to use an M-16.

"Okay," I say. Gnau is the leading petty officer. He would normally drive the boat, but I need to support his decisions. And I don't blame him. If we're under fire, driving the boat must be the worst feeling. You can't shoot back—you just have to sit there and take it.

I watch Gnau insert an ammunition belt, a chain of fifty-caliber, armor-piercing bullets all linked together. The tip of every fifth round is red—a tracer. It leaves a brilliant streak as it races out the muzzle, a visual picture of its absolute path of destruction. Gnau slips a white-phosphorous shell down the mortar tube. It'll be his first shot if we receive any fire.

Everyone starts pulling on flak jackets and helmets. PCF 27 is bobbing in the confused surf a hundred feet away. I watch the skipper getting ready. I didn't know they made flak jackets that big.

I suspect some of my crew offers a silent prayer, promising not to sin any more if they can just get through this day. I wonder how many times we can get away with that prayer.

"Viper Lee," Hoffman says over our radio, "this is Elbow Golf Six-seven. Radio check." I think Viper Lee is a great call sign for the army helicopters—sounds so much more virile and menacing than Elbow Golf.

"Orbiting—on station," Viper Lee replies.

"Elbow Golf Two-seven," I say over the radio. "Let's go." The skipper steps out of his pilothouse and gives me a thumbs-up.

A forest canopy borders each bank of the river, but the ground cover is not as dense as in the Bo De or the Duong Keo—it doesn't have that same foreboding look, that impenetrable veil hiding an ambush. Our two boats drive upriver toward Ben Tré, army helicopters leading the way, skimming over trees.

"Six-seven, this is Viper Lee. We're taking small arms fire," one of the pilots says over the radio. I'm surprised how casually he says it, as if a mosquito is irritating his skin. "I'm marking with white smoke. Request suppressing fire."

One Huey is in a steep bank, circling to the right, the door gunner firing down into the trees. A rocket is fired from the lead helicopter and it explodes. The cloud of white smoke spills out of the trees and spreads over the river.

"Elbow Golf Two-seven," I radio to the other boat. "VC target, white smoke, right bank. Give 'em hell."

"Roger," PCF 27 says. It's a crisp response; not happy, not excited, just acknowledgment.

"Gnau," I yell, "put your willy-pete into that smoke." Gnau launches his mortar round into the trees and it erupts into a dense billowy ball of white phosphorous, igniting everything around it. This chemical has its own oxygen; it can't be smothered and burns with intensity.

Our boat comes abreast of trees on fire and Taylor sprays the inferno with his twin-fifties. Hot red tracers flash into the forest. I look back at PCF 27; they're peppering trees with all the firepower they have.

Two Hueys are making strafing runs, one after another. I have no idea if any of us are hitting the VC—I'm not sure where they are.

Suddenly there's an eruption just beyond the river bank, a blast of black smoke shooting up—towering above treetops.

"Secondary, secondary!" Viper Lee announces over the radio. I realize we've hit something, maybe the Viet Cong's cache of ammunition. Seeing the secondary explosion invigorates my crew, bolstering confidence—they're on target. They keep pouring in our arsenal of fifty-caliber without pause. Four booming secondary explosions ignite one after another. Debris flies through the air.

"Shit, we're too close!" I say to Hoffman and he pushes our throttles to gain some distance.

Our boats and helicopters have been assaulting the VC for twenty minutes.

"About out of gas," Viper Lee says.

"Okay," I call back, "you're released." I'm not disappointed the Hueys are leaving—it's my excuse to get the hell out of this river before Charlie finds a way to counter-attack. I see nothing wrong with hit and run. "Turn around," I say to Hoffman.

"Let's keep going," Taylor yells from the gun tub.

"Not without air cover," I yell back. "Turn around," I repeat to Hoffman.

Our boats exit the river and drop anchor in the lee of the small island. We need to cover our guns and secure loose equipment before heading out into the turbulent seas.

Taylor throws his flak jacket onto the deck.

"What's that all about?" I ask, but I think I know.

"Could've kept going," Taylor says and turns away, jerking canvas over his guns.

I can't believe he wanted to stay in that river. I guess he feels invincible. I don't.

I feel exhausted. I'm not looking forward to our transit to Cat Lo. My ears are still ringing and gritty debris clings to sweat on my face and arms. I send a message to Sepia, reporting the river op is completed, and wait for a response.

"Gnau," I say, "we take any fire?"

"I don't think so."

"Did you see them, the VC?"

"No."

"It's Thanksgiving," Hoffman says as I peel off my flak jacket.

"What's for dinner?" I ask Suggs.

"Onan's busted," he says, as if I should have known, and begins rifling through boxes of C-Rats.

Our frozen steaks and French fries are now thawing and no way to cook them. I watch Suggs with amazement as he finishes his second can of corn beef that's packed in a gruesome looking jelly. I think adrenalin sparks his appetite.

I rummage through our box of C-Rats. Hoffman has taken the last can of Vienna sausage with beans. I find a can labeled "Turkey with Gravy." Hoffman refuses my offer to trade. I open the can of turkey and place it on top of the starboard engine, hoping to add some warmth to the gelatin glop.

As I sit waiting for my meal to heat, I remember another Thanksgiving. It was 1953 and Dad would be home from Korea in three days.

"Let's wait until your father comes home to celebrate Thanksgiving," Mom had said, and she gave a big smile to Randall and me. "We'll just have something simple tonight. Okay?"

That was Okay with me; I wasn't too interested in turkey anyway.

"Do you love me best?" I asked mom. She held my shoulders and looked straight into my eyes.

"No," she said, "I love you with all my heart, but your father will always come first."

Her answer hurt, but it raised the stature of my father. It made me want, even more, to be just like him.

On Friday, Mrs. Mash, my fourth grade teacher, asked all of us, "What did you have for Thanksgiving dinner?" Each kid described turkey, stuffing, cranberries, mashed potatoes with gravy, sweet potatoes with marshmallows and pecan pie.

When it was my turn, I said, "Tomato soup." I said it in a matter-of-fact way, not thinking to elaborate on why. Mrs. Mash didn't inquire further.

On Saturday the doorbell rang. Five women stood at the door, all holding platters and casserole dishes. They were all navy wives and said they just wanted to share some leftovers with a family they knew might need some help.

Mom was confused and embarrassed. She invited these ladies into our house and somehow they all figured out how this misunderstanding occurred. I caught hell from Mom that afternoon. On Monday, I caught hell from Mrs. Mash.

My can of turkey and gravy has warmed on top of the engine. It smells like diesel oil and I throw it over the side. Holidays in Vietnam seem to miss the spirit of sharing. Vienna sausage with beans would have been nice.

Daniel Taylor driving PCF 67

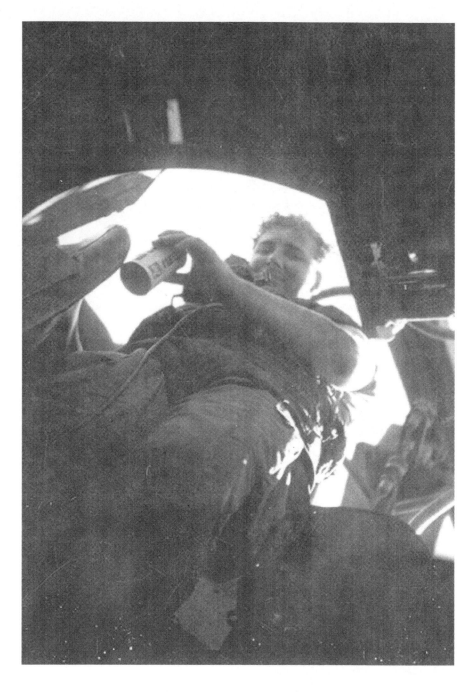

Moison in the gun tub, looking down into the pilothouse

Gnau on the aft-fifty

Off patrol and primping for a night in Vung Tau

Chapter Eight

Too Young To Die

The Mekong River begins as a trickle in the mountains of Tibet. Twenty-six-hundred miles downstream, the river is gorged in porridge-brown water, spreading into four fingers of the Mekong Delta. The rivers are called My Tho, Ham Luong, Co Chin and Bassac, and each one empties their discarded offal of humanity into the sea.

It is December and winds from the northeast have replaced the southeast monsoon. It's now the dry season. The ocean has turned mean, angry and unforgiving of poor seamanship. Our patrol for the next three days will be on the smooth Ham Luong River, but I'm not looking forward to the three hours it will take us to get there.

Our patrols have been lengthened to three days instead of one—we still only get one day off in between. I have a letter from Chantal, responding to my complaint of rough seas and long patrols.

"If you were French," she writes with teasing humor, "you would unionize and strike." But all I can say is *C'est la guerre*, it is war. Longer patrols are more efficient, more time in the rivers, less time transiting to and from Cat Lo, which in a way is a relief from the tormenting seas. I must be crazy, but I'd rather risk the possibility of being shot at in a river than the certainty of being seasick and bruised.

"We have another crewman," Gnau says. "This is Toi, our Vietnamese Navy liaison."

"Good to have you aboard," I say. "Have you been to the Ham Luong? Do you know the river?"

"Yes," Toi says, "I know the river—a little." Toi is barely five feet tall and thin, as if he never gets enough to eat. He has a nice smile and his uniform is spotless, a reflection of pride he must feel for the navy.

"Okay," I say to Moison with a measure of reluctance, "cast off. Time to go to work."

As Moison lets go the stern line, I see a man running toward us, waving his arms and yelling, "Wait up! Wait for me!" He's dressed in fatigues and carrying a small bag.

"Lieutenant Amerau said you're headed for the Ham Luong," he says, almost out of breath. "I need a ride to Coastal Group Thirty-seven. It's on your way. Any problem with that?"

"No problem," I say, "jump aboard." I think it's odd he doesn't have any insignia on his collar. "Are you an officer?"

"No, civilian contractor. Navy gave me these fatigues so I wouldn't mess up my clothes."

"Nice weapon," I say, admiring the .45 he has strapped to his waist. "More pizzazz than my .38."

"Just a precaution."

"Why are you going to the Ham Luong?"

"Military contract. My company provides diesel generators to the Coastal Groups. I'm doing a field report."

"Hey, could you take a look at our Onan? It's always crapping out."

"I'm just a rep. Honestly, I don't know shit about fixing 'em."

"Well, thanks anyway. It's nasty today; better hang on."

Our transit to the Ham Luong is rough and the seas are huge. Blue-gray clouds merge into the sea as if there's no horizon. We run into a stinging squall with wind gusting like hammers, walls of green water slamming our pilothouse and knocking our bow off course. Each wave, marbled with white foam, sounds like it's growling a warning: Beware.

Gnau is driving and I stand at the chart table, ready to relieve him if needed and ready to puke if not. I could use a triple dose of Dramamine. Everyone else onboard is gripping the sides of their bunks except our visitor. He's sitting in the main cabin on Hoffman's chair next to the HF radio, bracing his feet against the stanchion that supports our radar mast.

I'm dropped to my knees by a sudden shock as we're launched into the air by a giant wave, as if we were a seaplane trying to fly. I hear a loud bang behind me and turn to look into the cabin. Our guest is sliding on his back across the cabin deck and smashes his head into the aft bulkhead. The chair is following him—still attached to its broken pedestal—and slams into his chest.

"Grab that chair," I yell to Taylor. Taylor rolls out of the lower bunk and holds the chair before it slides away toward the bow. I step into the main cabin to help and I'm punched in my stomach, a body blow from the pillar stanchion, as if I'm in the ring with Muhammad Ali.

Taylor manages to tie down the chair and I help our civilian into Taylor's bunk. The hair on the back of his head is soaked with blood and I use a dishtowel like a turban to wrap his wound.

"I'm okay," he says. He gives me a grimace—then closes his eyes. I think he's passed out. "Just need to rest a bit," he mumbles. Taylor offers aspirin, but he shakes his head.

The seas along the coast are full of ugly curling whitecaps and savage rollers pounding the beaches. We enter the mouth of the Ham Luong and it's a rollercoaster ride all the way in. Our stern rises to a twenty-foot wave as our bow points down into the trough ahead. Our whole boat is lifted and accelerated, propelled by a giant wave, as if we're a surfboard caught by a tsunami. The rush of massive turbulent water makes steering a challenge, our stern yawing and skidding out of control.

"Don't get sideways," I scream at Gnau, "we'll get rolled."

"I'm losing it!"

"Anticipate, anticipate! Stay ahead of it. Stay ahead of the next wave."

Gnau struggles with the helm, spinning it left, then right, trying to keep control. We wallow for a second, almost motionless as each wave races by like a truck. Gnau adds more throttle, but it's not enough.

Another roller comes crashing toward us. I pray our stern will rise as each wave launches us again toward the mouth of the river.

"Thank God," I say as we enter the smooth, almost tranquil Ham Luong. "You did good," I say, smacking Gnau hard on the back. "Damn good."

"Hell of a ride," Taylor says, uncovering the twin-fifties.

"There's the coastal group compound," Toi says, pointing to a watchtower on the right. Gnau drives into a small creek and pushes our bow onto a sandy beach. A navy advisor attached to the outpost helps our passenger stagger up the beach. They disappear into the only building on this forsaken spit of sand.

"Taxi job's finished," I say to Hoffman. "Let's go."

"Wonder if his company gives Purple Hearts," Moison says, "for on-the-job wounds."

We wind our way upriver, inspecting sampans and junks. Our day job is controlling the rivers, inspecting sampans like traffic cops, as if we were stopping drunk drivers and looking for booze: "License, registration, and open your trunk please."

The tedium is unending. I remember my dad saying war is ninety percent boredom and ten percent unadulterated terror.

Rivers are forbidden to anyone at night. As curfew approaches, fishermen begin returning from the sea. Suggs, who has crammed our freezer full of steaks, notices some of the sampans have live lobsters, which are high on my hierarchy of need. With the help of Toi's translation, Suggs becomes adept at bartering.

"Steak for lobster, one for one," Toi suggests. Suggs keeps the lobsters alive in a bucket until dinnertime. We have two buckets. One is our toilet. No one wants to use the head, which is down in the crew's quarters below the pilothouse, afraid of being inside the main cabin while we're in the rivers—fear of B-40 rockets and things like that.

"Label the buckets," Gnau tells Suggs. They both laugh. It's good to hear them laugh.

Taylor has the watch, squatting on top of the pilothouse, scanning the river with binoculars.

"Skipper," Taylor calls out, "there's a large junk comin' upriver."

"Okay, standby for board and search," I say to the crew. It's not an enthusiastic command, but one of routine. I don't feel we're accomplishing anything, searching junks and sampans. Out of three-hundred searches this month, we've found only two suspected VC, one with too much money, and the other with a large stash of medical supplies.

As we close on the junk, Toi calls out over our loud speakers, "*Lai day, lai day*," Come here, come here.

The old junk is easily ten feet longer than our patrol boat, over sixty-feet, bigger than any vessel we've searched. Her brown weathered sails are furled and she's slowly making way with the putt-putt sound of a small diesel. A Vietnamese sailor tosses a line and we tie alongside.

An old man appears to be the captain. Toi asks for identification papers while Taylor and Moison leap aboard to begin a search. I stand near the aft helm, watching the old man. He's barefoot, wearing baggy black shorts that cover his knees and a filthy shirt three sizes too big.

Hoffman is crouched on our cabin top, Gnau on the fantail and Suggs on the bow, each with an M-16, the safety off, keeping an eye on the crew of the junk. To protect Taylor and Moison, they won't hesitate to shoot.

"Skipper," Taylor yells, "I've found something!" He waves to Toi and me to follow him. A dark mahogany cabin at the stern of the junk is wide with a low ceiling and we bend down to enter. There, lying on a woven mat is a young girl with a frail, delicate face framed in coal silk hair. Thin white linen is draped from her chest to her ankles. She seems sedated, not reacting to our presence, her eyes as if in a trance, just black pupils without tears staring at nothing.

Brown stains are seeping out through the cloth. Toi gently lifts the cloth. Her burns shock me. Her flesh is grotesque, tortured designs in shades of gray with thin white streaks of tissue drawn taunt like violin strings, stretching her young breast into unimaginable distortions, a startling contrast to her pale angelic face. Her chest, stomach and legs are oozing yellow pus. A foul putrid odor makes me gag and I fight the urge to vomit. I know it's a sign of infection, maybe gangrene.

"Toi," I say, "tell the captain we're taking her to the hospital in Ben Tré. Taylor, get our stretcher."

Taylor starts to leave and then pauses. "Mr. Erwin, this isn't our job. We'll be out of our patrol area for the rest of the day." Taylor's formality is a sign. Whenever he disagrees with me, he addresses me as "Mr. Erwin."

"Taylor, get the stretcher!" I repeat. Taylor bolts from the cabin, kicking the door, his body language conveying fervent disagreement. I can hear it in his voice as Taylor yells at Moison to search the cargo hold, and barks at Hoffman to get the stretcher.

The captain of the junk squats next to the girl and I kneel on the other side. As Toi translates, the captain becomes agitated, speaking fast and loud.

"He's refusing to let her go," Toi says. "He thinks we believe this girl is Viet Cong—thinks we are going to put her in prison." Toi pauses and then says, "Mr. Erwin, she might be Viet Cong, wounded in some battle."

"For crying out loud, tell him this girl is going to *die* if she does not get to a hospital! Tell him she's not going to prison. Ask him if this is his daughter." I watch the old man's eyes as Toi translates—I can tell when he hears my question. The old man looks at me and nods.

"Why is he refusing my help?" I ask Toi. "This is his daughter—a hospital can save her life."

Toi translates, but the captain just stares at me without responding. I wonder if he cares. I've heard the Vietnamese don't care about their children, that their culture is different. I now think it's true. I believe the years of war have made the Vietnamese callous to human feelings, an entire country just trying to survive; the task too overwhelming to worry about the life of one child. They can always have more.

Hoffman crawls into the cabin, pulling the canvas stretcher behind him. The father is startled, rising up to his feet, yelling, screaming at me with a vehement protest, spittle flying from his mouth.

There's no translation necessary. He's four feet away, his feet and arms spread; muscles tense—his whole posture says he's ready to fight, to sacrifice his life to prevent me from taking his daughter. I'm armed with a .38; the father with nothing but his body.

"He doesn't trust you," Toi says, "fears he'll never see her again."

Taylor comes back into the cabin with our medical kit. Toi translates as Taylor gives instructions for the burn cream, the sterile gauze and the morphine. The father begins to relax.

Taylor turns to me and whispers, "Junk's clean, no weapons, just fish and rice." Taylor pauses, and then says softly, "Skipper, please, let 'em go."

I want to help this girl—she's close to death, but all I can say is, "Okay."

The junk pulls away from our side and I watch it motor upriver. I wonder about Vietnamese values, about love for their children. Maybe I've been wrong; maybe they're just like me. I wonder what poison I've taken to fall under this prejudice. Maybe I created this image for my own self-preservation, the concept that no one will mourn if I kill someone. I'll be off the hook, no bad memories for taking a life.

I don't think the young girl will live. In my mind, I still see the father cradling her in his arms as she closed her eyes. I don't care if she is VC—she's too young to die.

Chapter Nine

Conviction

I remind myself we are here to protect civilians and defeat the Viet Cong, but it is hard to know who is Viet Cong and who is not. Taylor and I avoid discussing the differences we feel; we each have our own sense of purpose. Taylor wants to be aggressive, to engage the Viet Cong in do or die combat. I, too, hate the VC, but I don't feel a burning desire to be in a firefight.

I feel empathy for the South Vietnamese, caught in the middle of war. Maybe I should be more like Taylor, just stay focused on finding the VC and not worry about anything else. But I can't help thinking about the South Vietnamese and their simple way of life.

Each time we stop a sampan or junk, we give some gift, trying to earn their trust, offering bars of soap, cigarettes or sewing kits. We want to show we're not like the Viet Cong—we're not animals.

I enjoy meeting the fishermen, offering fishhooks, lures and nylon line. The fishhooks and shiny lures remind me of my mother's father. He was a butcher, a gentle man, small and thin like the Vietnamese. When Papaw smiled, the wrinkles in the corner of his eyes gave the impression he was laughing.

I remember evenings when I was eight years old, watching with fascination as Papaw sat at the table in his bedroom, spending hours creating beautiful and delicate dry flies. Papaw used rooster feathers and small bits of cotton, meticulously wrapping thin black thread around the feathers, binding them to a black fishhook held in a small vice.

Papaw talked out loud as he worked—how his flies would attract a Rainbow, a Brown or with luck, a Steelhead. I wasn't sure if he was talking to me or to himself. I try to imagine my grandfather standing in a cold mountain stream, morning sunlight glinting off his bamboo rod, dancing his elegant Mayfly over a swirling eddy. I smile, thinking of the conversation he would have with these Vietnamese fishermen, each arguing with passion over what lure works best.

I begin to think of Sepia as our mother. She's always sending us coded messages. I joke with Gnau during one of my sarcastic moods.

"Sepia will soon be asking if we've cleaned up our room," I say.

"Yeah," Gnau says, "she'll say be home by eleven."

"Or she'll ask what we did last night." We both have a laugh. Almost on cue, Mother Sepia sends a message in her sweet little code.

"Special op for tonight," Hoffman says, deciphering the scrambled gibberish.

Sepia's order is uncharacteristic of any caring mother I've known. Gnau joins me in the pilothouse and we plot the coordinates of a small canal across the Ham Luong from Ben Tré.

"Suspected VC crossing," I say, reading the message. "Wonder how Sepia got this information." Privately I wonder if Bob Anders, the lieutenant I met in the Vung Tau restaurant, sent this message.

"Set an Ambush?" Gnau asks, scanning the message. "Is that what I'm reading?"

"Seems like," Hoffman says. "This'll make Taylor happy."

At 2100 we anchor on the shoulder of a sandbar five miles downstream from the VC canal. I gather the crew on the fantail. We study the chart and talk about how we'll set our trap. This is new to all of us.

"We'll go in slow," I say, "beach in the mud or tie to a tree and shut down the engines. No lights. Hoffman, no smoking. Taylor, you'll have the Starlight."

Taylor grabs the Starlight from its case, a long spyglass with batteries that turns sinister night into green creepy daylight.

"I got the radar," Hoffman volunteers.

"Use the rubber hood; cover the scope," Gnau says.

"I know that," Hoffman snaps. "I know that.

"If we see a sampan," I say, looking at each man, "it'll be VC. I'll turn on our searchlight; if they don't raise their hands—open fire."

Each man checks his gun and puts a flak jacket, helmet and sound-powered phone close by. I watch them fidget with gear and gather extra magazines and ammo belts. I know what they're feeling—I feel it too, the thought of going into a canal at night. I'm really not looking forward to this.

"We'll go in at 0100," I tell Gnau. "Set a watch. Wake me at midnight." I doubt I'll sleep.

It's near midnight and someone is shaking my shoulder.

"Skipper, it's Suggs!" Moison says. "I think he's had a heart attack!" Suggs is lying on his back on the engine hatch, one leg twisted back where he's fallen. His eyes are closed and he's not breathing.

I begin giving mouth-to-mouth resuscitation, pausing to push hard on his chest and repeating the cycle. I don't know if I'm doing it right. I'm making myself dizzy blowing into his mouth. I'm doing it too fast.

"Take over," I say to Moison. "Gnau, get someone on the anchor. Hoffman, light-off the engines!" I call an LST that's anchored near Cho Lach.

"How long before you get here?" the LST asks.

"An hour."

"Okay, we'll have a doctor standing by."

We take turns, each man blowing into Suggs and pumping his huge chest as Hoffman drives us upriver. I can't tell if Suggs is responding. He feels cold and clammy like liver. I can't feel a pulse—can't tell if he's dead.

It's a long hour driving through the dark. The LST calls and asks where we are. I tell them we're still coming. This trip upriver is taking forever. We pull alongside the LST and they have a stretcher ready.

"What took you so long!?" the corpsman asks in a sharp rebuke. Suggs is whisked aboard, taken somewhere inside.

Sepia responds to my urgent report about Suggs. I'm advised to use my own judgment. We're short one man and we can't get into the canal on time.

"Tell Sepia we're aborting the mission," I say to Hoffman.

Taylor takes off his flack jacket, stows the starlight and lies down on the cabin top without saying a word. We remain alongside the LST, rotating a watch even though no one sleeps. We all wait to hear if Suggs is dead.

The sun is just beginning to warm the morning air as the corpsman steps aboard.

"Acute anxiety attack," the corpsman says. "He passed out. His heart rate and blood pressure are way too high and he's overweight. He could have a real heart attack next time. Recommend you take him off patrol for awhile."

We stay alongside until noon. Suggs is helped aboard by Gnau and Moison, and we start for home.

Getting back to Cat Lo is now the challenge. Our feared antagonist is no longer the Viet Cong with their B-40 rockets in narrow canals—it's the wind and twenty-five-foot mountains of water, cresting and crashing through the shallow mouth of the river. It is an unavoidable gauntlet before heading home through seas that are just as angry.

It is only by a slight margin easier to get into the rivers than to get out. Leaving the Ham Luong is like a game of bumper-cars, our twenty-three-ton boat being smashed by waves as if we are a toy, our bow lifting into the air, our twin propellers hitting sand bottom and in the next second, the rpm racing as our screws spin above water. God help us if we damage a propeller and it's not Captain Hoffmann I worry about. If we lose a screw, we won't have the power to escape these waves.

The hatches are closed, green water slamming into the windscreen with unnerving repetition. Moison installs aluminum braces. Suggs is in the lower berth in the main cabin. I see Toi kneeling next to him, watching him, keeping him steady. I wonder how Suggs is feeling as we slam through waves.

I relieve Gnau and take over the helm. I'm gritting my teeth, manipulating twin diesels, each one four-hundred-and-eighty horsepower, each one screaming when the screws lift out of the water. I throttle from full speed, to stop, to reverse and back again to full speed, trying to get into deeper water without being rolled over or flipped on our back—pitch-polled end over end. It is only this intense focus on survival that keeps me from barfing. It's hot and humid inside, but we can't risk opening hatches.

It has taken me an hour to get us past the sandbars and treacherous surf. Now we are beating through malicious, unrelenting waves, trying to make it home, hoping the pilothouse windscreens don't implode. We aren't afraid of the seas; it's just that they're so uncaring and cruel. The trip to Cat Lo is brain jarring; a pounding that continues without compassion. No one can stand, only lie in their bunk and hang on.

Moison relives me at the helm. Driving the boat is pure trial and error, maneuvering over the top of steep crests, pulling back on the throttles as we slide down deep troughs, trying to make headway and lessen the abuse, trying to stay upright and afloat—three hours of torture.

Moison maneuvers us alongside the Cat Lo Pier and Gnau takes Suggs to sick-bay. I walk to the Operations shack to check in with Hal and request taking Suggs off patrol. Suggs has a month before his tour is up. Based on comments from the corpsman, Hal agrees to transfer him to Base Maintenance.

"I'll find you another engineman," Hal says.

Every man aboard a Swift Boat has a critical skill: guns, engine, navigation, electronics or seamanship, each man cross-trained on the other skills. But to get underway without an engineman would be stupid.

I lay on my bunk in the officer's quarters. I keep remembering the girl with burns. She was so young. I'm angry that Taylor and her father were against me, angry at myself for giving up so easily. Where was my strength of conviction—to do what was right, regardless of what other people wanted?

I remember my dad trying to teach me about conviction. One of his pilots was having difficulty landing on the carrier. Dad grounded him. The pilot's father was a congressman and the pilot asked his father for help. The congressman-father contacted an admiral and a message floated down the chain of command. Dad was pressured to let the pilot fly. Dad backed down. On the pilot's first landing, he came in too low, flew into the stern of the carrier and died in a brilliant fireball as the plane dropped into the sea.

Dad said he still feels guilt for his lack of conviction. I think about that. If Dad had stuck to his guns, kept the pilot from flying, no one would ever have known he was right. I guess that's the hard part of convictions.

I wonder if that girl is still alive.

Chapter Ten

Backdoor to Cat Lo

It's my day off and sit in the Officer's Club with two other skippers, D.C. Current and Bob Emory, drinking beer and talking about the god-awful weather, each of us sharing sea stories, each story more dramatic than the last. We've lost some men and three Swift Boats to the heavy seas. Some broached and rolled under, and one pitched-polled end-over-end. The heavy Vietnam seas are without clemency and there's no appeal.

Bob Emory is skipper of PCF 51. His call sign is "Baby Fats." It's easy to see how he got that name, with his round soft cheeks and innocent looking eyes.

"Thanks for transferring Gnau to my boat," I say to Baby Fats. "He's a good quartermaster."

"Yeah, it was hard to let him go."

Baby Fats and D.C. Current, "Short Circuit," are studying a chart of the Mekong Delta. I again notice the scar above DC's eye, reminding me of the Bo De. I would hate to get hit in the face.

"We're trying to devise an alternate route from the rivers to Cat Lo," Baby Fats says.

"Instead of going downriver and punching out through the surf," DC says, "we can head upriver—follow this canal from the Ham Luong." He traces the canal with his finger. "We go past Ben Tré, cross the Ba Lai River and get into the My Tho. It's then a short run to Cat Lo past the Rung Sat."

"You ever been in that canal?" Baby Fats asks.

"Only from the Ham Luong to Ben Tré," DC says. "Should be okay from Ben Tré to the My Tho."

"I've been on the Ba Lai," I say. "We found a VC ammo cache."

"My next patrol is on the Ham Luong," Baby Fats says. "I'll try this backdoor on the way home—let you know how it goes."

As I listen to these guys, I realize it is incredible we prefer exposing ourselves to VC ambushes, B-40 rockets and Claymore mines to the sea's ruthless indifference. But it's our choice. We'd rather be in a calm canal with only the *possibility* of a firefight, to the certainty of being pounded by a relentless ocean.

I head down to my boat to check on the crew and show Gnau and Taylor the backdoor plan.

Gnau walks his dividers across the canal from the Ham Luong to the My Tho. "Twelve miles," he says.

"Half hour," Taylor adds. "Piece of cake."

We're interrupted as Michael Stancil, Engineman 3rd Class, reports for duty to replace Suggs. He's twenty years old. Stancil has keen sharp eyes, soft spoken in a shy, well-mannered sort of way, and neatly trimmed hair. I sense his eagerness from the way he keeps shifting his feet while we talk.

"You just arrive in-country?" I ask Stancil.

"No sir. I've been on Lieutenant Hudson's boat up at Cam Ranh Bay."

"Shit, he and I were in training together. How is he? Did he ever get his sea bag? How's his tan?"

"He's good, sir; a good skipper."

"What's his call sign?"

"Ichabod."

"That fits."

Gnau introduces Stancil to the crew, and then introduces Stancil to the two V-12 GM diesels with their injectors, hydraulic clutches and reduction gear. I watch Stancil climb down into the engine room, smiling as he runs his hands over the blowers and manifolds, as if stroking an old friend. Stancil looks too young to act so confident, rummaging through the tool box as if a surgeon searching for his stethoscope. I like Stancil already.

"We're getting underway tomorrow morning," I say, looking down through the engine hatch. "If you want a hot meal on patrol, fix that damn Onan generator."

Our next patrol is on the Bassac. As we approach the river from the north, I spot another Swift Boat coming from the south heading toward us. I call repeatedly on our Prick 25, but there's no response. PCF 44 enters the shelter of the river mouth and pulls alongside.

The skipper, Lieutenant Kerry, says his radio is out. He's coming from An Thoi, transiting to Cat Lo.

"Just got assigned to you Black Cats," Kerry says. "Guess they're giving me a break."

"Rough patrols?" I ask.

"Yeah, you don't want to go there."

"Been there, couple of times."

"Try it, day in, day out."

He talks to me as if I'm a newbie, as if I've never been shot at. I resent his aloof demeanor. I'm not disappointed our conversation is brief. As Kerry departs to head north to Cat Lo, I wonder how much worse it has gotten since our forays into the Bo De and the Duong Keo.

We begin to patrol our sector of the Bassac and boredom sets in as Toi checks identification papers, boat manifests, and the crew passes out fishhooks and sewing kits. At midnight, we anchor in midstream near a village and set a watch. Moison is in the gun tub with the Starlight scope, Stancil on the fantail and Gnau is in the pilothouse. He periodically checks the anchor to make sure we're not dragging.

The current is seven knots and our bow wave is creating a wake that burbles in a trail behind us. We rotate the watch every four hours. We sleep on deck or on top of the cabin when not on watch. No one sleeps inside the cabin.

It's 0650 and I'm on watch. Half the crew has another hour before I wake them for the day. The morning sun is already hot, its red-orange glow coloring the treetops while the small village, a hundred yards off our starboard side, is still in cool shade. I sip my fifth cup of coffee while scanning the river.

A few fishermen have already passed by heading out to sea, their black nets folded in the bow of their sampans, their long-shaft motors hardly working as the current carries them downstream.

I see an arching trail of smoke headed toward our bow, coming from the starboard bank. I'm too startled to react. The explosion in the water shakes me out of my daze. "Incoming!" I yell. "General Quarters, get underway, fast!" I stare at the tree-lined bank, expecting another B-40 rocket.

Taylor wakes up and scrambles to the gun tub. Gnau lights off the engines and throttles up in less than a minute, driving us ahead into the current. We pass over our anchor and Moison pulls in the line as fast as he can. We're lucky the anchor line doesn't foul the screws. Gnau maneuvers our boat farther away from the bank.

"Hold your fire," I say. We can't shoot back; risk of hitting the village is too great. It's probably why the VC fired from that spot.

My adrenalin is still coursing through my body. I wonder how that B-40 could miss us while we sat motionless at anchor. I heard a story about an Army pilot reporting that he had just landed and was shutting down his engine. A Viet Cong jumped up out of the bushes and unloaded the entire magazine of his AK-47, pointing his gun some fifty feet ahead of the helicopter. The door gunner cut him down.

The pilot and door gunner inspected the corpse. Carved on the wooden butt of the AK-47 was a diagram: a stick-man holding a gun, dotted bullets intercepting an X, ahead of a crude helicopter sketch—a simple instruction on how to lead a target. Someone failed to tell the young budding VC guerrilla that the helicopter needed to be moving.

I wonder if the VC thought we were underway. He was simply leading the target. Regardless of how he missed, it was like a spitball in the eye, objecting to our presence, letting us know we can't relax.

It's December 18th and our relief, PCF 28 enters the Bassac. We pull alongside each other, nose to tail, for a patrol briefing. The skipper is Lieutenant Zucker, call sign "Boston Strangler," but I always call him by his nickname, Zeke, which I think is a cool name. I tell Zeke about the B-40 rocket and Zeke tells me the latest news.

"Fifty-one got hit yesterday. B-40 or recoilless rifle," Zeke says. "Penetrated the main cabin—shrapnel all over the boat. Engineman Hartkemyer was killed, Baby Fats and Bud Kittle were wounded."

"Where'd it happen?"

"On a canal off the Ham Luong. Baby Fats was on a joint op with DC."

"Using the backdoor?"

"Don't know what that is."

It's depressing news. I sense Gnau is taking it hard, hearing about Hartkemyer, Kittle and Lieutenant Emory. Gnau just transferred off PCF 51 three weeks ago.

We use the grueling ocean passage to get home. PCF 51 is tied to the Cat Lo Pier. A hole the size of a basketball is just aft the pilothouse door where the round entered. The center pilothouse window is blown out, the port window shattered and the main cabin is strewn with debris. DC is standing on the bow.

"What happened?" I ask. "Were you guys using the backdoor?"

"No. We were going to later. There's another canal on the left side of the Ham Luong, directly across from the backdoor, from the Ben Tré Canal. We were on an op with two 'Death Dealer' Cobras covering us. I was in the lead, the OTC was in the ninety-six boat and Baby Fats was last.

"The canal runs parallel to the Ham Luong. We had almost run the whole length of the canal, about seven miles. Figured we were done, so the

OTC released the Cobras. Baby Fats was supposed to broadcast a PsyOps tape as we exited the canal. Hartkemyer was in the cabin turning on the tape player. That's when they got hit—recoilless rifle. Hartkemyer didn't feel it—decapitated. We shot up the place, then I towed the fifty-one into the Ham Luong. Baby Fats and Kittle were medivaced."

"Shit. I had orders to set up an ambush in that same canal. We had to abort."

"Lucky you," DC says. "Don't talk about the backdoor. Streuli got wind of our plan. He put out an edict, no one uses the backdoor."

PCF 51

Chapter Eleven

Christmas Eve

It's now Christmas Eve as we again patrol the Ham Luong River. I didn't buy any presents for my crew. In fact, I forgot about Christmas.

I think about Chantal and pull out her letter, reading it for the tenth time. I remember while I was on the destroyer, *USS Berry* (DD 858) in the Mediterranean. We surfaced a diesel-powered Russian submarine, staying with her until she had to come up for air. As our reward, the commodore of our destroyer squadron ordered us to take liberty in Palma, Mallorca off the coast of Spain.

It's where I met Chantal. She was on holiday in Palma. Her smile was the first thing I noticed, and then the beauty mark on her left cheek. Her blond hair fell to her shoulders; it was soft and curled at the ends. She was wearing a blue silk dress that came to her knees. The dress had a white collar buttoned close to her neck and white cuffs on long sleeves. Chantal portrayed the image of innocence. Her dress unsuccessfully hid a perfect figure.

We had two evenings together. I was infatuated by her charm, her French accent and her stunning beauty. I was captured. No, I surrendered without even considering evasion. Two evenings were enough to know there was mutual attraction.

"Can I see you again?" I asked, hoping for encouragement.

"I would like that. When?"

"Give me your address, I'll find a way." We started writing and she invited me to visit her home in France.

The *Berry* returned to Newport and I asked my skipper for two weeks leave.

"Where are you going?" Captain Dermody asked.

"France."

"Oh shit," he said and then laughed. "A girl?"

"Yes sir, we met in Palma."

"Don't make any hasty decisions." He laughed again, telling me he thought I was delirious. I was. I booked a flight to Paris. Chantal lived with her mother, who owned a small hotel at a ski resort. It was in Le Mont-Dore near Clermont-Ferrand, three hours from Paris by car.

Each morning Chantal would bring a cup of coffee to my room. She'd give me a kiss and it was electric. And then we would go skiing. She was an experienced skier and I struggled to follow her as she raced down black-diamond slopes. I fell on my face a lot. In the afternoon we helped her mother prepare dinner. We shopped for sausage in one store or live trout in another, and wine in the next.

After two weeks I was sure this was the girl I wanted to spend the rest of my life with. I asked Chantal's mother for permission to marry her daughter. Chantal's father had deserted the family many years before. In such a short time, her mother seemed to trust me.

"*Oui*," her mother said. She gave me a hug and then she started to cry. She launched into a long lecture, none of which I understood, which is probably good.

"Will you marry me?" I asked Chantal.

"*Oui*," she said and wrapped her arms around my neck, and then cried just like her mother. I returned to my ship and we continued to write, making our plans.

I wrote to Chantal that I'd volunteered for Vietnam. She didn't understand my decision, but she didn't ask me to justify it—she simply offered her love and hope.

"I'll wait for you," she wrote. "Keep that promise close to your heart."

Now I stare at Chantal's picture, at her exquisite figure as she was lying by a fireplace after our last day of skiing and after her mother's dinner of rabbit that I thought was chicken. I can feel the heat of that fire while I patrol this sultry-brown river.

Hoffman decodes a message from Coastal Group 37. It's an invitation to any Swift Boats in the area to join them for Christmas Eve dinner.

At 1600 we pull into the small creek next to the Coastal Group compound. Just beyond their beach, I see massive waves breaking over the shallow Ham Luong River mouth where two unrelenting forces are at battle. The strong river current pushes to escape; the ocean's flood is determined to come upstream, each refusing to concede. I'm thankful we're not trying to get home—we'd be caught in the middle of a turbulent brawl.

Two Swift Boats are already anchored in the creek. We tie alongside PCF 37 and Richard Holleran's boat, PCF 53. "Rocket" Holleran is fun to be around. I think a better call sign would be "Wild Man." Rocket is short, built like a small fullback, full of life, always telling jokes, laughing, smiling.

The navy lieutenant I met earlier, the Coastal Group advisor, is dressed in camouflage fatigues and he gives us a tour of the compound. It's not a long tour—they only have one building, a wire fence and a watchtower. The lieutenant's job is to coordinate activity between the US and the Vietnamese Navy. The Vietnamese Navy patrol rivers in Yabutas, wooden junks with slow diesel engines and not much firepower. It takes guts to patrol rivers in a Yabuta.

I suspect being an advisor is a lonely job. He's the only American at this base and seems elated we have responded to his invitation.

"How's that civilian contractor, the generator salesman?" I ask.

"Oh him, he's okay," the lieutenant laughs, and then gives me a wink. "But he doesn't sell generators." It doesn't take a lot of imagination to guess who this guy works for and why he carried a .45, and why he didn't have any insignia.

"CIA?" I ask. The lieutenant just winks again and nods his head. I fantasize about what mysterious things this man must do for a living.

The lieutenant directs our crews to join the Vietnamese sailors. He tells the officers to follow him up a rise above the creek to a shack made of bamboo and dried palm fronds. The small shack is sparse with a low wooden table and straw mats on the floor, but the atmosphere is warm from the glow of a kerosene lamp. Already seated are a village elder and a Vietnamese Navy officer. There's still room for the lieutenant and the three of us boat drivers.

We sit on the mats with our legs crossed, our knees against the table. It's not too comfortable. Introductions are made with toasts to each. We clink our jelly-glass jars of San Miguel beer and more is poured with each toast.

The village elder is squatting on his haunches Vietnamese style, his knees pressed against his chest. He must be our host, as he's at the head of the table. I don't think he's ever seen a dentist, but his smile seems genuine. He begins to serve our bowls from a large wok heated on a bed of coals. I stare at little square pieces of food just larger than dice, wrapped in green leaf and held together by tiny shoots of spring onion.

"What is it?" I ask the lieutenant.

"I think it's dog, maybe monkey—one or the other; try it, it's good."

I remember my Vietnamese training in Coronado: Don't insult your host.

I look over at Rocket. He's staring at me, hesitating, and we both laugh.

"Dip it in nuoc mam," the lieutenant suggests, pointing to a bowl of black fish oil. Nuoc mam is the most foul-smelling sauce in the world, akin to the aroma of diarrhea, only worse. The lieutenant hands me a shot of whisky. "Belt this down, then try the sauce. Your nose will be anesthetized. I promise."

I'm surprised; the dog or monkey is good; a little chewy, but good. The nuoc mam odor annihilates the nerves in my nostrils and I begin to relax. I toast our host, drink another whisky and start to enjoy the meal, eating everything I'm served, all dipped in hot spicy nuoc mam. I try the fried fish paste. I swallow hard and wash away the taste with more beer.

The dinner is over and I try to stand. My legs are cramped and my stability is questionable. It is pitch black outside. I have no idea what time it is; my watch is out of focus and I stumble to the boat. Gnau is in the pilothouse.

"You smell pretty bad," Gnau says, "kinda like shit."

"Set up a watch rotation with the other crews," I say, ignoring his comment. "We need at least one man awake on each boat." I'm too tired or too drunk to stand watch and crawl into the lower bunk.

I wake to a Christmas hangover, my face pressed against the hull. It's a struggle to climb out of my bunk and I realize our boat is listing to port. I jump up thinking we are taking on water and run to the fantail. We're not sinking; we are hard aground. And not just aground, but thoroughly beached. The creek is ten feet behind our stern. I hear laughing and search for my crew. They're on the beach with the other crews playing tag football.

"Hey, Mister Erwin," Stancil yells, "Merry Christmas."

Rocket calculates the tide.

"Another three hours before we're afloat," Rocket says.

"Never seen the tide drop this far, over ten feet," I say. "Was anyone on watch last night?"

"Thought *you* had the watch."

"Have you sent Sepia a report, about us being aground?" I ask, hoping he hasn't.

"No," he laughs, "I just reported we're guarding Coastal Group Thirty-seven."

I notice Taylor isn't playing football. He's sitting in the gun tub with his arms crossed. I suppose he's pissed about missing another day looking for VC. I don't care what he thinks; my head hurts.

Our three-day patrol in the Ham Luong is over. The crew is eager to return to Cat Lo to see if Santa has left anything in their stockings. I'm looking forward to a sober day off. My body is numb as we reach Cat Lo. After three hours, pounding through brutal seas, I stagger like a Christmas drunk as I walk off the pier.

Somehow, it doesn't feel like Christmas. It's just another day in Vietnam.

Virg Erwin in the BOQ Quonset hut

Left to right: Ked Fairbank, Chuck Mohn and Richard Holleran

Chapter Twelve

Bassac River

It is early morning and the hot clammy air feels like a sauna. We're patrolling the Bassac River, part of Operation Sea Lords, inspecting sampans and looking for VC.

"Turn on the tape," I tell Hoffman. Orders require us to broadcast a *Chieu Hoi* tape at least one hour each day. I hate playing this tape. It frequently draws sniper fire or worse. It's the same tape Baby Fats was going to play.

"Shit," Hoffman says as he goes below to turn on the tape player. He doesn't linger in the cabin. We blast out a message over loudspeakers, encouraging the Viet Cong to surrender.

"Stay in the middle," I tell Stancil, who's sitting at the helm. The Bassac is wide. Staying beyond range of B-40 rockets is a good idea when broadcasting this tape.

"Something in the water," Taylor says from his perch in the gun tub. I see it, floating toward us in the current. A bloated body, head bent forward underwater, elbows pulled back, bound by a bamboo pole across his back.

"Victim of neutrality," I say with as much sarcasm as I can convey, "dumped in the river like trash." This sight makes me loathe the Viet Cong.

"VC don't honor a white flag," Taylor says.

"That's okay with me. I don't plan to wave one." My images of the Viet Cong are men without principle, not even men, but sadistic animals belonging in a cage. The VC crawl into villages at night and brutally murder anyone supporting the Saigon government, or kill them for not supporting the VC. Neutrality is not an option.

The Viet Cong sometimes chop off the head of their victim and place it on a pole in the village; a warning, cruel intimidation, forcing people to accept communism to stay alive. Whether this war is noble or not, I will kill VC with commitment and passion.

At noon Taylor and Toi board a sampan. They discover hidden drugs: two quarts of sodium chloride, a quart of dextrose and forty-five thousand Piastars.

"That's about two hundred dollars," Gnau says.

"They look too old to fight," I say.

"Maybe tax collectors," Toi says.

"At least sympathizers," Gnau says. I look at their faces, wondering if they are secretly Viet Cong.

"Look at their hands," Moison says. "See if their hands are rough, like fishermen or farmers." Their hands are soft.

"Wonder if they're sorry for their dead countrymen—floating in the river," I say. We bring them aboard and turn them over to the Coastal Group for questioning.

We stop a sampan returning from the sea. The old man has a toothy grin and his clothes smell like they were marinated in nuoc mam. In the bottom of his boat are ten, maybe fifteen, sea snakes. They're not like the big brown and yellow one that wanted to bite me; they are thin and black, twisting and slithering over each other.

"Gnau," I say, "check out that sampan."

"I inspected the last one," Gnau says.

"I helped him," Moison quickly adds.

"I ain't puttin' my hands in that sampan," Taylor says. I always thought Taylor was so macho.

I look at the man's face. Trust is a relative thing. He looks innocent and his hands are rough.

"His ID's okay," Toi says.

"Let him go," I say. I hate sea snakes.

"Got a message from Mother," Hoffman says. "Gotta pick up some doctors and nurses in Binh Thuy, take 'em to a village along some canal."

"Medical clinic," I say, reading the message. "We'll stand by for protection."

"Shit," Taylor says, "baby-sitting."

We pull into Binh Thuy and I walk to the hospital to meet personnel that will be going. I'm lost, asking for directions, going from one building to the next. They are small one-story buildings, raised a foot off the ground, the walls painted green with white roofs. The buildings look peaceful, tall nippa palms offering shade and warm hues of hibiscus drawing attention away from their purpose—they're all hospital wards.

I enter one of the wards and realize I've come in the backdoor. I'm not prepared for what's inside. As I walk toward the other end of the ward, I pass rows of beds on each side filled with men, women and children, all Vietnamese.

Most of the patients seem unaware of my presence, but one man smiles at me and I stop. I can't move and I can't look away. Even if I try, I don't think I can make my vocal cords work. He has no arms or legs, just white bandages covering four stumps. He smiles again.

How can this man smile? There's a glass of water with a straw on the table next to his bed. I walk over and offer him a drink. I can't stop my hand from shaking.

"Thank you, but I'll do that," a nurse says. Her sharp voice makes me feel I've done something wrong. I leave, walking to the other end of the ward, but now not looking to either side, only straight ahead. I can't look anymore. I can't wait to get out of this building—can't stop thinking about this man who smiled.

This man reminds me of words from a poem by D. H. Lawrence: *I never saw a wild thing sorry for itself. A bird will fall frozen dead from a bough without ever having felt sorry for itself.* This man without limbs showed no self-pity. He is one of the bravest men I have ever seen.

I find the American Army doctors and nurses, and they board our Swift Boat as if it is a Sunday outing. They seem happy, as if taking an afternoon trip on the Mississippi River. Their laughter surprises me. I'm worried about their safety and yet they seem carefree, as if some invisible shield protects them.

"Must be newbies—they haven't got a clue," Taylor says.

"I don't know," I say, "I've seen the wards."

One of the nurses must have perfumed herself to hide the sweat we all endure. Her scent is like gardenia. I wish she hadn't done that. Her aroma arouses feelings that compete with my need to stay alert.

"Have you seen a young girl?" I ask one of the doctors. "She's got severe burns on her chest, stomach and legs. About fifteen. She was aboard a junk. Would have been about a month ago."

"Do you know how many patients we have like that?" He looks at me as if I am an idiot. I guess I am. It was a dumb question. I hope she survived.

We arrive at the village and beach our boat on a muddy bank. My crew remains alert, watching for any sign of an ambush. There are five huts of bamboo with thatched roofs in a small clearing. The village looks quiet and peaceful. Villagers begin to crowd at our bow, looking at us with inquisitive eyes. Taylor remains in the gun tub griping the twin-fifties, watching the trees.

The clinic goes well. We have boxes of medical supplies stacked on our deck and boxes with bars of soap, toothbrushes, plastic cups, bowls and school kits. I'm impressed with the planning of this army medical team.

I watch Gnau, Moison, Stancil and nurses offering small gifts to the children. I've been told in my training that the parents and elders will step forward and take their share before letting the children receive anything. There's none of that. Parents in this dirt poor village stand behind the kids, smiling, enjoying the sound of children's laughter as each kid receives a coloring book and crayons.

"Seems bizarre to see crayons in a war zone," I say to Taylor.

Looking at these Vietnamese, I realize I have been dehumanizing the entire country, believing everyone has lost any semblance of respect for life. I've been wrong.

Hoffman turns on our loudspeakers. He doesn't put in the *Chieu Hoi* tape, the one encouraging the Viet Cong to give up. He puts in Simon and Garfunkel's "Homeward Bound."

For a moment I forget the war. Maybe everyone does—for just a moment.

We drop off the medical team in Binh Thuy, refuel and head home to Cat Lo.

The Cat Lo volleyball court is between two Quonset huts and an intense game is in full swing. The tallest players, Chuck Mohn and Ked Fairbank, square off on opposite sides of the net. Doug Armstrong would be at the net too, but he's on patrol. Steve Hart, D.C. Current, Matt D'Amico, me and others, rotate serving from the back of the court.

A washtub of beer and ice prevents dehydration in the ninety-degree heat. The ice doesn't last long and neither does the beer. Hal Amerau referees. I think Hal aspires to the State Department. Each time there's a foul, Hal says, "I didn't see it."

After a brown water shower, we all head into Vung Tau. We each go in different directions, agreeing to rendezvous at the Grand Hotel for an after-dinner Saigon Tea. The streets are crowded. I see soldiers and sailors standing in front of shops that sell reel-to-reel tapes with the latest music from back home. "Marrakesh Express" is blasting out from speakers next to one of the shops. I love Crosby, Stills and Nash. It would be a great tape to play for the VC. I'm sure they'd love it more than the *Chieu Hoi* tape.

I watch Vietnamese women shopping. They're wearing *ao dais*, white high-necked tunics that fall below their knees with slits along each side. The tunics flap over baggy black cotton pants that seem too long, the cuffs dragging in the dirt. The Vietnamese women have an odd style of walking, scraping their sandals in short shuffling steps. They're wearing conical hats tied with a string beneath their chin. They each carry a straw basket as they shop at rows of outdoor markets for vegetables, fruit and fish. Fish too long in the sun permeate the air.

Old men with stained teeth wear billowy shirts and black shorts. They sit squatting on their haunches, smoking cigarettes in front of butcher shops that have chickens and pigs hanging by their feet.

I spot a vendor selling watchbands and buy a wide leather band with snaps to hold my watch on top. It looks unique and rebellious, like something the Hells Angels would wear. I'm sure Taylor will be impressed. A group of kids surround me, begging for money and clawing at my arms.

"No," I say harshly. In seconds they're gone. So is my watch. The easy snaps were an invitation they couldn't resist. I wonder if these kids are orphans. They look ragged and dirty.

The watchband with snaps is not a good idea and I throw it away. I'm very pissed off. I bought that Omega watch from the ship's store aboard my destroyer. I'll miss it.

As I fume at my misfortune, I feel a tap on my shoulder. It's Bob Anders, the lieutenant from Sepia headquarters.

"Sorry about your watch. I'll buy you dinner," he offers.

"I guess your weather reports aren't so bad." We laugh and decide to be friends. Bob weaves us through the crowd to his favorite Thai restaurant. It's obvious the owner knows him and we're seated at the only empty table.

"I've never had Thai food."

"I'll order for us. Two Tiger beers," he says to the owner.

I'm served spring rolls filled with cabbage, strong tangy ginger, black mushrooms and glass noodles. The next course is a large bowl of steaming broth with curried shrimp, onions and peppers. The peppers ignite a flame in my stomach that I can't put out. Two more bottles of Tiger beer do little to help.

Bob tells me about his duty at Sepia and what he's learned about the Vietnamese.

"Land," he says, "it's all about land. They don't own the land they work. They got nothing to fight for."

"I don't understand."

"The farmers are paying rent to absentee French landowners and taxes to Saigon. Not much different from what the Viet Cong demand. They're only dissimilar in how the money is collected."

"I've seen examples of that."

"You guys got some river ops coming."

"How do you know?"

"I see plans formulating, questions about how many boats are available, about LST positions, Seawolf detachments, that sort of stuff. I'll let you know what I can, if I learn any more."

"Thanks. Always helps to know what's coming."

"I got an apartment in town. Want to see it?

"Thought you guys had a BOQ up on the hill."

"I do, but I prefer the apartment."

We walk over to see it. His attractive Vietnamese girlfriend is in the kitchen cleaning dishes.

"We share this apartment. I pay the rent and she fixes dinner most evenings."

"I teach English and French at the elementary school," she says. Her English is perfect.

As we sit in the kitchen sipping beer, Bob notices the time.

"It's nearly curfew," he says. Bob offers a couch to sleep on, but I have a patrol in the morning. I run to the Grand Hotel for the rendezvous and discover the Bronco is gone. I've missed my ride to the base. There's not a navy or military jeep in sight. I feel panic, but I have no choice and start walking the fives miles to the base.

It's dark and I'm worried, walking alone on this road. I don't have a gun. Uncomfortable scenarios flash through my head, all of which have something to do with the Viet Cong. I'm now less worried about missing my patrol or even a nasty message from Captain Hoffmann; I just want to make it back to the base.

Motor scooters are whizzing by, everyone trying to get home before curfew. I stick out my thumb. A Vietnamese soldier stops and motions me to climb on.

"Cat Lo," I say and he nods. "Thank you," I say and he nods again. I'm not sure he understands, but he's headed in the right direction. I wonder what I'll do if he dumps me off in the middle of this dark lonely road, still miles from the base.

The number of scooters dwindles as we head toward the base; the number of street lamps drops to zero. Now we're the only scooter and his headlamp the only light. I remember my first night in Vietnam on a bus. I was scared. I'm scared now.

Out of habit, I look at my wrist to see the time and regret I don't have a watch. I feel this ride is taking longer than it should and I wonder if we're on the right road. I'm fighting to stay calm and realize I'm squeezing the waist of the soldier.

I see watchtower lights up ahead—the base! My rescuer pulls up at the gate and I climb off, thankfully offering some money for the ride. I'm impressed that he declines the money. He gives me a salute and turns around, heading back in the direction we came. I realize he's gone out of his way.

Chapter Thirteen

Nha Be

It is January 17th as I step aboard PCF 67. Our next patrol will be in the Rung Sat canals near Nha Be. I tell Gnau about my motor scooter ride last night.

"Should've stayed in Vung Tau," Gnau says and laughs.

"And miss all the fun?"

"Onan's purring," Stancil says, and he gives me a big grin. Stancil is a genius.

"Good job, Stancil. Hope we find some lobster. Okay," I say to Gnau, "let's get 'er underway."

"Cast off," Gnau yells to Moison. Taylor uncovers the twin fifties, and Moison pulls in the dock lines and fenders.

We cross the bay beyond Vung Tau and head into the Long Tao River. The Long Tao meanders through the middle of the Rung Sat Special Zone. I think about my first orientation ride and how scared I was. The Rung Sat doesn't look so scary in daylight, even knowing the VC are hiding in its maze of canals and its Louisiana-like swamp. We continue on, following this river toward Saigon. It is forty-five miles to Saigon, but we won't go that far.

Taylor is the gun tub and spots a small navy boat up ahead. "MSB," he says. "Minesweeper."

We pass the minesweeper, giving it a wide berth. The MSB looks top heavy for its size, which is not much longer than our Swift Boat. The MSB is towing two torpedo-shaped floats with little flags on top. I give the skipper a wave as we pass by.

"They're dragging the bottom," Moison says. "Those floats have cables with steel blades. Supposed to cut loose VC mines anchored underwater."

"Sounds like a fun job," I say, but I know it's more like fishing for sharks. What do you do when you catch one?

It's 1800 as we pull into Nha Be, a navy base located where the Long Tao joins the Soi Rap River. Saigon is only another half hour farther upriver. We are now reporting to "Game Warden" instead of "Market Time."

"Won't have to listen to Sepia on this patrol," Hoffman says.

"This is PBR territory," Moison says, pointing to boats tied to a pier.

"First time I've seen them," I say, looking at green fiberglass boats about thirty feet long. They have a canvas roof, twin fifties forward and another gun aft. "God, I'm glad I'm not on a PBR."

"They're fast," Moison says. "When they're up on step, they can race over six inches of water. Our heavy ass needs five feet."

"PBR sailors think their boats are faster," Gnau says, "but I doubt it."

Stancil and Moison top off the fuel tanks, but we don't really need it. I report to the Operations shack to check in and get any news on local activity.

As I walk out of the Operations hut with a handful of notes, someone yells, "Hey, Black Shoe, what the fuck are you doing on my base?" I spin around, ready to take or give heat, depending on the rank of some SOB. It's the smiling face of Lieutenant Bruce McFadyen. It's a great surprise. I know he's ribbing me for requesting destroyer duty—the "Black Shoe Navy"—but to me it's a compliment, serving on a greyhound-of-the-sea.

Bruce is a good friend from officer candidate school. We were both going to be experts in explosive ordinance disposal, but I backed out.

As a kid, I fantasized about being a Frogman, a clandestine secret agent blowing up enemy ships. I was fascinated with firecrackers and bottle rockets, and I loved to swim—a Frogman seemed the perfect fit. My brother, Randall, and I would plant M-80 firecrackers underneath toy tanks, light the fuse and then crouch down in our improvised bunker. The toy would be blown to pieces and we would roll on the ground in giddy laughter.

While at officer candidate school, Bruce McFadyen and I attended a lecture on EOD, Explosive Ordinance Disposal. The speaker promised a career of daring excitement. A test would be required. There were only a few EOD positions available, but I didn't think that would be a problem— it's rare to see a line of men at the door, all wanting to disarm bombs.

"From the men who qualify," the speaker had said, "only the elite will be selected."

"Let's do it!" Bruce said. He talked non-stop all the way back to our barracks. "If we both make it," he said, "we'll room together at EOD School." I was swept up in his enthusiasm. I liked the word the speaker used: *elite*.

On the following day, Bruce and I sat in our swimsuits next to the pool with ten other guys, listening to an instructor talk about the test. The test began with swimming laps that were timed. Bruce and I were fast without showing off. We were shown how to assemble a set of pipes into a specific configuration. We were given a chance to practice. A weight-belt was placed around our waist, we were handed a net with the disassembled pipes and given a blacked-out face mask. For once, my poor eyesight would not be a problem. We were led to the pool, told to jump in and reassemble the parts in the correct order before coming up for air.

I jumped in and sank to the bottom of the pool. I could hold my breath for three minutes and putting the parts together was a piece of cake. I received written acceptance within a month. Bruce got one, too. I thought I was going to become a modern day "Frogman" and do something as daring as flying jet fighters like my father. Bruce and I started making plans to room together at EOD School and we joked about disarming M-80 firecrackers.

"What happened? Why'd you change your mind about EOD?" Bruce asks as we grab a Coke in the Nha Be O' Club.

"My dad talked me out of it. He's career navy. Said EOD will never lead to command of a ship. He convinced me to go for destroyers; said the smaller the ship, the more responsibility I'd have. He said as an ensign, I'd be in charge of a coke machine on an aircraft carrier. But on a destroyer, I could be Officer-of-the-Deck, in charge of the entire ship while underway."

"And how was it?"

"He was right about destroyers. But sometimes during those two years, that coke machine sounded pretty good. And what about you? What's EOD like?"

"Best duty in the Navy. I get extra pay for EOD and on top of that, combat pay for Vietnam. I do six months in-country, six months in Guam. Even get combat pay while in Guam."

"Shit, I couldn't do it—too scary."

"After eighteen months of training, learning how to disarm bombs, we always detonate—we never disarm. When we find a booby trap or VC explosives, we attach a satchel charge, light the fuse and run like hell. It's a piece of cake. And more fun than M-80s."

It's great to see Bruce. I tell him about my collision at sea and about the Bo De River, and he tells me about the bars in Guam. We agree to get back together whenever possible and we exchange addresses.

"Shit, I got a patrol!" I say. "My crew is probably wondering what happened to me." We say our goodbyes: a fair wind, a following sea and all that navy stuff.

"Where you been?" Taylor asks. "We got a sector to patrol." I can tell he's pissed. The only thing worth telling the crew is that "Moon River" is the call sign for our Officer-in-Tactical-Command.

"OTC is a lieutenant commander," I say. "Nice air-conditioned room—full of radios and charts."

Hoffman gets us underway and we head into the Rung Sat. Taylor is in the gun tub, Gnau on the aft fifty, Stancil and Moison behind the cabin. The Dong Tranh River is narrow, like a one-lane road, hardly a river. The banks are covered with trees and the depth is shallow. It's dark; we could easily get lost in this maze of twisting narrow rivers and mangrove swamps. I'm starting to feel like a target.

I see a brief flash of orange light on the dark horizon, then hear a heavy boom that rumbles for a long second. I'm alarmed by the sound, but it stops. It's not like aircraft dropping bombs or the beginning of an attack.

"What was that?" Hoffman asks from the pilothouse.

"Taylor, see anything?" I call.

"Back toward Nha Be," Taylor says.

"This is Moon River," I hear over the Prick 25, "set General Quarters." I don't understand who Moon River is calling.

We head back to Nha Be at full throttle. As we approach the base, I smell smoke. I see bright floodlights on the pier and the helo-pad. I see men with stretchers as we pull alongside the fuel pier.

Mike Haecker is a Yeoman, 3rd Class.

"A PBR found a six-foot mine floating in the channel," Mike says. "Commander Knowles had jeeps form a semicircle and shine headlights toward the beach while the mine was pulled out of the water. EOD personnel were called. At least four, maybe six Seabees brought more lights. An EOD officer opened a cover on the mine to check it out.

"I just reached the helo-pad when the mine exploded. I froze and my boss, Walker, pulled me down to the ground. Took a piece of shrapnel in my leg. Seconds later, water spray came down, then sand, then bigger chunks. Everything started hitting the helo-pad. Chunks of metal started landing right near us. It was tops and hoods of jeeps. When things quit falling, we both got up and ran toward the smoke.

"I was first to reach one of the jeeps. The driver was moaning, but he was mostly okay. I used the jeep's radio to call 'Moon River.' The OTC already sounded General Quarters, thinking we were under attack. I ran down to the PBR piers and managed to get some help bringing stretchers. We put the PBR commander into one of the stretchers and headed to sick bay.

"The 'Doc' was freaking out, trying to administer to a dead sailor. A corpsman had to shake him out of it. Men were suffering from the concussion of the blast. At least seven men—sailors, EOD, Seabees—basically vanished."

I hadn't seen Bruce in two years, and now he's dead.

"He was so relaxed," I say to Gnau, "happy, joking two hours ago." I want to turn back the clock, warn him, remind him of what he said: we *never* disarm.

"There's nothing we can do," Gnau says.

"VC are watching," Taylor says. "They're somewhere nearby."

We resume our patrol, eager to find any VC lurking in the Rung Sat. Taylor is ready to shoot anything that moves. So am I.

I've never known someone that died. I don't understand the feeling, the tightness in my stomach. I keep thinking about Bruce's comment, "We always detonate; we never disarm." I wonder what changed his mind. I think about career decisions, some already past, and I suppose some yet to come.

Chapter Fourteen

Admiral Zumwalt

It's 0500 and PCF 67 is waiting for me at the dock. I've only had four hours of sleep since returning from Nha Be. I stayed up too late, thinking about Bruce and thinking about today's operation, going back into the Ca Mau.

Moison pulls in the tire fenders as we get underway with other boats. Our three Swifts are headed south, a long transit to rendezvous with the *Washoe County* off the Ca Mau Peninsula. PCF 59 has the lead and Rocket is OTC in PCF 53.

"Got some stuff for the ninety-five boat on the way down," Gnau says.

I spot PCF 95 at 0630 off the Ham Luong River mouth and we pull alongside to transfer mail and engine parts. Ked Fairbank is the skipper. I'm not sure which he wants most, the mail or the parts. We continue on with the other boats and rendezvous with the *Washoe* for fuel.

"Special op is cancelled," Rocket says. "New orders. We're going to the Bassac—blockade operation at Dung Island." Taylor acts disappointed, but I'm not. The Ca Mau is not a fun place, but neither is transiting the coast, another three hours back the way we just came.

Before we pull away from the LST, I'm ordered to embark a reporter, Liz Trotta from NBC. I can't believe the reporter is a woman, here in a combat zone. She seems so young and unafraid. She's wearing green fatigues, white tennis shoes and she's going with us. My crew goes out of their way to make her comfortable as we head north. They're excited to talk to a round-eyed American woman.

I feel relief as we slip into the river after the pounding seas. The Bassac splits into two channels with Dung Island in the middle. I call it "Shit Island," but I don't tell our reporter that. Our three boats split up and surround the island, making sure no one can escape while a Vietnamese Army force, call sign "Arabian Knight," searches the island from north to south, as if beating their drums in the jungle and driving a lion toward a net.

"Intelligence report," I say to Liz, "says Viet Cong have a prisoner of war camp on the island. Maybe they're holding Americans. This is worthwhile."

We maintain our position, watching for sampans and waiting for something to happen. Liz is sitting on an engine hatch, scribbling on a small notepad. I think she's bored. It's now dark and we're directed to slip into the Tran De, a small canal winding through the island.

"Do not fire unless fired upon," I say to Gnau and Taylor. "We got friendlies and maybe POW's in the area." I dread the thought of a firefight with our own men. We throttle down to five knots, hoping our engines can't be heard. I feel claustrophobia from the narrow banks and thick trees, like being in a smelly closet that has too many clothes.

I try to act brave in front of this female reporter. Liz has a nervous laugh. I think she's gotten over her boredom. I give her credit for courage, being here with us.

"Shut down the engines," I tell Hoffman. We drift in a weak current. It's near slack tide and we come to rest against a tree branch sticking out from the bank. Taylor has the Starlight scope up in the gun tub, watching for sampans or swimmers. The absolute quiet is unnerving. I need to pee, but I'm afraid Liz will see me. I think I hear something in the bushes. I realize it's my whiskers rubbing on the collar of my flak jacket. The radios are turned down as low as possible. I depress the Prick 25 mic just to hear the "click" to make sure it's on.

The darkness heightens my senses. I smell a brief whiff of something sweet. It's orange blossom or maybe honeysuckle. Maybe it's Liz. Seems strange to notice little things when I'm scared.

It's 0545 and the tide is ebbing. The current pulls us away from the bank and we light off our engines and exit the river. Another night of quiet tension. No firefights and no POW's.

Rocket detaches us to refuel and we transfer Liz to his boat. My crew shakes her hand, wishing her luck. She has remarkable courage.

We find the *Mercer* (APB 39) anchored thirty miles upriver in the Bassac. She's a self-propelled barracks ship, offering bunks for men when they're not out chasing the VC. The *Mercer* is busy nursing a host of river boats: PBRs and Mobile Riverine craft, all filling up from this waterborne gas station. They're out of ice cream.

As we prepare to return to Dung Island, Mother calls. She gives us something else to do, another canal, another night looking for VC. At midnight we sneak into a canal, our engines at low rpm. We're trying to be as quiet as possible and reach what we think are the right coordinates. It's impossible to know for sure, but it looks right on radar. It's damn dark.

We push into the mud, shut down the engines and take turns on the Starlight scope. Its eerie green light takes getting used to, but we can see anything and everything as if it were broad daylight. The scope destroys night vision. I only use my left eye when it's my turn, so my right eye can still see in the dark.

Taylor has the scope now, sitting in the gun tub. Taylor refuses to let anyone take his place on the twin-fifties. Stancil is sitting with his M-16 in the bow rope locker, his little foxhole. No one else wants that position and neither does he; it's lonely up on the bow.

I'm at the chart table and Hoffman is sitting at the helm watching the radar. Thick foliage pushes against our hull. I hope it's too thick for a hand grenade to find its way aboard. I feel the VC are near—afraid they're sneaking up on us. The feeling grows with each hour.

Taylor squats down in the bottom of the gun tub and whispers, "Sampan crossing—right to left."

"Wait," I whisper, "watch for more."

"I see 'em!" Hoffman says, looking at the yellow sweep of his radar. "Halfway across—moving fast." I reach up and switch on the searchlight.

"Taylor, don't let 'em get away—shoot!" Taylor's fifties light up the air in front of me, tracers following the beam of light. I can see an orange muzzle flash coming from over the pilothouse. "Hoffman, light off the engines! Let's go!"

Hoffman backs us into the canal and floors the throttles, heading toward the crossing. It's more than seventy-five yards away, almost the length of a football field. We weren't close enough.

We reach the crossing and slow to a crawl. I shoot pop-flares, one after another. The light illuminates an empty sampan drifting in the canal.

"VC jumped overboard," Taylors says. Taylor and Gnau unload a devastating assault into the trees on each side. Stancil riddles the sampan until it sinks. I'm sure the VC are close, but they don't shoot back. We loiter only a minute. With flares drifting down, we are now a very bright illuminated target.

"Get us out of here," I say to Hoffman. He spins us around and heads for the river. I switch off our light, thinking any minute we're going to be ht. As Hoffman drives through the canal, I have to remind myself to breathe.

We reach the Bassac, drive a few miles upriver, drop anchor and wait for morning.

"I hate ambush operations," I say to Gnau. "Kept wondering if the VC knew we were there, wondering if they were sneaking up on us."

"Impossible to be in the perfect location," he says, "—to be close enough."

"Any closer—might have been us ambushed."

It's a relief when morning light comes. It's January 21st and Mother sends a message.

"Return to base," Hoffman says. "Message is not just to us; it's to all of Coastal Division 13."

"Is the war over?" I ask Gnau.

"That'd be nice, but I doubt it."

We exit the river and head north. I see another Swift Boat exiting the Co Chin River. Matt D'Amico is the skipper and we run together, talking on our private frequency, questioning the message. We see another Swift Boat coming out of the Ham Luong, but it's too far ahead for us to catch up.

The Cat Lo docks are crammed full—fifteen Swift Boats—like a department store parking lot the day after Thanksgiving. I've never seen this many Swift Boats at one time. A duty yeoman is telling the officers to meet at the O' Club. It's the only space large enough for all of us. Rumors are flying, but still no one knows anything.

"We've been ordered to stand-down for twenty-four hours," Commander Streuli says. "Tomorrow morning we'll take two of our boats to Saigon for a meeting with Admiral Zumwalt."

The O' Club has never had so much business. Cigarette smoke is thick as men bang dice cups on the bar rolling for drinks. The rowdy din of conversation is nearly incoherent. We're happy to have a day off, but we still don't know what this meeting is about.

We're underway at 0700 and cruise up the Long Tau toward Saigon. We pass two minesweepers dragging the river. As we pass Nha Be, I give a quiet salute to my friend, Bruce McFadyen, a man with more courage than I will ever have.

Our decks are crowded with officers in khakis. I hope we don't get into a firefight. With this many officers, all used to giving orders, I'm sure we would confuse the crew. It would be a Chinese fire drill.

Our meeting with Admiral Zumwalt is at his residence. The expansive living room is empty of furniture except for rows of folding chairs. The tiled floor and bare walls echo every sound. We mill about waiting and then boat drivers from An Thoi arrive—Coastal Division 11. It's great to see Bob Elder, the first time since we parted in Cam Ranh Bay.

"Where's Harwood?" I ask Bob.

"You haven't heard?" Bob says, and then he pauses. "Jim got hit in a firefight—lost a leg."

I don't know what to say and just stare at Bob's eyes. I can't believe I'm hearing this. We all trained together, came over together, Jim, Bob, Doug, Mike and me.

"When?" It's all I can think to ask.

"November, on the Bo De. It was bad. Five Swift Boats—the VC were waiting. Harwood was on the seventy-two boat. Two other guys were hit: Joe Ponder on the thirty-one, a gunner's mate, and Bob McGowan, quartermaster."

"When was it? In November?"

"Twenty-fourth."

Bob walks away as I stare at the floor, thinking about what it would be like to be wounded, to lose a leg.

I hear, "Attention on deck," and all thirty-five officers snap to attention. In walks not just Admiral Zumwalt, but General Creighton Abrams, commander of all Allied Forces in Vietnam. I realize this is a pretty high-level meeting. In my opinion, only the president could make it higher, but then—maybe not.

The general begins speaking, telling us how important our job is and how well we are doing. I realize I'm only half listening, thinking about Jim Harwood. He was wounded three days after I was on the Duong Keo. That seems eons ago. God, I don't want to lose a leg.

I try to focus on what the general is saying, but he's finished. He steps down from the podium and I think this is incredible, a man of his rank, just here to warm up the crowd.

Now Admiral Zumwalt is speaking. I can tell he's not referring to notes, his words flowing with confidence, without pause. I am startled by the contrast between the admiral and the general. The admiral is talking to us as if he doesn't realize he is a god, as if he's just a mere mortal like us. I listen to his voice as much as his words. I feel he has genuine empathy for the risks he asks us to take.

"You are fighting the VC on their terms," Admiral Zumwalt says, "on their schedule, in their choice of rivers and canals." I appreciate his honesty, acknowledging the frustration we have, the difficulty in finding the enemy before they find us.

"Hanoi," Admiral Zumwalt says, "is boasting they control the Ca Mau. We are going to demonstrate they control *nothing*. We are going to continue engaging the VC on every river and canal. We are going to annihilate their sanctuary—pacify the Ca Mau. We are going to make it safe for the South Vietnamese to return to their homes."

Although I don't like my role, waving the flag and acting like a target, I hold this admiral in the greatest esteem; he's not making excuses, not apologizing, not lessening the risk or failing to recognize the loss of lives we have endured. This man has the strength of his convictions.

I now realize this meeting's purpose. It is not to announce a new strategy; it is to say that the course we're on will not change, and I suspect it will intensify. I am only disappointed that Admiral Zumwalt has not given us some concrete plans, some high-level strategy or low-level tactics that I can hold on to.

Captain Hoffmann takes the podium and presents statistics: ammunition expended in November compared to December and this month so far. He's saying our numbers are down and suggests we can try harder. I have to admit, my morale has suffered and my enthusiasm for harassment and interdiction has been slack. The frequent messages telling me what targets are now off the list and then a week later they're back on has confused and frustrated me. I feel the White House is acting like these brief overtures are doing something more important than simply giving the VC an opportunity to regroup and rearm.

I move my head behind the boat driver sitting in front of me, trying to avoid direct eye contact with Captain Hoffmann, afraid he'll suddenly ask me to stand as an example of poor navigation.

One of the Swift Boat skippers tells Captain Hoffmann that we could use more firepower.

"I'll see what I can do about that," Captain Hoffmann says.

It's quiet as we head back to Cat Lo. I keep thinking about Harwood. I wonder how much it hurts when you get hit, if morphine helps, if the pain stops when you go into shock.

We're all tired from months of patrols—so tired. This day off is nice, but tomorrow we're underway again. Nothing has changed.

Chapter Fifteen

R& R

Everyone's talking about Tet, the big Viet Cong offensive in February '68. Fortunately, I missed that. I heard it was rough. The VC and North Vietnamese Army launched surprise attacks throughout South Vietnam.

The Paris Peace Talks are in the news.

"Hanoi's talking about a truce," Gnau says. "February 15th to the 22nd. Maybe we could take a few days off."

"It's in honor of the Tet lunar holiday," Toi says.

"It's a ruse," I say. "VC don't have anything resembling a code of honor. I don't think they'll go along with Hanoi's plan."

"That's still two weeks away," Stancil adds, "and the Onan died again."

"Can you fix it? I'm tired of heating C-Rats on top of the engine block."

"Can't get parts."

"Out of beans with Vienna sausage too," Hoffman says.

Baby Fats has recovered from his wounds and is now the maintenance officer. While I'm pissing and groaning about spare parts for our Onan, the duty yeoman hands me a page labeled, "Rules of Conduct for US Servicemen on Rest and Relaxation."

"Where do you want to go?" the yeoman asks, ticking off R&R locations.

"When?" I ask.

"Depends on where you want to go. It's like a lottery."

"Hawaii."

"Nope, that's only for married men. Where else? Hong Kong?"

"No, I want to see round eyes."

"How 'bout Sydney," he says and gives me a wink. "They got round eyes."

"Okay, put me down for Sydney. When do I go?"

"Depends; it's a lottery. What's your second choice, just in case."

"San Francisco. If that doesn't work, surprise me."

"San Francisco's not on the list, but Cam Ranh Bay is." He laughs as if he's heard some stories about trips to CRB. Yeoman humor.

As I walk out of the office, I see Chuck Mohn, a Swift Boat skipper, walking toward me wearing green fatigues and tropical boots. I almost laugh.

"What the hell you doin' in jungle greens?" I ask. "Goin' on a special op?"

"We got orders to wear these, all Swift Boat crews. You too. You better get over to supply before they run out of extra small sizes."

I can't find anyone who knows why we are switching from khakis and blue jeans to greens and jungle boonies. Everyone has an opinion.

"It's to keep the VC snipers from knowing who is skipper of the boat," Matt D'Amico says.

"My crew has that same question," I say, but I think this is strange.

I get my new outfit, *medium size*. I've just been promoted to full lieutenant and the base tailor, an old Vietnamese man, sews black lieutenant bars on the collar. He gives me a smile and calls me Dai Uy that sounds like "Die We."

"Step up from 'Trung Uy'," Toi says. "You're a big man now."

I like my new two-tone jungle boonies; they're lighter than my "Black Shoe" boondockers. They have patches of green fabric—lets my smelly socks get some air.

"What do you think of my new outfit?" I ask Gnau. "Pants got neat little pockets on each leg."

"Can't think what to put in 'em," he says, looking at his pants.

Our boats are given new outfits too; rope boarding nets for the bow.

"They're ugly," Moison says. "Make us look like tugboats."

The nets, together with our greens and boonies, drive the rumor mill into high gear. None of the rumors are attractive. I'm beginning to think D.C. Current's theory about carrying troops was not so farfetched.

I see Taylor smiling. I haven't seen him smile very often.

"Look what we got," Taylor says. He points to two M-60 machine guns. I realize Captain Hoffmann didn't forget a request for more firepower.

It's my day off and I call Sepia headquarters. I plan to rendezvous with Bob Anders in Vung Tau for a Thai dinner. Bob is dead, bludgeoned in a

Vung Tau alley two nights ago. That's all anyone knows. I feel like getting drunk and go to the O' Club. I wonder if Bob's death was an act of war or murder. I'm not sure it makes a difference—he's dead.

"Are South Vietnamese worth American lives?" I ask the bartender. "Do they want us here, fighting for them? Do they care who wins this war?"

"Pipe down," someone yells at me.

I think about the Vietnamese army soldier giving me a ride to the base the last night I saw Bob.

"Maybe he saved my life, maybe *he* cares," I say. But no one knows what I'm talking about.

"Think you've had enough," the bartender says.

"We get orders—areas to avoid," I say. "Next week, they're high priority targets. Who's running this war?"

Two boat skippers lift me off the bar stool.

"Think I'm gonna be sick," I say. I feel my body being rushed out of the bar. "Not just good guys against bad guys," I say, and then I throw up.

I wake with an enormous hangover. I feel embarrassed for the verbal diarrhea I spewed last night. I'm glad my crew didn't see me. After voluminous cups of coffee, I scribble a note to Dad. "Did you ever feel confused about war?" I rave about my impressions of Admiral Zumwalt, but omit anything about Bob. It's too appalling to describe. I don't mention Bruce either. I don't want to confirm that his advice about EOD was so foretelling. I want his advice, but I don't want him to be right all the time.

My day off is over. It feels better to be standing in the pilothouse, underway, away from Cat Lo and away from Vung Tau. Seems strange to be wearing fatigues and new boonies, even stranger to be wearing clean clothes.

Our patrol on the Co Chin River is routine, busy inspecting sampans all day. Stancil is now a hero; the Onan is working, our galley functional. Gnau tries baking a chocolate cake. It comes out flat.

"Think I forgot something," Gnau says.

"Yeast?" Moison offers.

"Oh yeah, yeast."

We eat it anyway.

"It's like chocolate pizza crust," Taylor says.

Board and search operations are interrupted—new priority orders from Mother: "Rendezvous with two Swift Boats, embark Vietnamese army troops." She gives us the coordinates. I chat with two other Swift Boats on the Prick 25. All of us have been diverted from patrols.

"We've already been on patrol three days," one of the skippers says.

"*Xin Loi*" I say. ("I'm sorry" in Vietnamese, "Tough shit" in Mother Sepia talk.)

We arrive together at the rendezvous and beach our boats to a welcoming of Vietnamese soldiers and US Army advisors.

"Now we know for sure," I say to Moison, "the reason for bow nets."

The troops look clumsy, climbing the nets with full packs. Moison and Stancil help pull them aboard. Our fantail is packed with fifteen Vietnamese soldiers as we head farther upriver. Gnau reminds them to keep their heads below the fifty-caliber barrel as we enter a canal single file.

"What's our objective?" Taylor asks.

"We're just a water taxi with guns," I say.

Stancil is sitting in the bow rope locker, manning his new M-60. Moison has the other one perched on top of the cabin. Someone radios a command and each boat beaches in the mud. The troops jump off and sink to their bellies. They're mired in a thick-gooey muck, like black Mississippi mud.

"Someone forgot to check the tides," Gnau says. The mud stretches thirty feet from the water to high ground. At first it's humorous, but it's not.

"If the VC catch us like this," I say, "these men won't have a chance." The soldiers can't move; they can't even turn around; they're stuck like tar babies in a briar patch.

In a slow creeping struggle, some men make it to dry ground and begin cutting stalks of bamboo and nippa palm leaves, laying them out over the mud for men to crawl on. Stancil throws a line to one soldier to help pull him loose from the mud while Moison squirts water from our saltwater hose to help break the suction.

I have a sudden diarrhea attack. I run back to the fantail and grab a bucket. I need to be close to the radio and return to pilothouse. I sit on the edge of the gunnels, balancing the bucket underneath me and holding onto a railing. I feel humiliation with my pants pulled down like this. My crew and the crews of other boats can see me, but there is no way I will use the head down below, not in this canal. Fear of a B-40 rocket is stronger than dignity. Hoffman is sitting at the helm. I know he can hear my flood splashing into the bucket.

"Oh shit, Mister Erwin," Hoffman says, "you got the wrong bucket. You got our lobster bucket."

"*Xin Loi*" I say. "It was urgent. Just grabbed the first bucket I saw."

It's taken an hour for the Vietnamese soldiers to assemble on the bank. It is an understatement to say the element of surprise has diminished. Perhaps in an effort to not lose face, the troops with their command and advisors move off into the jungle, and three Swift Boats return to designated patrol areas. I'm not sure where the soldiers are going or how they plan to get back to their base.

Two boats plead with Mother for relief and we search for the VC—and a new bucket.

Our three day patrol is over and we return to Cat Lo. My temporary orders and travel vouchers arrive for rest and relaxation. Officers without boat assignments will rotate as skipper aboard PCF 67 while I am away.

"Don't worry skipper," Gnau says, "we know the routine."

Moison has R&R too. I think he's going to Hong Kong. Allen Cott, another Swift Boat sailor, takes Moison's place. I catch an Army Caribou from Vung Tau to Ton Son Nhut Airport, and then a jet to the land of round eyes. I fall into quiet dreams and only wake as the wheels screech on the runway and the engines reverse.

I feel I've landed in San Francisco. It's hard to believe I'm in Sydney. Six-lane concrete freeways with on-ramps, off-ramps and overpasses are identical to home. Traffic signs have that same green color with white lettering. But it is alarming to be driving on the wrong side of the road. I fight the constant urge to yell at my taxi driver to watch out.

The overnight contrast from jungles, tropical heat and brown muddy rivers is a culture shock. I keep finding my mouth open, like a child at Disneyland.

My hotel room is simple, but to me it's a presidential suite. It has indoor plumbing and a huge bathtub. I can't resist the bathtub and fill it with steaming hot water. It's not muddy. The water is so hot that my skin turns red. I fall asleep as I soak. I towel off, turn on the TV and take another bath. And then a third. I feel an absolute compulsion to keep returning to the immaculate bathroom for another bath.

I call room service for more towels. I know it is strange, but I can't fight this need to feel clean. My civilian clothes seem foreign, as if they belong to someone else; I haven't worn them since San Diego.

The hotel bar fits my image of an Irish Pub: black and white tiled floor, a dark wood counter with huge handles for the beer and ale on tap, stools at chest-high tables, glasses hanging from brass rails, a mirror with an ad for Guinness Stout etched in the glass and the rosy cheeks of a rotund barmaid with a strange accent.

As I sip a glass of Guinness, a local patron strikes up a conversation.

"Are you on R&R?"

"I&I," I say. I explain the meaning. The barmaid laughs and buys me a local lager called Tooheys. It's nice.

"We got men in Vietnam too," the man says.

"And proud of 'em," the barmaid adds.

It's 5:00 p.m. and the barmaid introduces me to some of her female friends as they stop in for a drink. I guess my loneliness is obvious and one attractive lady accepts an invitation to dinner. I enjoy her company, the conversation about life in Sydney, conversation about anything except war.

"You have beautiful round eyes," I say. They're green and she has short black hair, a slim figure and a silky dress that clings to her best features. She smells like lavender. I feel more than casual attraction.

I think she feels some empathy for a guy who is a long way from home. Maybe she just wants to offer comfort to someone a little lost, as if I were her brother. For her it might be a small thing to share an evening; for me, it is therapy. I just want some company, not to be alone in a strange city. We have dinner and we part with nothing more than a hug.

I think about Chantal. I wish she could be here with me, but it's a long way from France. If we were already married, we could be in Hawaii. I don't think Hawaii is any closer to France. I feel so alone.

Maybe because I've been taught some manners or because I didn't make her uncomfortable, my only date in Sidney accepts another dinner invitation for my last night of R&R. She looks at me with sad eyes, as if she is wondering what my fate might be. The restaurant is quiet and the wood paneling has a warm, comfortable feeling.

"Are you afraid to go back?" she asks as we sip coffee and brandy.

"No, just wish they had clean water and bathtubs in Cat Lo."

Her gaze makes me uncomfortable, as if she has a supernatural premonition of my fate. After dinner, I walk her to her apartment door. We say farewell, *adieu* and I head back to Cat Lo.

I stare out the airline window as we approach Saigon. Sunlight glints off rivers and canals of the Mekong Delta. I feel a shiver run through my body; I'll be back on patrol tomorrow. I wonder if I'm afraid.

There are no flights this afternoon from Ton Son Nhut to Vung Tau and I'm given a bed at the BOQ, the Bachelor Officer's Quarters. I take the opportunity to find Colonel MacVey. He's a good friend of my dad's and he's like a second father to me. I know he is in Vietnam, attached to Air Operations.

The desk sergeant at the BOQ makes some calls and then hands me the phone. On the other end is Colonel MacVey. He seems overwhelmed with excitement and gives me directions to his office.

Colonel MacVey's greeting is exuberant. I feel slight embarrassment, seeing his staff sergeant grin. I'm a Navy Lieutenant, gripped in a tight

embrace by a full-bird Air Force Colonel, but I think the sergeant understands we are "family." And we are. The colonel lived across the street from
our house in Colorado Springs. He and Dad are both fighter pilots. I loved
listening to their stories as they drank Bloody Mary's on Saturday morn-
ings, sharing stories I long ago memorized. The stories grew with each
telling. I watched them use their hands to dramatize aerial feats of combat.

Colonel MacVey releases me from his bear hug.

"Goddamn, a full lieutenant," he says.

"As I recall, you tried to recruit me."

"To the better service! We're going to dinner." We ride bicycles from
his office to the O' Club.

"Are we winning this war?" I ask after the first drink.

"Hell yes," the colonel says with a booming voice, "and it'll be over
before you know it—if the politicians stay out of the way. We're being told
what targets to hit, which ones to avoid. Christ, we can't run a war this way."

"I haven't figured out where the Vietnamese stand. Do they want us
here?"

"Damn right they do, least the ones here in Saigon do. How is it on the
rivers?"

"Some do, I guess."

"I mean your patrols."

"We're just a target to draw 'em out," I say. "Cat and mouse game."

"I know. I've kept tabs on you for your dad, checking Sea Lord
reports. I talked to your dad not long ago—over the Mars net. Call him if
you can, and talk to your mom; she's worried."

"She'll be more worried when she hears my news. I met a girl."

"Well, that's a good start."

"She's French. I met her on shore leave while I was in the Med. I flew
back over to see her and to meet her mom. We're engaged."

"Congratulations! That calls for another drink."

"Not sure how Dad will feel. He's pissed at the French, their lack of
support for NATO."

"Shit, give your dad credit. He's pissed at the French government, not
pretty girls. But think about your career. It's hard being a navy wife; hardest job in the world. You'll be at sea—she'll need to be strong. More careers
are made or broken by the strength of a wife. Your dad and I know. Think it
through." Colonel MacVey sounds so much like my dad, skimming over
emotion, basing decisions only on objective criteria.

There are no streetlamps and it's dark as the colonel leads me to the
Officer's Quarters. My little bicycle headlight is useless. I'm drunk and
struggling to keep up as he makes a right turn. I cut the corner. My front

wheel goes down into a ditch. I hurl through the air and land on my back with a loud thump. I'm fighting for breath.

"Hey sailor, you need training wheels?" he says and laughs. It's a great evening. It feels good to see someone from a place I remember as home.

I have a very sore back and too hung over to look out the window on the flight to Vung Tau. The first thing I learn in Cat Lo is that my boat is in the skids being repaired.

"While you were enjoying R&R," Hal Amerau says, "PCF 67 was patrolling a canal off the Co Chin. Submerged mine was detonated under her keel."

Allen Cott was filling in for Moison while Moison was on R&R. Allen said he was sitting in the bow hatch.

"When the mine detonated," Allen says, "I got catapulted into the water like a circus cannon." Allen was recovered, wet, shaken and bruised, but otherwise just upset that someone was trying to kill him.

I hear another part of the story from Stancil. The large saltwater strainer for the starboard diesel ruptured from the explosion. The engine room was flooding; PCF 67 was sinking. Stancil was ingenious. He closed the through-hull valve, shutting off the gush of water. He kept the engine running, and the cooling pump kept sucking, pulling saltwater from the bilge and pumping it over the side. It gave the crew enough time to beach the boat at nearby Coastal Group 35 at the mouth of the Co Chin.

Swift Boats always monitor a common radio frequency on the Prick 25. PCF 22 heard the call for help. She immediately came to the assistance of PCF 67, making sure the crew was safe and protected from VC attack.

"After the flooding was controlled," Hal says, "PCF 57 arrived and escorted your boat back to Cat Lo."

There is a casual feeling between Swift Boat crews: When you're on patrol, you're on your own. But when a boat is in trouble, saving her is a singular priority. It is unwritten, unspoken, a feeling we all share, an instinct to protect one another—as if we are siblings.

I inspect the hull of my boat and there's no sign of damage. I'm impressed that the hull is so clean—not one barnacle. The bottom is not painted with "red lead" like other Swifts; it's an experimental tan-colored paint.

"Don't never completely dry," a maintenance sailor tells me. He rubs his hand over the paint. "Stays soft; don't give them barnacles somethin' to hold onto."

I look at the polished brass propellers. There's not a nick in them. I see Taylor approaching, smiling as if he's glad to see me.

"You missed a lot while you were gone," Taylor says.

"Yeah, I heard."

"You missed Tet. The base was mortared. Scared the shit out of everyone. No real damage though."

"It's great to be back," I say. "You should see the bathtubs they have in Sydney."

PCF 67 is repaired and she has a new one-year warranty. Our first patrol is in the Co Chin. We pull into Coastal Group 35 and talk about the mine.

"Local Ruff-Puffs captured a thirteen-year-old boy," the Coastal Group advisor says. "Intelligence Group got his confession. VC planted the mine in the Tra Vinh Canal. Two wires were led up the bank and into the trees. The boy was told to sit by a twelve-volt battery and wait. When a Swift Boat passed a point that lined up with two trees marked with cloth, he was to attach the wires to the battery. Failure to do this meant death to his father."

"What happened to the boy?" I ask.

"I don't know."

"I love my father. I would have done the same thing."

"Yeah, me too."

"Bow nets make us look like tugboats."

Mississippi Mud

Stuck like tar babies in a briar patch

Chapter Sixteen

Irma La Douche

Rivers and canals are critical to the Viet Cong's need for mobility, stealth and speed, to move men and supplies throughout the Delta, to organize and control their operations. Their sampans are powered by two long-shaft motors mounted side by side and their speed is impressive, crossing a river in minutes, a canal in seconds. If we're not looking, they're gone.

We hunt VC at night, patrolling rivers to convert their secret alleys into barriers. The Viet Cong counter with ambushes, hiding in mud bunkers or concealed in a blind as if waiting for mallards. Their patience is a tactical weapon, especially with B-40 rockets. I often wonder who is the hunted. But if the VC don't shoot or if they don't run the rivers, we never see them. So we accept our role as paper targets, and we keep looking.

Typhoon winds and intimidating storms of the dry season are gone and the wet southeast monsoon has announced its arrival with days on end of torrential rain. Hot humid air is unbearable. Mattresses on PCF 67 are vinyl-coated. Gross pools of sweat collect in the depression my body creates on the mattress. My green fatigues are like damp dishtowels and Gnau's paper charts are starting to mildew. Taylor bitches about keeping his guns and ammo dry, and he bitches about trying to catch the Viet Cong.

"Let's set up our own ambush," Taylor says.

"Where?" I ask.

"Some canal, hide in the bushes. Gotta get creative." He points to a small canal on the chart. "Here," he says.

Gnau looks at the chart. "Don't know about this," he says, shaking his head. "Pretty tight." The canal looks narrow, but I think Taylor's idea is worth a try.

"Okay," I say, "we'll do it tonight."

There's no moon on this airless night as we patrol the winding Vam Co River, a tributary of the Soi Rap. Even though it can't be seen, the moon's gravity has pulled brackish water upstream from the bay of Vung Tau. These two elements of nature, rain and tide, have raised the Vam Co nine feet; the riverbanks and rice paddies have disappeared under water.

Our Decca radar is incredibly acute at capturing the sharp image of anything floating on a smooth river, such as a clump of vegetation, a swimmer or a VC sampan. But it is useless for navigation tonight. The swollen Vam Co no longer resembles the chart—our radar can't tell us where the river is deep.

"Slow to five knots," I tell Hoffman. He watches the fathometer, feeling his way over the dark river bottom. We creep into the canal Taylor suggested. Hoffman kills one engine, but the clinking metal flap covering the exhaust still makes too much noise, like a clapper ringing a dinner bell for the VC.

Water level in the canal is so high that branches normally above Taylor in the gun tub are pushing in through the pilothouse door, creating a floral arrangement on my chart table.

"Shut 'er down," I say to Hoffman.

"Lasso that branch," Gnau tells Stancil. We sit patiently buried in trees along the bank, watching for VC. Taylor peers through the green light of the night scope. I take turns with Hoffman, watching the amber sweep of our radar.

Muggy heat suffocates the pilothouse. Rank odor leaks from my sweat-soaked flak jacket, as if some decaying rodent was inside. I have my face buried in the boot covering the radar—the inverted rubber cone hiding its light. The small opening stinks with sweat from my face. It seems hours have passed. I fight fatigue, shaking my head like a Labrador Retriever stepping out of a lake.

"Something's coming," I say softly.

"What?" Hoffman asks.

"Sampans! One, two, shit! A whole string of blips," I say. Wet hair on my neck is electric.

"Sampans! Get ready," Hoffman whispers to the crew over his phone.

"Wait!" Taylor says, "I see 'em in the scope; it's a mobile riverine force. HOLD YOUR FIRE!"

"Shit," I say, "what if *they* fire? Turn on the running lights."

Hoffman flips a switch and little red, green and white lights sparkle around the gun tub. I make a radio call on the only common frequency I can think off.

"This is Elbow Golf six-seven," I say. "I have running lights on, M-R-F unit approaching me. Acknowledge."

"Roger, see ya. Out." The radio voice is so casual, like not a care in the world. Thank God they answered my call.

Goliath monsters emerge from darkness. They're painted black-olive-green. These mobile riverine vessels look like Civil War Monitors with huge gun barrels. They're sheathed in welded rebar armor and they're low to the water; their bow waves a bare ripple. The canal is narrow and I stand on the gunnels as they creep pass our port side, a mere ten feet between us. The only sound is a deep throated rumble, like a grizzly sleeping in a cave.

I don't see any faces. Where is the driver; where are the men? It's as if they're empty ghost ships. They keep coming and coming, passing in a slow, single-file formation. One after another they pass, and not a voice is heard, not a "howdy," nothing.

"Doubt we'll see any Viet Cong tonight," Taylor says.

"Not with that flotilla around," Gnau says.

I don't go to sleep, but my pucker factor drops several notches.

Morning light captures rivulets of water draining from the bank. The moon-driven tide has ebbed. Our bow line to the tree branch is nearly straight up and Taylor stands on top of the pilothouse to untie it. We leave the canal in the same direction as the silent armada last night, and enter the Vam Co. I'm eager to be relieved from patrol.

"River's at least nine feet lower than last night," Gnau says. Rice paddies are still draining and now covered in rich savory mud.

We're driving downriver at twenty-five knots and I spot an apparition, like a painting by Salvador Dali. It's a distorted image, but I know what it is: a Swift Boat in a rice paddy, easily fifty feet from the river and nine feet higher than the water. It's sitting in the mud like a cake decoration. It's both comical and obscene, bringing a chorus of sorry laughter from my crew.

We look at this pathetic sight, a beautiful gunboat built for speed, now mired in mud. Hoffman maneuvers our bow into the bank. It seems odd to stand on top of the pilothouse in order to be eye level with the Swift Boat skipper who's knee deep in muck.

"Need any help?" I ask. I laugh, looking at this stranded sailor on the side of the river highway, as if he's blown a tire and doesn't have a spare. The skipper is Ensign Doug Martin. He smiles, but I can tell he's trying to deflect the greatest embarrassment of the century. I see a water buffalo grazing near the bow of his boat and the local militia standing in the distance, a defensive perimeter guarding PCF 98. The militia soldiers are smoking cigarettes and laughing.

"We had a blip on the radar," Ensign Martin says. "Thought it was a sampan. Maybe our radar was on the wrong scale. We were going pretty fast."

Without him telling me more, I can visualize the scene, his face in the boot of the radar scope, the image of the river looking narrow and normal. A flip of the range dial would have alerted him, would have told him that something was wrong with the banks of a small river now seeming to be over a mile wide. Checking the range dial would have told him the rice fields were flooded.

"I guess the blip you were chasing last night," I say to Martin, "was that dangerous and ferocious water buffalo." We both look at a young boy leading the buffalo away.

"VC buffalo for sure," Taylor says.

"Tax collector," Gnau adds.

Going aground is not uncommon for Swift Boats in Vietnam. In some cases it reflects on navigation, as it reflected on me when I hit a shallow reef. In other cases it's from inexperience or aggressive behavior. Last night I suppose it was all three.

"How is he going to get his boat back in the water?" Stancil asks.

"Won't be easy. Almost fifty-thousand pounds," Moison says.

"Maybe wait for another high tide?"

"Won't be enough."

"Can't wait to see the message he gets from Captain Hoffmann," I say.

"Maybe a free ride in a "Bug-smasher," Moison suggests.

The Viet Cong build bunkers along the rivers, constructed of massive tree trunks, packed and covered with mud. The mud dries and these bunkers become virtually impenetrable. Fifty-caliber machine guns and flame throwers have little effect.

The Mobile Riverine Force is close at hand. They present a unique solution to the ensign's dilemma: They have "Irma La Douche." The name is a play on words: *Irma La Douce* was a movie about a Paris prostitute who had a passion for everything that makes life worth living. That certainly fits the attitude of the Mobile Riverine Force. Someone changed Douce to Douche. It's both French and English, a word for taking a shower or cleaning a body cavity with a jet of water.

Irma is different from the "Zippo." The Zippo is a napalm cannon that shoots a stream of liquid fire. Irma shoots water. It's an incredible weapon: A water cannon. Irma has two massive pumps that suck water from the canal, each through a six-inch hose. The pumps blast a stream at 3,000 psi through a two-inch Titanium nozzle. The piercing torrent dissolves mud bunkers as if sandcastles on a beach and the water velocity could rip a man in half.

Irma is called up to the frontline to save the stranded Swift Boat before its guns, propellers and rudders are stripped by VC, as if it were parked in a Detroit alley.

The water cannon carves a trench in the mud below the stern of the Swift Boat and a steel cable is attached to her stern. Irma pulls with twin diesels, while a constant stream of water lubricates a channel, breaking the suction as the Swift Boat is inelegantly pulled backwards into the river.

The sight is not befitting this lady, a graceful Swift Boat with a passion for life, being dragged by her derrière through mud as if punishment for adultery. The scene could only be worse if rice farmers stood by, stoning her hull.

We head back to Cat Lo. I can't wait to get to the O' Club with some wonderful stories to share. I enjoy a day off, but I'm exhausted from retelling my water buffalo story as each skipper comes in from patrol. It's time to get underway before I get a sore throat.

Chapter Seventeen

Co Chin River

The Mekong River is a cultural solvent, a highway of commerce and the Mekong Delta is downtown, a big downtown. Swift Boats and the smaller PBRs are the traffic cops. Like all traffic cops, our work is ninety percent boredom. We check water taxis full of people commuting to work, fishermen coming home from the sea, farmers taking rice to market, women shopping for vegetables, and we look for the Viet Cong who are trying to slip by, moving men and supplies, and collecting taxes in their brutal and fanatical way.

Narrow, ungainly sampans fight the current with their long-shaft outboard motors. The current is strong, at least six knots, sometimes more. We have to watch our wake to prevent capsizing the fragile Vietnamese craft as we speed through the river. The sampans are often overloaded and too heavy; easily rolling over and losing precious cargo, like husbands and wives and children.

We have become a bit lazy patrolling the Co Chin River and anchor midstream, just beyond range of VC rockets. It's easier for everyone. We use our siren and arm waving to hail the traffic, telling the sampans to check in. Sometimes a shot across the bow is needed to get their attention.

My crew has become like family, more than just combat sailors living together on a fifty-foot patrol boat. It's early morning and I decide to treat them to a special breakfast, a little morale boost. I need a kitchen utensil, something I can use to cut a small perfect hole in a slice of bread. A shell casing is the answer.

I load the M-79 grenade launcher, aim in a deserted part of the river and fire the round. I watch it arch like a softball. The grenade explodes in the river, leaving a white frothy patch on the brown water. Taylor leaps out of the pilothouse and swivels his head in every direction, scanning the river.

"Where'd it come from?" Taylor yells as he scrambles up to the gun tub.

"*Xin Loi*," I say. "Sorry. It was me, just needed this shell casing."

"Jesus, Mr. Erwin," Taylor yells, "let us know when you're going to do that again." It was dumb to shoot the grenade without warning my crew. I realize I'm starting to act nonchalant, too casual with the power of weapons. I'm not acting like an officer, more like a teenager playing with M-80 firecrackers.

I think Taylor is more pissed about sitting anchored in the river than about the M-79 explosion. He'd probably rather be in some murky canal, looking for trouble. Well, he won't be pissed much longer—his tour is up in a week. He has refused to take a job on the base. Maybe he wants one last gunfight with the VC before heading home.

The grenade explosion has disturbed the local traffic. Sampans— those that were about to slip by without stopping—are now headed our way, worried I might fire another round. I can tell we're going to be busy, flooded with customers and checking ID's.

Taylor sits in the gun tub looking grumpy while Gnau, Hoffman, Stancil and Moison handle our visitors. I should be on deck with my crew, but instead I go into the galley to prepare a breakfast treat. I lay out six slices of bread and cut a hole in the center of each one with the empty shell casing. I save the little circle of bread. The skillet is hot and I plop in some butter, brown the bread and drop an egg in the hole of each one. In a second I flip them over and in a minute they're done: A fried egg in the center of toasted bread. I fry the six center-cut pieces in butter and breakfast is ready.

"Who wants an 'Egg-in-the-Basket'?" I yell. I'm not overwhelmed by a rush of comers. I think everyone is still upset with my cavalier attitude, shooting without warning. Gnau is my second-in-command. He saves my embarrassment, forcing everyone to eat, whether they like it or not. As we sit eating, sampans keep coming alongside, interrupting our meal. I hate cold eggs. We should have a sign on our railing that says, "Closed. Out to Breakfast. Come back later."

At noon we pull up anchor and spend the afternoon patrolling the river. I see some kids in a sampan. Each one has a paddle and they're laughing as they struggle in the current, trying to get back to the riverbank. They remind me of kids back home. I have a quiet laugh, wondering if their dad knows they have his boat out for a joy ride.

It's now dark and we anchor again. I wonder what's for dinner. My evening is interrupted by the radio and Hoffman deciphers the message. Mother has sent new orders.

We rendezvous at an outpost at 0500. It's still dark as we pull alongside a small wooden dock. A strange, fierce-looking team of Asian soldiers with a SEAL advisor clamor aboard. SEALs are the most dangerous combat fighters the US has ever created. Their name is from the environment they operate in: sea, air and land. The SEAL officer briefs me as we head toward a canal.

With his painted face and shaved head, the SEAL looks as battle ready and hardened as any man I've ever seen. He moves his body with liquid motion as if walking on a spongy mat, and he talks to his men in a cryptic language. I don't think it's Vietnamese. I can tell Taylor is impressed with the SEAL leader, the way Taylor stands close to him during our briefing, the way he looks at the .45 and grenades this man carries. Taylor would make a good SEAL.

I stare at the men the SEAL has brought aboard. They're wearing green-black camouflage fatigues, small packs at the back of their waist, and bandoleers across their chest with hand grenades. They have canteens at their waist and machetes in a scabbard at their hips. They're not wearing flak jackets or helmets, only wide-brimmed camouflage hats with a loose string hanging at their neck.

"Vietnamese?" I ask the SEAL, nodding toward his team.

"Chi-com mercenaries," he says, "and a few Montagnards. They're mostly father-son pairs. Best fighters that money can buy. If shooting starts, they don't drop to the ground; they first look to see where the firing is coming from, then they attack. They're smart; they don't make a frontal assault. They flank the enemy or attack from the rear."

"They look tough," I say, and realize it was an absurd understatement.

"These guys collect ears," the SEAL says, "not numbers for some body-count record. I tried to stop 'em, but they think that's how they're paid."

"Is it?"

"No. They get the same pay every month. They hate the Vietnamese, but they hate the VC more. Maybe that's really why they take the ears. VC are scared shitless of these guys."

I notice one of the soldiers has a strange-looking machine gun with a handle on top of its barrel.

"What's that?" I ask.

"Stoner," the SEAL says. "Thousand rounds per minute. Nice to have when we need it."

"What do you want us to do?"

"Just insert us where I tell you, then get out of the canal. We'll find our way home. If I change my mind, I'll call."

We enter the canal as a weak morning sun begins to heat the air. Hoffman looks nervous, chain-smoking and fidgeting with the radar. Gnau and Moison have not said a word for the past hour. I can see the back of Stancil's head through the pilothouse window as he sits on the bow with his M-60, scanning the trees. If anyone has a reason to be scared, it's Stancil. It's likely the first rounds from an ambush will come from ahead.

Every canal we go into is different and every one is the same. Like all other canal operations, I worry about the depth and being able to turn around, and I worry about what I can't see beyond the trees, ferns and bamboo that push out over the banks. I feel like I'm in a forest of repulsive spider webs, ready to snare the unwary. And like all the other canals, I'm scared of being ambushed.

But this canal op feels different—ominous, serious. The canal has a foul stench, like a rotting compost of wet, cut grass. I'm sure the VC are close or we wouldn't be taking these fierce mercenaries into this canal. The SEAL keeps looking at his map and then at my chart, and then at the radar and then all over again. This man is precise. He wouldn't let his men be dumped in the mud.

"Pull onto that bank," the SEAL says, pointing to a small clearing on the left. The bamboo is thick like a barricade, but fewer bushes. For once we can see at least fifty feet beyond the bank. I watch the SEAL and his men jump off the bow, but they're not running. They're moving slow, and like the SEAL they move with purpose and stealth. Not a word is spoken as their camouflage blends into a green jungle and they disappear like phantoms.

I feel a shiver. I'm glad these fathers and sons are fighting for us. I doubt they have a sense of duty to anyone besides their own tight-knit family—their temporary loyalty to the highest bidder.

"Wonder where they live in the off season," I say to Taylor.

"*Is* there an off season?"

We've carried so many squads and troops into canals and then they disappear. We seldom see them again. I wonder what happens to them and how they get back to their base. Maybe sometimes they just become someone else's collection of ears.

I'm exhausted. Every time we go into these canals, adrenalin tenses every muscle in my body. We loiter in the river just beyond the canal in case we're needed, but no one calls.

No one calls but Mother Sopia.

"Jesus," I say to Gnau, "one of these days I'm going to smash that radio. Mother never calls just to ask, 'How are you doing; are you okay?' "

"Another mission for tomorrow," Gnau tells the crew. "Another Swift will join us."

I'm designated Officer-in-Tactical-Command, my second time to be in charge of an operation. It's first light as we rendezvous with the other Swift Boat midstream in the Co Chin. We tie alongside each other and drift in the current as we study the chart and talk about the operation.

"Standard op," I say. "Explore the canal, show the flag, take targets of opportunity under fire and exit." The skipper and I review the "what ifs." Actually, we only discuss one "what if" —an ambush.

"Canal's dead-ended," the skipper says.

"If ambushed," I say, "we'll run through it, get clear, turn around and come back full bore—no hesitation. Okay?"

"Sounds good, but might need tweaking."

"One last thing," I say. "Unless we're taking fire, no shooting without my Okay."

The canal is as wide as my boat is long and curves like a serpent; I can't see beyond each bend. A jungle forest hugs each bank, too thick to see more than twenty feet past the water. I wonder if anyone lives here. We're single file with my boat in the lead, trolling at ten knots.

Hoffman is sitting at the helm, gripping the throttles. I'm betting he'd like to be going faster. It is dangerous to go slow and dangerous to go fast. At ten knots, we're an easy target, but the VC have started stretching wire across the canals, just about throat level to a man sitting in the bow hatch. Stancil hates being on the bow.

We come to a bend to the left and reach a fork where two canals come together. It is now wider where the two join, more room to turn around if needed. A clearing has been cut and a small village is clustered on the far bank. Five bamboo shacks with thatched roofs are clustered in a haphazard fashion in the center of the small clearing. The village looks deserted, but two sampans with long-shaft motors are beached in the sand.

"Stop," I tell Hoffman. I wave to the other Swift Boat to hold up. We sit at idle for a minute, scanning the village.

"See any bunkers?" I call up to Taylor.

"Don't see any."

I don't know what to do. If we were taking fire, I'd know what to do. This stillness is unnerving.

"I see smoke," Taylor says. "Got to be someone there."

"All right," I say to Hoffman, "take us in slow. Beach to the right of the sampans."

I call the other Swift on the Prick 25. "We're going to pull up to the beach. Stay back and cover us. If a firefight starts, don't fucking hit us."

"Roger that," the skipper says.

Hoffman slips our bow gently onto the sandy beach and we sit. I can hear Taylor rotating his turret from one side to the other and back again. I'm guessing his trigger fingers are as sweaty as mine.

"What are we doing?" Taylor asks. He keeps swiveling his twin-fifties. It's a good question and I'm not sure, but I don't say that.

"Gnau, Moison," I say, "grab your M-16s. We're going to take a closer look." The three of us jump off the bow, spread out abreast and walk in a crouch toward the center of the village. I step on the porch of the hut to the left and look inside. There are several beds, a low table and some clothing. I turn around. Gnau and Moison are gone.

"Gnau, where are you?"

"Over here," he calls, but I can't see him.

Moison comes trotting from around the far side of the hut on my right. He opens fire, raking the hut waist high with his M-16.

I drop to my knees. "Where are they!" I yell.

"Didn't see anyone, just hosing it down," he says.

"Cease fire, cease fire right now!" I'm livid. "Gnau, you okay?"

"Yeah! Who's shooting?" I spot Gnau crawling on his stomach from the far side of the hut that Moison was shooting at.

"Moison," I say, my voice shaking in anger, "you could've killed Gnau!"

I study the path that Moison's bullets must have taken. Bamboo huts don't stop bullets. Gnau is lucky he's not dead. This is dumb; we weren't trained for crawling through villages. I look back at my boat and wave to Taylor, then stick up my thumb: we're okay. The other Swift Boat has pulled up to the beach. The skipper and two men are running toward us, two with M-16s and the skipper with a shotgun.

"You okay?" the skipper yells. His men are fanned out to the right and now down on one knee, their guns pointing at the shacks. They look disciplined.

"We're okay; hold your fire."

I hear hysterical yelling and crying. In a second the village is flooded with women and children, all crowding in close, surrounding us. There must be at least twenty and more keep coming.

"Where'd they all come from?" Gnau asks. Kids are screaming. Mothers are yelling at their kids and yelling at us. It's a madhouse! Our crews are spinning around in circles, scared the VC are among this throng or somewhere ready to pounce on the chaos. This scene is out of control.

"Shut up, shut up!" I yell, but the raucous racket grows with more intensity. The mothers are pushing up against us, kids clinging to their black pajamas. I raise my M-16 and fire a round into the air. "Shut up!" I yell again.

The screaming grows louder. It's total pandemonium. I have no control over this mob of women and children.

"Back to the boats," I yell over the mayhem. "Slowly, walk slowly, cradle your guns." We walk backwards, keeping our eyes on this frantic village of frightened women and children. They follow us toward the beach, as if a reproach for scaring them for no reason.

We scramble aboard and back our boats into the canal. We spin our stern around and race away from the village at full throttle, banking into each turn of the canal, each hull up on-step as they plane through the water. No one is looking back. God, what a cluster-fuck. It is a miracle no one was shot or killed.

We reach the wide Co Chin River and I begin to breathe normally again. We pull our two boats together as we had done before. I call the skipper into my pilothouse.

"That was the weirdest, scariest situation I've ever been in," I say.

The skipper laughs. "Virg, you dumb fuck, what did you think you were doing, getting off your boat?"

"I haven't a clue, and I'll never do it again."

"Where'd all those women and kids come from?"

"Spider holes, tunnels, who knows?" I say.

"There weren't any men. Think we should've checked the tunnels?"

"Are you serious? You gonna crawl down into one of those?" We both laugh, a feeling of relief, glad to be out of the canal and away from those screaming kids.

"Think it's a VC village?"

"Maybe," I say, "but how would we know if no one is shooting. This op is over." I pause to think. "Okay, I'll write up the report and you are released. Go scrounge up some lobster."

We pull away from each other and Hoffman steers us into the current as the other Swift Boat heads downstream.

"I have no idea what to say in my report," I say to Gnau.

"Maybe skip the part about going ashore?"

"Good advice."

"Skipper," Taylor says, interrupting us, "there's a sampan, drifting toward us—looks empty." There's an outboard motor at the stern, but it's not running; its propeller shaft out of the water. The sampan is being carried by the current.

"Could be a trap, loaded with explosives," Taylor says. "Want me to hose it down?"

"Wait," I say.

Taylor stands on top of the pilothouse, trying to get a better look.

"Some people in it," he says.

We maneuver alongside, each man with an M-16, ready to shoot at the slightest provocation. Four people are lying down, head-to-foot, the full length of the sampan, a man, a woman and two children. Moison and Stancil lean over the side and grab the side of the hull, holding it alongside. The woman mumbles something we can't understand. I wish Toi was with us. The kids look afraid. The man at the rear has his eyes open, but he doesn't move.

"Must be sick," Gnau says.

"I'll get 'em," Stancil says as he climbs into the sampan. He lifts the children, one at a time, and Gnau pulls them aboard. It's awkward, trying to hold the sampan steady and not tipping over. It's clumsy getting the woman aboard. The man is almost lifeless. Stancil gets him to a standing position. Taylor leans down and lifts the man aboard as if he were a feather.

One child, a boy about five, has on dirty white pajamas and a scarf over his head. The girl, maybe a year older, is wearing a black blouse and black scarf.

"Dehydrated," Moison says, and gives them some water as they sit on the engine hatch. "Kids look better off than the father."

"Maybe malaria," I say. "Where were they headed?"

"Who knows," Taylor says. "Guess the outboard ran out of fuel."

"Cast off the sampan," I tell Moison. The women starts crying, pointing to the sampan as it drifts away. I regret we let it go, but a sampan seems insignificant right now.

We head downriver to Coastal Group 35 and drop them off for medical attention. Taylor and Gnau carry the old man in a stretcher. Hoffman and Stancil carry the kids. The father seems close to death.

If Taylor hadn't spotted them, the sampan would have drifted in the river and out to sea. I look at the two children. I doubt they would have survived very long without water.

This war seems so crazy: mercenaries, screaming kids, drifting sampans and always wondering: Who is the enemy?

We have a day off in Cat Lo and I have a letter from Dad. He's impressed with my description of Admiral Zumwalt. He mentions his good friend, Admiral Jim Holloway. "He helped my career," Dad writes, "gave me support for duty assignments, maybe even with promotions. I asked Holloway for a personal favor, to help your brother attend the Naval Academy. Randall has just been accepted, thanks to the admiral's recommendation."

Dad offers some unexpected advice. "Regarding your thoughts on a career in the Navy, this is something you must decide alone." And then, out of the blue, he writes, "Separations can in some cases save a marriage; in others it can be fatal to happiness. In your case, the one it will affect most has not been selected. Whatever you do, the most important decision you will ever make will be the choice of a wife. Her influence will be reflected throughout your life. Why do I have to get on a soapbox every time I talk to you? I think the last time I wrote to you, I was about to hire a marriage broker."

I read this paragraph over and over. What is behind his advice? I wonder if Colonel MacVey has told Dad about Chantal. But Dad writes that my choice for a wife has not been selected. Maybe he still doesn't know.

"Hal Amerau left while you were on patrol," Steve Hart says.

"Regret not saying goodbye," I say. "He was a great XO. Who replaced him?"

"Matt D'Amico. Turned over his boat to a new skipper."

"I like Matt. Conscientious."

"Nervous energy," Steve says with a laugh.

"After almost a year, everyone gets that way, edgy, extra attention to detail."

"Being off patrol will probably help him relax. It would sure help me."

Hal is not the only one who has packed his going-home box. I join my crew on the boat and sit on the ready-service locker. It's a comfortable seat, even though it's full of mortar rounds. The crew is milling about, doing odd jobs that don't need doing, hosing the deck, coiling a line, cleaning the cabin, all looking restless. Everyone is aboard but Taylor. It's a day I haven't been looking forward to. I sense the crew feels the same way.

"He's up at the ops shack," Gnau says, "getting his orders and travel vouchers."

Taylor comes back to the boat to say goodbye. He's stoic as always, as if he's wearing an iron mask, but I suspect he's going to miss his shipmates. Maybe he'll even miss me. We've had our differences—about how aggressive we should be in the rivers and canals. Taylor is a fighting man and a man who wants to win this war. I respect him for his courage, for his reverence for navy tradition and for his smart military bearing.

"You're as fine a sailor as I have ever met," I say, shaking Taylor's hand.

"Take care of these guys, skipper." We all shake his hand and he's gone. Goodbyes are hard for men.

Swift Boat crews, as small as they are, become family, knowing the intimate details of one another's life, the idiosyncrasies that can't be hidden, the good and the bad, like knowing who snores or who hates Gnau's chocolate cake—things like that.

Under any circumstances, it is difficult for someone to step aboard a small boat and be immediately accepted as part of the crew, especially a crew that has experienced combat, canal operations and boredom together. It takes time.

It's even tougher to replace someone who is especially missed, like Taylor. Dan Hudson, a gunner's mate, steps aboard facing all these barriers, whether he knows they exist or not. It is to his credit that he seems to be aware that shared trust is something that evolves. It can't be rushed—it just happens at some point in time.

Michael Stancil, driving from the aft-helm

Turning around in a tight canal takes patience

Chapter Eighteen

Death of a Swift Boat

The faces of my men look tired. Beads of sweat are dripping off tanned shoulders and backs as they load ammunition belts into their guns. I'm proud of these men, a crew I trust with my life, and I'll trust them again today. We're preparing for the largest operation I've been a part of since arriving in Vietnam seven months ago.

This scene must look like an armada, thirteen Swift Boats rising and falling in ocean swells alongside our mother ship, a Landing Ship Tank. She's anchored ten miles off the Ca Mau, a peninsula infested with Viet Cong guerrillas. The LST has two Seawolf helicopter gunships on her deck, poised to launch when needed. I watch twenty Vietnamese Marines on our fantail look for someplace to sit without being in the way.

Thirteen Swift Boats. Three is the largest number I've seen for an operation.

"Not a lucky number," Stancil says.

"Should be twelve," I say. "The forty-three boat wasn't scheduled to join us."

Don is skipper of PCF 43. His boat is tired, needing repair. But Underwater Demolition Team Thirteen, another ominous number, with their thousand pounds of C-4 explosives, has mistakenly boarded PCF 43. Or maybe Lieutenant Don Droz encouraged them. It doesn't matter now, they're aboard. Don is arguing with Captain Hoffmann, saying his Swift Boat is okay.

"Hell, take my place," I think to myself, and then laugh out loud at my morbid humor.

"What's so funny?" Stancil asks.

"Enthusiasm." Stancil waits for me to say more, but I let it go. Stancil squints his eyes at me, as if acknowledging I'm a little off balance, and returns to his task, loading an ammo belt into his M-60 on the bow.

"You know, skipper," Stancil says, "this rope locker wasn't designed for a gun position."

"I need you on the bow. Need another gun facing forward."

Stancil hates being on the bow, afraid he'll be the first to get hit because he's the farthest forward. The crew has always looked out for Stancil, maybe because he's the youngest. Taylor cumshaw'd—as we call stealing in navy—some old flak jackets and lined the inside of the rope locker to give Stancil a feeling of protection, at least for his legs. I wish Taylor was still with me now.

Stancil and I hear Don Droz pleading with Captain Hoffmann to let him go.

"Going to be a big operation," I say. "Guess Don doesn't want to be left behind."

"I saw Captain Hoffmann an hour ago," Stancil says. "He said to a bunch of us, 'You men are the scruffiest group of sailors I've ever seen, and the most effective.'"

"Captain Hoffmann is only tough on the outside."

A thick cloud of diesel exhaust from so many idling engines is making me gag. This is the dry season and the afternoon heat is depressing. If we can just get underway toward the river, I'll feel better. The fumes, the heat, the waiting are intolerable.

"All right, God damn it, you can go," I hear Captain Hoffmann tell Don. "But you drop the UDT guys at the first insertion—then you get the hell out of that river."

Capt. Hoffmann knows Don from operations in Cam Ranh Bay. I think he likes Don's professional demeanor and his gusto. Capt. Hoffmann, with his deep gruff voice, rules his Swift Boats with intense scrutiny. He has over eighty Swift Boats and a skipper for each one, and more than 350 enlisted men manning his boats. Hoffmann has a penchant for details, details most officers wish would go unnoticed, such as how much ammunition we expend or when we go aground. Hoffmann knows the name of everyone wounded and everyone sent home in a box. Too many names. Captain Hoffmann knows our weaknesses, our strengths and our drive to win. He wants to win this war. I think Don does too.

Captain Hoffmann gives the command. All thirteen boats pull away from our nest, the *Westchester County* (LST 1167). Finally, we're heading for the Duong Keo River. It's late afternoon, April 12th.

I remember being in this river five months ago. We were naïve back then, and luckily, no one was killed in the brief firefight. But now we have thirteen Swift Boats, ten UDT guys and 240 Vietnamese Marines from the 6th Battalion. And we have two Seawolf gunships ready to scramble from the deck of the LST. We are loaded for bear. This armada seems virile—not invincible, but damn formidable.

"I wouldn't want to be the Viet Cong today," I say to Gnau.

My boat is third in this long, single-file column, stretching out a half-mile as we head in at fifteen knots, slowed by the heavy load we all carry.

It's tricky getting into this river, maneuvering at the entrance to avoid sandbars in the shallow water. We've slowed even more, now just a crawl. There's no doubt in my mind that Charlie can see us coming. This would be a good time for the VC to hit us as we struggle to find deep water, like blind men with white canes, tapping the bottom to find our way in.

"Lead boat hit a sandbar," Hudson says from the gun tub. "Next one too."

We creep past them, taking the lead. Hoffman watches the fathometer and steers a wide 'S' turn, following an invisible channel into the river. With his seventh sense, Hoffman can tell just when to turn left or turn right. I watch each boat follow our course, my anxiety urging them to get closer. I don't want to go into this river alone.

"Check your guns," I yell to Hudson in the gun tub and to Gnau back on the fantail. I hear Hudson cock each barrel of his twin-fifties. Two rounds clink as they drop to the bottom of the tub. I knew his guns were already cocked. I reach back into the tub and toss the rounds over the side. Live rounds can be dangerous if hot brass rains down on them. They can "cook off" from the heat—a little explosion and maybe some shrapnel.

"Water just got deeper," Hoffman says. "Twenty feet, now twenty-five, still getting deeper. We're in."

I feel that pucker factor, that feeling I get each time when I'm first to enter a river. I try to rationalize. The VC usually hit the second or third boat in a column, almost never the first. Maybe this is a smart move.

"This is Dipsy-Doodle." I'm startled by the sound of the radio. "First five boats, beach—port side."

Dipsy-Doodle is the call sign for Commander Yost, our OTC, our Officer-in-Tactical-Command. Someone creates these god-awful call signs, making it harder for the VC to say the words, harder for them to send false messages from their own radios. I've heard 'em try. I laughed as they tried to pronounce a call sign last month, saying "Brack Widow Spryer." Hearing their voice almost makes them sound human.

Hoffman spins the helm and we push our bow into black mud on the left side of the river. Four other boats beach to my left. Vietnamese Marines jump off our bows, run to the edge of the tree line and set up defensive positions. Other marines explore beyond the clearing and crawl through the trees. There's no gunfire and I begin to relax.

"Who's Dipsy-Doodle?" Hoffman asks.

"Coast Guard Commander," I say. "He's a newbie, still cherry. He's on the thirty-one boat."

All the skippers and crews on this operation are experienced in river operations. It seems strange—Dipsy-Doodle, a Coast Guard Commander with only a week in-country is leading this river incursion. I'm not sure I could be OTC today. My largest command has been three Swift Boats. I gave simple commands: Go into the canal, show the flag, act like a target, return fire—lick your wounds. Piece of cake.

Yost, using his comical Dipsy-Doodle call sign, just sent his message in the clear, no code to disguise our movement.

"Virg," Jack Chenoweth yells from his boat, "I just spent a day with Yost. He picks up the mic and sends out messages in the clear. I told him he should encode those messages. Know what he said? Says to me, 'Takes too long.'"

"Guess we don't need any codes."

"Christ," Jack says, "Yost is broadcasting our intentions to the entire Viet Cong."

"I don't think the VC needs a radio to know we're here."

While I and four other boats sit beached in the safety of mud, eight Swift Boats pass my stern, continuing up this brown-ugly river.

"What's going on?" Gnau asks.

"Pincer strategy," I say, half believing I understood the morning briefing. "We got a hundred marines ashore right here. Those eight Swifts will insert their marines farther upriver. If our intel is right, the marines will have the Viet Cong boxed in on two sides. We prevent a river escape. Seawolf gunships will fly in, close Charlie's backdoor. We are gonna tighten the noose today!"

Gnau and I watch the eight Swift Boats head upriver. Bill Shumadine's boat is now in the lead. Bill's a good skipper, has his shit together. Don Droz on PCF 43 is tail-end Charlie, his boat struggling to keep up. Don has either forgotten or is ignoring orders to drop off the UDT guys and exit the river. I watch Don's boat disappear around a bend in the river. There's nothing for me to do now but wait.

I compose a letter in my mind to Dad, describing this awesome sight of so many Swift Boats gathered to engage the Viet Cong. I know he'll appreciate this image. It will remind him of sitting in the cockpit of his F9F Panther with the canopy slid back, waiting to launch into the wind toward North Korean targets. He'll be proud of me. Keeping this letter from Mom will be my only risk. She always worries.

I keep looking at my watch. The minute hand seems stuck. It's 1730. I hear distant explosions and crackling gunfire, now more explosions and constant gunfire. The radio speaker erupts with screaming—high-pitched voices, all trying to talk at once, voices cutting each other off in mid-sentence. Someone just keyed their microphone to talk, machine gun fire in the background blotting out any comprehension of what's being said. Voices are yelling, conveying total confusion.

"You hear that?" Gnau asks. "What's happening?"

"Quiet!" I say. "I keep hearing that same voice. Someone's trying to get through." I hear a boat calling for help, but she's getting interrupted. It's a weak garbled signal; radio discipline is nonexistent.

"Everyone's talking on the same frequency," Gnau says.

Twice I hear, "...the forty-three boat..." No one is responding to this call.

"Christ," I say, "am I the only one who can hear this?"

"Can't just sit here," Gnau says.

"Let's go, get 'er underway!" I say to Hoffman. He backs us into the river, pivots our stern and slams the throttles to full rpm. Thank God, Chuck Mohn is pulling his boat into the river with me. Our two boats are now racing toward the firefight. I'm scared. I know we are heading into certain hell. For the first time since arriving in Vietnam, I put on flak pants. I'm already wearing my flak jacket and helmet. I continue to monitor the radio as we race upriver.

"Dipsy-Doodle, this is Seawolf 14," I hear one of the pilots say. "We're orbiting overhead." I'm surprised how fast these helicopter gunships have reacted.

"Seawolf 14, this is Dipsy-Doodle. We have some wounded. I want you to medivac my wounded."

"This is Seawolf 14; we're heavy. We'll have to unload our rockets before we can take on any wounded."

"This is Dipsy-Doodle. Uh, understand, just unload 'em anywhere north of the river." I imagine a chaotic scene of crippled boats and wounded men from the constant, urgent radio voices. Dipsy-Doodle must be feeling overwhelmed. He has two Seawolf gunships with rockets and M-60 machine guns flying overhead, but he hasn't ordered a strike at the ambush site.

"...fifty cal...one mile...high and dry... over."

"There it is again," I say to Hoffman. "You hear that?" This crackling voice is trying to get through, broken sentences begging to be understood.

"This is Dipsy-Doodle; understand one mile from this position. Which way and what is it? Over."

I hear the voice call again, repeating the message.

"This is Dipsy-Doodle; understand we have the forty-three boat, one mile back, high and dry, is that correct? Over."

"Affirmative," a voice says, confirming Don Droz is in trouble.

"Okay, we'll send someone back to tow her out."

Now I have the full picture. Chuck and I are almost there, minutes from the ambush. Shit! A B-40 rocket just passed behind our stern, exploding in the river. I hear Gnau on the aft fifty, firing into the trees. We keep going.

"Dipsy-Doodle, this is six-seven with the one-oh-three," I say over the radio. "We'll be there in two minutes." I'm not sure I'm heard. Radio transmissions are frenzied, confused.

"Six-seven and one-oh-three," Dipsy-Doodle says, "return and pick up your marines, then come upriver. Insert them short of the ambush."

Chuck is in the lead. I watch him bank to port as he turns around. He's heard the message. We've been ordered *not* to dive into this maelstrom of death. Following this order is wrong. Don is in trouble and we're almost there—we can help him.

Should I turn around? Following orders in the heat of battle is paramount. I wait for Chuck to pass down my left side. I'm scared.

"Turn around," I tell Hoffman. I know I will live with this memory, accepting an order that should be ignored—and guilt for feeling grateful.

I hear an excited voice from one of the Seawolf gunships over the radio: "Fifties, fifties, quad-fifties. Jesus, we're taking fifties!"

"Dipsy-Doodle, this is Seawolf 16," a calmer voice says. "We're taking fire– request permission to unload in that area." He's following the "Rules of Engagement." Rule Number Two: Get permission first—then unleash your fury.

"This is Dipsy-Doodle; we have a boat high and dry, one mile back. Can you provide cover?"

"This is Seawolf 16, roger, I see him—I'm over him now."

I hear Seawolf 14 and 16 talking to each other, identifying the Swift Boat and the VC location. One of them says something about green smoke. Maybe one of the men on Don's boat has thrown a smoke grenade to mark their location.

"Okay, let's hose 'em down," one of the pilots says. I hear pulsing machine gun fire over my head and over my radio.

I listen to the radio as Chuck and I race back to pick up our marines. Dipsy-Doodle is trying to organize a rescue for Don's boat. He asks Bill Shumadine and the skipper of another boat to go back and help.

"Need a minute," Bill says. He's trying to transfer the dead and wounded onto the riverbank. The other skipper declines; too many wounded to man her guns.

Chuck and I beach our boats. I stand on the bow looking at Vietnamese Marines sitting in a large circle. Each man has a bowl of rice in his hand, calmly eating with chopsticks.

"Get aboard, now! Now!" I yell, franticly waving at them. They barely look up, ignoring me as they continue to eat. I'm shocked by their indifference.

I spot an American Marine advisor and scream, "Get these assholes aboard my boat—*now!* There's been a fucking ambush!"

The American Marine says something to his Vietnamese counterpart and then yells back, "They won't move without direct orders from their senior officer. He's upriver with Dipsy-Doodle."

"Well, call him, goddamn it, call him!"

Chuck is having the same problem. I hear him call Dipsy-Doodle over the radio to get someone to command these Vietnamese Marines to board our boats. Radio messages are flying back and forth between Dipsy-Doodle, the US Marine advisors and the Vietnamese command. Nothing is happening. I listen to the exchange with disbelief.

Five fully functional Swift Boats sit useless; one hundred marines sit eating lunch, all of us sit without direction while Don and his crew fight for their lives. There's nothing for me to do but endure a vicarious firefight over the radio.

I hear Bill Shumadine report he is headed back to help Don.

"Wait," Dipsy-Doodle says, "I don't want you to go alone."

It's been twenty minutes since Dipsy-Doodle told Chuck and me to turn around. My attitude is evolving into bitter resentment. Clearly, I'm rationalizing guilt for my lack of conviction, but I'm angry.   Maybe Dipsy-Doodle feels guilt, too. I hear him talk to Bill as they head back together to rescue the forty-three boat.

I hear Dipsy-Doodle report they have recovered the wounded from Don's boat. I hear him requesting a medivac.

"Dipsy-Doodle, this is Dread Advice. Where do you want me to put down?"

"Come along my port side," Dipsy-Doodle replies as if responding to a boat. He has no idea who he is talking to. Dread Advice is a medivac helicopter. Someone, maybe a radio operator on the LST, called for airlifting the wounded. I hear one of the Swift Boat skippers take over, coordinating the evacuation.

"This is Latch," a voice booms over the radio. Christ! Latch is Captain Hoffmann's call sign. He's onboard one of the Seawolf helicopters. I listen in as Latch and Dipsy-Doodle exchange options.

Dipsy-Doodle suggests a retreat to the LST. "Do you concur?" he asks.

"PCF 43 is on fire," Latch says. "There's risk passing by if she explodes."

Dipsy-Doodle says maybe it's better to spend the night in the river. Each time Dipsy-Doodle proposes an idea, he says, "Do you concur?"

It's uncomfortable to hear Dipsy-Doodle, our officer-in-tactical-command, sound so undecided, to hear each proposal end with, "Do you concur?" Dipsy-Doodle tells Latch he is uncertain what the marines want to do. That's been clear to me for an hour. I hear someone say the wounded have been evacuated by shuttles of Dread Advice helicopters. Dipsy-Doodle decides to remain in the river and hunker down for the night.

Gnau and I avoid looking at each other as we listen to Seawolf pilots describe PCF 43 erupting like a volcano. They announce the event over the radio as if watching a fireworks display on the 4th of July. Their voices sound exuberant with descriptions of an awesome scene as a thousand pounds of C-4, mortar rounds and fifty-caliber ammunition explode in multiple detonations. It is the death of a Swift Boat.

I stare at Vietnamese Marines bivouacked on the beach in front of my bow. I wonder how they can be so nonchalant about what has happened today. This is their country. I wonder if they care who wins this war. If they don't care, why should I?

Gnau sets a watch rotation, someone manning the twin-fifties all night. I'm emotionally exhausted, but sleep is fitful. I keep waking up, thinking I hear gunfire and then realize it's a dream.

It's early morning and already it feels like a sauna as five Swift Boats motor upriver to provide assistance to our raped sisters. As we arrive at the ambush site, I see a melted aluminum skeleton lying on its side, as if the bleached bones of a whale, her ribs and backbone twisted by explosion and fire. It is the disfigured remains of Don's boat, Patrol Craft Fast 43, beached high on the river bank, the scene of yesterday's carnage. Each Swift Boat passes the remains in a somber procession.

I watch Vietnamese Marines combing the ambush site, looking for bodies. We find seven Swift Boats all huddled together where they spent the night. Stancil tosses a line to a sailor on PCF 51 as we pull alongside. She's lost both engines from a rocket into her stern. All of her windows are blown out from another rocket into the cabin.

Lieutenant Russ Puppe is the skipper. His face is pale. He looks like he's in shock, ready to collapse from exhaustion. Russ tells me his quartermaster, Thomas Holloway, was killed. Gnau was once the quartermaster on this boat. He left in December, just before Hartkemyer was killed. I wonder what Gnau is thinking now.

"I saw what's left of the forty-three," I tell Russ.

"Droz was killed," he says and then turns away.

We pass PCF 43 for the last time as we tow Russ's boat downriver. Progress is slow, like dragging a barge full of twenty-three tons of concrete. I hail another boat to come alongside. We tie ourselves together and the two of us tow the crippled Swift Boat out to the LST.

Twelve boats nest alongside the *Westchester County*. We're like babies in the arms of a wet nurse. I look at the faces of men. Their expressions are somber, everyone avoiding eye contact as they toss empty shell casings over the side and begin cleaning guns. One sailor sits on a locker full of mortar shells, his feet on the lifeline, gazing at the horizon. The smell of depression is as strong as diesel fumes.

It is the scent of survivors' guilt.

Captain Hoffmann assembles the officers in the wardroom of the LST for a debriefing. Bill Shumadine, skipper of the lead boat, describes the ambush.

"Claymore mines exploded from the riverbank," Bill says. "A Vietnamese Marine was decapitated. The explosion wounded my gunner. Another marine lost both legs." Bill trashes my theory about the third boat always getting hit first.

The next skipper says his boat took a B-40 rocket into the stern quarter, penetrating the hull as if it was tinfoil—shrapnel exploding in the engine room. The next two skippers report their bow gunners were hit from AK 47s. I hope Stancil doesn't hear this.

One of the skippers says speed was the only evasive action in the narrow river, but everyone in the room knows that a boat going twenty-miles per hour can't outrun a rocket. Each boat was trying to suppress enemy fire, all eight boats trying to stay together. No one said they thought of stopping short of the ambush or turning around; it just wasn't an option.

Each man gives his report in stoic monotone, as if recounting a meaningless dream. I listen, staring at the floor, wondering if I have the right to be in the same room with these men.

Tom Gilbert, skipper of PCF 38, isn't present to give his report. He was hit, taken out by Dread Advice.

"I saw Tom on the fantail after they exited the kill zone," Bill Shumadine says. "He was still conscious, in charge of his boat. I saw a crewman put a tourniquet on Tom's ankle. Crew was using their emergency tiller."

One of Tom's crew gives a report.

"PCF 43 was following us, last boat trying to get through. We saw her launch onto the riverbank. Our skipper turned us around. We headed back and got hit by two B-40s, one into the main cabin, one into the pilothouse.

Skipper was hit—miracle he wasn't killed. He tried to take control from the aft helm, but the steering was jammed at full left rudder and we lost the port engine. We just circled left."

They rigged the emergency tiller and got out of the kill zone a second time. They were unable to reach Don's boat in this devastating onslaught, but an unsaid message was clear—there was chaos. Chaos in battle is not extraordinary, but heroism is. I think about the incredible courage it took for Tom and his crew to turn around and go back into hell. If this had been an Audie Murphy movie, they would have annihilated the Viet Cong and rescued the stranded men. But this was real life on the Duong Keo River and it just didn't happen that way.

Only Tom and his crew knew that Don's boat was aground and their radio was damaged. I remember hearing their weak signal, their broken messages trying desperately to tell someone, anyone, that PCF 43 was in extremis.

A UDT officer who was aboard PCF 43 talks about their fight for survival.

"We had fallen behind. Everyone had already cleared the ambush. We got hit by a B-40. Our corpsman, Worthington, was killed, two of our team wounded. Second B-40 hit the pilothouse. Droz was killed. We were out of control and careened onto the bank directly in front of the VC bunkers. Boat was out of the water, engines still running full throttle. We were canted hard over to starboard. Couldn't use the twin-fifties in the gun tub or the fifty on the fantail. We set up defensive positions in the mud next to the hull. Had our M-60s; that kept the VC in their bunkers. We were exchanging hand grenades with the VC.

"Tom's boat came back, but got hit before he could reach us. Bill Shumadine and Dipsy-Doodle came in later and pulled us out. Lost two men, twelve wounded."

The wounded and dead on PCF 43 were evacuated, but the two diesel engines were still screaming at full throttle without cooling water. Fire erupted in the engine room. She was loaded with a thousand pounds of explosives that UDT 13 brought aboard. Rescue was only twenty minutes before she exploded.

It's my turn to add to the debrief. I begin to describe my frustration with Vietnamese Marines refusing to board our boats. I'm interrupted.

"I already understand why that happened," Dipsy-Doodle says. He says he doesn't need my report and the debriefing ends. We walk through a passageway toward the helo deck.

"Got our butts kicked," someone mumbles.

"Lost that battle, but we're winning the war," another voice says.

"Fuck you!" someone yells.

We all return to our boats to check on our crews. They could use some rest, but there's little chance of that. I wish I could talk to my dad, talk about yesterday, share my thoughts about war and about guilt.

I suddenly remember a carnival he took me to when I was ten years old. There was a Ferris wheel, a merry-go-round and cotton candy. There was a wooden counter under a tent and little boats moving across a painted ocean at the back of the booth. Dad paid a quarter and a man handed me an air rifle. He loaded five pellets.

The gun made a "pop" each time I fired. I thought I was shooting real bullets. I hit three boats and won a stuffed teddy bear. It wasn't a very masculine prize and I gave it to Randall; he was only three.

Patrol Craft Fast 43

Duong Kco River

Vietnamese Marines aboard PCF 23

VN Marines ready to jump off the bow of PCF 31

PCF 51 being towed out of the Duong Keo
Bob Gnau is on the right

Chapter Nineteen

Impressions of War

I remember my first impression of war. It was two years ago, June 5th, 1967. I was an ensign on the *Berry*, an old destroyer. We were steaming near Greece when the 1MC speakers announced: "General Quarters, General Quarters! Man your battle stations! This is not a drill, repeat, *not a drill!*" I raced to the gun director perched above the bridge. My helmet and sound-powered phones were there waiting for me.

I received calls from Mount 51 and then Mount 52, both reporting "Manned and Ready." These were our big guns, five-inch barrels. The gun director was a turret that rotated like a miniature gun. I sat inside and could point the big guns, automatically feeding information on where to shoot.

After an hour the skipper, Commander Dermody, addressed the crew on speakers located throughout the ship.

"War between Israel and the Arab States has begun," he said.

We stayed at General Quarters for another five hours. With fatigue a concern, the skipper downgraded us to Condition II, twelve hours on and twelve hours off. Weapons were manned and ready at all times. We were prepared to fight, but fight who?

That evening I couldn't sleep and visited the bridge. Commander Dermody was sitting in his chair on the starboard wing, staring at a dark horizon. There were only dim red lights on the bridge. I approached him with caution, not wanting to disturb his thoughts.

"Captain, request permission to ask a question." I was being as formal and polite as possible. I thought maybe my question would be dumb. He just barely nodded without looking in my direction.

"Sir, whose side are we on?" He took a minute to acknowledge my question and then looked me straight in the eye.

"I don't know," he said, and then he turned away. My life, the life of our entire ship, depended on his judgment. His answer was honest—but not comforting.

The next day I was sitting in the gun director, standing my twelve-hour watch, looking out at the beautiful azure Mediterranean. The sea was a mirror and reflected my feeling that this war had nothing to do with me.

Combat Information Center reported an approaching aircraft, nationality unknown, no IFF signal (Identification Friend or Foe). We knew it wasn't one of ours. I trained the gun director to the reported bearing and quickly spotted the plane. Using the fire-control radar, I locked onto the target. I flipped a switch and automatic controls took over.

The director slowly rotated, following the plane's movement. I had not engaged Mount 51 or Mount 52. If I had, our guns would also be locked on, trained on this plane. We didn't know whose side we were on. There was no sense being overt or provocative. I am sure that plane knew it was being tracked.

It was an Israeli Air Force plane, a slow, multi-engine, propeller-driven flying boxcar with camouflage paint. I felt no threat. She was not an attack aircraft. After circling a few times, she disappeared in the direction from where she had come.

The next morning, June 8th, the *USS Liberty* (AGTR 5) was attacked by Israeli aircraft. The lead attack was from Mirage fighters armed with rockets and 30mm cannon. They raked the *Liberty* with precision. The next wave was from Israeli swept-winged Dassault Mystyre jets with not only 30mm cannon, but napalm, a jellied gasoline that had devastating results. The third attack came from torpedo boats. A direct hit amidships left a giant bleeding hole in *Liberty's* starboard side.

In response to cries for help, the aircraft carrier *Saratoga* launched four F4 Phantoms. For reasons I will probably never know, they were ordered to return before coming to *Liberty's* defense.

We were immediately dispatched to go to *Liberty's* aid and relieve the *USS Davis* (DD 937), which had already arrived and taken the wounded aboard. We escorted the *Liberty* to Malta for temporary repair and to offload the dead. There were 172 American sailors wounded, thirty-four killed.

As we steamed alongside the *Liberty* en route to Malta, I was startled at the grotesque damage. A gaping hole exposed her insides. I felt stunned, as if looking at something I was too young to see. I was awestruck, seeing what enormous destruction can be wrought from weapons of war. The *Liberty* was an unarmed vessel, a spy vessel no one disputed, but totally defenseless; an easy target. I have never learned why she was attacked and assume it was a tragic mistake.

I stared at this crippled vessel and realized it could have been us. We could not have successfully fended off such an attack without receiving horrific damage. We had no surface-to-air missiles. Shooting down a jet with shore bombardment guns, even with fuses set to explode in the air, would have been a real trick. We were designed to hunt submarines, not fight jets.

The Arab-Israeli War lasted six days. This war in Vietnam is lasting longer. I compare in my mind the total destruction of PCF 43 to the crippled *Liberty*. My first impression of war in 1967 was ugly and unglamorous. My impression has not improved.

Mail is my biggest morale boost. It's the first thing I think of as we pull into Cat Lo. I have a letter from Dad. "Try to get orders to Destroyer School before you leave Vietnam," he writes. It's great to have his advice, the same advice Commander Streuli gave me.

I start to write a letter to Chantal, describing the conflicting feelings I have about the Vietnamese, about the violence on the Duong Keo, but halfway through the page I tear it up. I can't tell her about this, I can't tell anyone who wasn't there. They wouldn't be able to comprehend what this war is like, and they wouldn't want to.

Chapter Twenty

Tears

Patrolling the My Tho is comfortable, a short run from Cat Lo. The afternoon is warm and I realize the heat doesn't seem to bother me as much anymore. I've stopped taking salt tablets. I hear music over loudspeakers as we pass by an Army base and guess it must be a USO show. I've never seen one of those and wonder if anyone would notice if we pulled onto the beach and joined the party.

I drop my fantasy idea. I can't see the stage and I know it's too far from the river to leave our boat and join the fun. With my luck, our boat would be stolen by the Viet Cong. Now *that* would be an interesting court-martial.

We head upriver to refuel from an LST anchored not far from the USO show. I spot another Swift Boat who is already maneuvering along-side the LST and we slow our engines to wait our turn.

The LST doesn't have a floating platform to tie up to. Instead, she has a large steel boom, about forty-feet long and a foot in diameter. The boom is swung out ninety degrees from the deck of her port side with lines hanging down to secure to the bow of her visitors. The boom is about fifteen feet above the water.

I watch with interest as the Swift Boat ahead of us swings in alongside the LST. I'm unsure what the helmsman is planning to do. I can see it's an officer. The current is dragging his boat backwards toward the boom. I guess he's impatient, because he puts his engines in reverse to back down even faster.

This young officer is so focused, looking backwards at the boom, he doesn't notice that the height of the boom is somewhat lower than the height of his radar mast. The rear of the Swift Boat passes neatly under the boom at a good rate of speed and then the sixteen foot radar mast strikes the steel boom with a loud crack. The mast breaks off cleanly at the cabin top and falls into the river.

Moison, our expert boatswain's mate, approaches the boom bow first and we tie up alongside the dismasted Swift Boat.

"Need any help?" I ask the ensign.

"No thanks," he says. "We'll get it repaired, don't worry."

"Oh, I'm not worried. By the way, have you ever been in Cam Ranh Bay?"

I think it is a deplorable state of affairs that the navy has allowed ensigns to have command of a Swift Boat. I am sure the Secretary of Defense, Robert McNamara, is responsible for this unpardonable ignorance of how worthless a navy ensign is. This fits another of his miracle wonders: the single screw destroyer escort. McNamara is not only smearing the sterling reputation of Swift Boat skippers and Greyhounds-of-the-Sea, he pretends to be a military strategist, designating our targets with incompetent precision. I sometimes wonder if McNamara has stock in an automobile factory in Hanoi. We top off our tanks and resume our patrol, leaving the ensign to help clean up his mess.

I check the patrol assignments in the operations office each time we pull into Cat Lo. Our next assignment is not a good one. Matt D'Amico, the new XO, has my boat going back down to the Ca Mau. We load our boat with as many extra flak jackets as we can scrounge.

It is May 19th as we drive south on a smooth sea. I see innocent clouds on the horizon casting shadows, each one with dark flat bottoms and puffy white tops. The warm sea breeze feels good. My crew is sprawled out on deck in shorts, reading letters from home. Gnau is sitting at the helm, driving us south at twenty-five knots to rendezvous with an LST while I sit on top of the pilothouse and daydream about Chantal. I try to imagine the two of us on a sailboat on a day like this. I fantasize that we're off the coast of Spain where we met.

My daydream is interrupted. I spot two navy vessels through binoculars. They both look like LSTs. As we draw closer, it becomes clear one vessel is different. I'm not sure what it is.

While Moison and Stancil take on fuel from the LST, I scale the cargo net to check in. I'm told by the OTC that we'll remain alongside for the night and go into the river in the morning. I ask about the other vessel anchored nearby.

"That's the *USS White River*," the officer says. "She's an LSMR."

"What's an LSMR?"

"She shoots rockets. She's here to soften up the area before we go in tomorrow."

"What's new?" I ask.

"PCF 51 got hit today. Keith Evans is the skipper. He lost Robert Thompson, his boatswain's mate. The fifty-one has had it rough. Engineman Decker and Gunner's Mate Stindl were killed last week."

I wonder if Gnau has heard this news. PCF 51 was his old boat. PCF 51 has had the worst luck of any boat I know: five killed, four wounded, all since December.

At 1705 there is a sight to behold and I have a ringside seat. If there is such a thing as a banshee, she is not only wailing and screeching, she is anchored before me, a nautical ghoul launching her fire-breathing wrath with such vehemence as to shake Zeus from the sky. Hundreds of rockets in rapid succession are flying off the deck of the *White River* without pause. Not just one at a time, but volleys of Roman candles scream into the air, arc into the jungle and explode with awesome destruction. Just the sound alone is enough to frighten a poltergeist. It can't be a comfortable evening for the Viet Cong.

It's 0800 and I still marvel at the thrill from last night. But this morning is another troop insertion, just like the others, day after day. We're tired from the numbing repetition of canal operations.

We're like dirty gray shadows in a dark alley, three Swift Boats creeping single file into this narrow canal. Dank humid air carries the odor of rotting vegetation. Green palms, bamboo and thick bushes reach out over the water like claws. It's claustrophobic, like a tunnel, hiding anything and everything behind it. Clumps of leaves are floating past in the ebbing current, water escaping to the ocean, the muddy bottom getting closer.

"What's our depth?" I whisper to Hoffman. I can smell the stink of my sweat. Hoffman is on my right, sitting at the helm, his left hand on the throttles, ready to jam us to full speed.

"Ten feet, skipper. I'm watching it." Getting stuck on the shallow muddy bottom could be fatal if we are caught by the VC and need to run. The width of the canal is less than our fifty-foot length. Turning around is not an option in the heat of a firefight.

The VC still own these rivers, these backwater canals, these muddy waterways full of claymore mines hanging in trees. It's not a healthy place—not for boats, not for men, not for trees.

Morale is fading, too many friends wounded or killed. Stancil is on the bow with his M-60, Hudson up in the gun tub, Gnau on the aft fifty. Moison is aft of the cabin with another M-60. I'm standing in the pilothouse watching the bushes.

"Stay alert," I say, as if that was necessary.

"Tell that to the gooks," Hudson says, looking back at the South Vietnamese Marines crowding our stern. Each boat has ten Vietnamese Marines. Sometimes Hudson calls them "Slope-heads" or "Zippers." I use the same slang—we all do. I wonder if we are trying to denigrate the Vietnamese or hide compassion, because that's what men do during war. Empathy shows weakness—it's not masculine.

"Seems odd to call 'em gooks," Hoffman says with a soft laugh, "if we're willing to die for 'em."

"Knock off the chatter," I say. "Stay alert."

I can sense my crew's bitter feelings. We're near the Duong Keo River where we were hit in an ambush last month. We had thirteen Swift Boats, two Seawolf helicopters, and 240 Vietnamese Marines. I felt safe then.

We lost men that day. PCF 43 was destroyed in a cataclysmic explosion. Forty-six men wounded. I was infuriated by the Vietnamese Marines—their indifference to Americans being slaughtered. It was not a good day.

Today we have three Swift Boats and thirty Vietnamese Marines. Not good odds.

I arrived in Vietnam with naïve expectations about the Vietnamese. I thought this would be a noble war, fighting communism, defending the South Vietnamese, but all those lofty ideals are now dead. Maybe some suppressed prejudice is beginning to surface, clouding my thoughts.

I remember Rodgers and Hammerstein's *South Pacific*. John Kerr played the role of Marine Lieutenant Joe Cable. He said, "You've got to be carefully taught, to hate all the people your relatives hate." It reminds me of my father's parents.

I was ten years old, sitting in the front seat of my grandfather's Packard as we returned from Sunday Service. My grandmother's fleshy arms were pressed against my face, the smell of her lilac powder suffocating me.

"There goes some of those Jews," my grandfather said as we stopped at a crosswalk. I perked up, looking at everyone crossing the street, straining to see a Jew.

"Grandpa, where? What do they look like?" He just laughed and ignored my question. To me, I only saw everyday people.

As we returned home from their Baptist church, we passed another church. I felt exciting vibrant sounds penetrate my whole body, inviting me to come in. I squirmed in my seat, wanting to get closer to those voices singing with such rhythm and feeling.

"Why don't we go to *that* church?" I asked.

"That's a colored church," he said. "We don't go there."

On command of the OTC, each boat swings to the right, our bows sliding into the soft muddy bank as far as the hulls will allow. Fingers of thick palms drape over the foredeck completely engulfing Stancil, and more ferns push in through the pilothouse door. Vietnamese Marines and the American Marine advisor jump off our bow, their camouflaged fatigues and painted faces melting into the dense jungle. They disappear in less than a minute.

Each Swift Boat shuts down the engines. It's now quiet as death; no one talks and no one smokes, not even Hoffman. As I sit waiting for something to happen, I wonder if the South Vietnamese care who wins this war.

"Never judge people by the color of their skin," Dad had said, "by what songs they sing in church, or by the language they speak."

"That's not what Grandpa thinks."

"He doesn't know any better. Things happen that open your eyes. One time I had to ditch my plane in the drink, didn't have enough fuel to reach the carrier. A destroyer got as close as they could, but the water was so cold, I couldn't hold the lifeline. A black man jumped in to attach a harness— nearly cost that man his life."

Dad moved us every two years from the East Coast to the West and back again, repeatedly traversing the dry land between Chincoteague, Coronado, Falls Church, Pensacola, Alameda, Newport, Naples and Colorado Springs. I was immersed into one new neighborhood after another. My need for acceptance infiltrated my sub-conscious, becoming imbedded like breathing; it dominated my behavior, like trying to grasp a lifeline.

Preston Parker was my best friend in Italy. He was a black kid. We were on the high school track team and we did everything together, like sneaking out of study hall to go to a bar where we listened to a jukebox. We sang along with Sam Cooke's "You Send Me," and the Marcels' "Blue Moon." It didn't occur to me that his black skin was more exceptional than my freckles or my coke-bottle glasses.

But now I'm in Vietnam, not Naples or Chincoteague, Virginia. I'm feeling a different prejudice in the middle of a war. It's not religious or racial, I don't know what it is. I thought I was above prejudice, but after the Duong Keo ambush, I'm not.

My body jerks! A startling burst of violent concussion waves reverberate through the trees. And now more gunfire—coming from the left.

"This is Leatherneck!" a radio voice says. "Request covering fire, north of smoke—identify color."

"Hudson," I say, "see any smoke?"

"No."

"Smoke is red," one of the Swift Boats says over the radio.

"This is Leatherneck, roger red, cover-fire now!"

Fifty-caliber machine guns open fire from the Swift on my left. I duck out of reflex, my eyes transfixed on tracers flashing into trees, branches cracking and dropping to the ground, a constant pulsing stream of bright red magnesium penetrating everything in its path.

"Cease fire, cease fire!" I can barely hear urgent screaming over the sound of machine guns. "This is Leatherneck," a radio voice screams. "Cease fire, cease fire! You're shooting at me." Then silence. I'm looking into trees, looking for movement, my hands shaking from adrenalin. A blue-gray cloud of cordite drifts into my mouth. It tastes like acid.

Two fifty-caliber barrels deliver eleven hundred rounds per minute. It was a short burst, but still hundreds of armor-piercing bullets have streaked over a mile in two seconds—if they didn't hit something first.

"This is Leatherneck," our radio squawks. "You got friendlies comin' in; hold your fire." It's a calm, professional voice, an American Marine advisor, out there somewhere, hunkered down in the trees.

Two Vietnamese Marines emerge from thick bushes carrying a man between them. The man's head is bent down, his limp legs dragging as the three come toward us. Now two more Vietnamese Marines are bringing another wounded.

Gnau yells from the bow, "*Lay dai, lay dai*, come here, come here. Stancil, Moison, give me a hand!"

Vietnamese Marines wade into chest-deep water alongside our boat, carrying their wounded comrades to where we can pull them aboard. There are no angry words, no insults shouted, just empty faces looking for a place to drop their wounded before returning to the bush. I feel bitter anger for the crewman that fired his twin-fifties in the wrong direction—and sympathy for the guilt he must be feeling.

"We're taking them out to the T," I yell to the other skipper. The LST has medical facilities anchored five miles off the coast. "Hoffman, get us out of here."

Hoffman jumps into the pilot house and punches ignition for the engines, throttling up the rpm and shoving the gears into reverse. Hudson climbs into the gun tub, sunlight glinting off his sweaty arms. Gnau mans the aft fifty. He looks overweight with his flak jacket and bulky helmet covering his earphones. Seems strange to notice these things at a time like this.

Hoffman backs us into the river as Stancil helps me carry one of the marines into the main cabin. I kneel on the floor cradling the marine. His small body feels light, almost a child in a jungle uniform. I can feel the throb of our engines accelerating. I'm afraid to move him, afraid if I let go, he will simply fall apart. I can't believe he's still alive.

I should be in the pilothouse directing our course and giving orders, but there are none to give. Hoffman will have no problem following this canal to the river and back to the ocean.

"Hoffman," I yell, "stay in middle and the depth will be okay."

I stare with disbelief at the gaping hole in this young man's chest. A fifty-caliber bullet creates a hideous wound. Red bubbles are foaming up through the shredded hole each time he tries to exhale. A nauseating vapor permeates my nose and the back of my throat. The stench of his sweat is like dirty wet wool and his jungle-green uniform is coated with sticky blood. Saliva is pooling in my mouth. I fight an urge to puke.

His eyes are looking into mine, maybe searching for some sign I can save him. I feel his blood soaking into my pants from the hole in his back. It turns cold as it dries. I feel useless holding a gauze pad over his chest. I can put my whole fist inside this dark visceral crater of raspberry mush. He starts to close his eyes.

"Hey, look at me!" I say. It doesn't matter if he can't understand my words, it's only important he hears my voice. Stancil injects a shot of morphine into his leg. I'm not sure he needs it, not sure if he still feels pain. I offer a canteen and he shakes his head no. Somewhere I heard you shouldn't give water to someone hit in the chest or stomach. I wonder if he knows that. How could he know, to be aware of anything with half his chest missing?

"Friendly fire" seems such a benign phrase. Fifty-caliber bullets are anything but benign, no matter who pulls the trigger. I think of the small thirty-caliber bullet that just missed me in the Bo De. Taylor pried it out of our pilothouse door and gave it to me as a souvenir. It was no larger than the end of my small finger. A fifty-caliber bullet is over two inches long and half an inch wide.

It is such a long way to the LST. I look back through the aft cabin door and see our wake spilling over the top of the bank as we race through this narrow canal. I see Stancil and Moison holding the other marine. Stancil still isn't old enough to drink. I wonder how he is coping, tending to disintegrated flesh

We're going as fast as our engines can take us. I know we can be hit at any time as we head for the safety of the ocean. We're alone. If any VC are watching, we're a tempting target.

The main cabin is the last place to be while in Ca Mau. B-40 rockets. It's not good to be inside. For some reason this doesn't seem important. I can't move. Just holding this marine is all I can do. My leg is starting to cramp. I don't want him to die. I can't figure out how to bandage his gaping wound, the damage so great and my skill just too fucking insignificant.

"Skipper, we lost him," Stancil says through the aft cabin door. Moison is still kneeling next to the marine on the engine hatch. I just nod to Stancil. I look at the clock on the bulkhead. It's been twenty minutes.

"We got wounded coming in," I hear Hoffman call over the Prick 25, alerting the LST—it doesn't matter how many.

I can tell we have left the canal, the bow rising and dipping as we push through ocean swells. Salt spray filters through the cabin, a relief from the gagging odor. We're safe now, at least some of us. The boy's head is beginning to jerk from the hammering motion of our hull. I tighten my arm around his neck. He looks like a boy, but he's man. He's defending an ideology of freedom. I hope he believes in it—he's on the frontline of commitment.

He's stopped breathing. Still I can't let go; I can't put him down. I refuse to accept what I know. I want to rock him in my arms, see him open his eyes, see him smile.

Hoffman brings us alongside the LST. I lay the boy down and come out into stark sunlight. My legs feel numb. I keep losing my balance as we bob alongside. Dark bile erupts from my stomach. I'm retching. A brown-yellow stream spills out, over and over until nothing is left but the taste.

Sailors on the LST are looking down at us as if this were some fucking car accident. I watch a corpse being hoisted in a wire basket up the side of the ship. The metal basket scrapes the ship's hull. I want to yell, "Easy, be careful," but that would be stupid. I want to yell at these sailors, "STOP LOOKING! You've got no right to look."

I have never seen a man die before and I never want to see it again. But there are no tears. Dad taught me at an early age: men don't cry.

Ca Mau Canal

Chapter Twenty-one

Stealing Cars

As we sit alongside the LST off the Ca Mau, I think about endless canal operations still ahead. I begin to fantasize about the feasibility of escape from Vietnam. I consider our speed and how far we can get before P2Vs begin reporting our position, before destroyers intercept our course. I'll report over the radio, "We're on a secret reconnaissance mission."

I calculate the distance to Kuala Terengganu, Malaysia. With our fuel tanks topped off at 830 gallons, it'll be a piece of cake. It's 210 nautical miles to Kuala from the LST. At 2000 RPM we can make 23 knots in calm seas, over 200 miles in ten hours. We would still have a hundred gallons of fuel when we reach Malaysia. I wonder if customs and immigration officials will be sympathetic to a man burned out from war.

Gnau sees me drawing a line on a chart with parallel rules and measuring distance with dividers. He interrupts my fantasy daydream.

"What are you doing?" Gnau asks.

"Just goofing off," I say. "You ever been to Malaysia?"

"You okay?" He's looking at me like I'm ready for a tight fitting jacket with extra long sleeves that tie in the back.

"Yeah, I am. This is just my way of letting off pressure; mental masturbation."

Gnau doesn't laugh. Maybe he thinks I'm serious.

The seas are calm as Stancil sits at the helm driving us north to Cat Lo. Hoffman is sitting on the bow, smoking. The Onan generator is dead and Moison is in the galley rummaging through our box of C-Rats. I lay on the roof of the pilothouse, scanning the horizon without really looking for anything, not daydreaming about anyone, just something to do until I fall asleep.

We pull into Cat Lo and I check in with Operations. I discover Matt D'Amico has returned to the "World," gone after two months as XO. Like Hal and Matt before him, Tim Guard has had his last patrol. He turned over command of his boat and is now the new XO. It's all Commander Streuli's plan, to take men off the boats and off patrol as they get close to the end of their tour. I wonder if my turn might come someday.

New guys, cherries, fill open slots on the boats. Ked Fairbank is now the Readiness and Training Officer, making sure the new guys are prepared before going into the rivers. I bet he takes them to the Rung Sat at night for their first orientation, just to make an impression.

I have a package from Mom. It's almost like Christmas, opening her present. She has sent two large cans of corn-wrapped tamales, a can of refried beans, a block of cheddar cheese that's a bit green with mold, a big can of tortillas and a bottle of Tabasco.

"Mexican party tonight," I announce to the guys in the Quonset hut. Ked Fairbank is assigned to find some Tequila and limes. Chuck Mohn says he'll create a salsa with tomatoes and onion. Everyone is excited, thinking of what they can bring to the party.

It's nice to have mail after a long patrol, something to take my mind away from constant tension. I have a letter from Dad. "Deacon Barker came for a visit," he writes.

Oh Deacon, what a character he is, a pilot from Dad's squadron in Korea. Deacon has a great belly laugh, a short crew cut, and a southern accent from Vicksburg, Mississippi. No one would think he could be a fighter pilot from the way he talks and the way he says, "Y'all." I think he must be related to Bird Dog.

While we lived in Naples, Deacon came for a visit and stayed in our apartment. Deacon was the pilot for an admiral, the Naval Attaché to Saudi Arabia. Deacon said things to me like, "Somala-ala-cum, kay-fallic-sadeek—Y'all." Then he'd say, "That's muh greetin' for them *southern* Arabs."

He wore gray slacks and gray socks, the socks embroidered with the Confederate flag. He had a roly-poly swagger and did a funny little shuffle in his black penny loafers, making it look like he was walking forward while sliding backwards.

He has always been like an uncle to my brother, Randall, and me. I'd see him scribble in his little black notebook. Mom said he was jotting down ideas for someone's birthday or Christmas present. I thought that "someone" could only be Randall or me. I felt shock and disappointment to learn years later that Deacon was an uncle to more than just my brother and me;

he treated every pilot's kid like they were the only kids in the world, all of us believing we were unique in Deacon's life. I know now it is Deacon that is unique.

That evening in Naples, while Mom, Dad and Deacon sat in the living room drinking too much Italian wine, I stole the car keys to Dad's 1958 Thunderbird and snuck out. I did this a lot. My friends, Ward and Preston, always went with me on these joyrides. We took turns driving. It was just innocent fun, but this night we were stopped by four motorcycle Polizia, the Carabiniere. They were riding revved-up Moto Guzzis. The Carabiniere were impressive with a white sash across their breast and black leather boots that came up to their knees, and serious looking guns in fancy white holsters.

Ward, Preston and I were seventeen, not old enough to have an Italian driver's license. The Carabiniere told us to get back into the T-bird and follow them to their station. Two motorcycles led the way and two followed. Ward was driving and he panicked, turned left and sped away. The Carabiniere clocked us going 160 kilometers per hour down a one-way street— the wrong way. The Carabiniere were smart enough to turn around, making us think we had gotten away so we would slow down and not kill anybody. They already had our license plate number and tracked down the car, my dad's phone number, and made their calls. Not a pretty situation and I had no diplomatic immunity, at least not from my father.

Deacon answered the phone when the Carabiniere called. Deacon told me this was a serious offense, that I was jeopardizing my father's career. This incident was quickly known by all the senior NATO staff in Naples. Dad was chief of staff to an admiral and worried he would be sent back to the States if this happened again.

I was brought to the police magistrate's office in the center of Naples.

"You are going prison," the magistrate said. "Driving without a license, speeding and reckless driving. Your father is being returned to the US and there is nothing the navy or your American president can do to help you or your father." He paused to let this sink in. "However," the magistrate said, "I will give you a second chance. I will suspend your prison sentence and let your father remain here, but if you violate any more Italian laws, you will immediately go to prison and your father will be sent home in disgrace."

I didn't know it at the time, but Dad arranged for this fake "hearing," a theatrical performance to scare the shit out of me. I didn't know he had scripted the Magistrate's speech. Naples was a rough city. I imagined what their prison would be like, but worse, I dreaded the thought that I had damaged my father's career. And I had lost Deacon's respect.

I stopped stealing Dad's keys. And anyway, it was Ward's turn.

There is a beehive of construction activity on the Cat Lo base. A new BOQ, the Bachelors Officer's Quarters, is under construction and from the looks of it—each officer will have a private room. This will be like a Hilton compared to the Quonset hut we have now. And a new O' Club is being built. It's my day off and I join Tim Guard and others, pouring concrete for the floor of the new club. I trowel the concrete smooth. It feels calming, like therapy, only thinking about this simple task. When no one is looking, I use my finger to carve "Virg" and "PCF 67" into the wet surface.

My job every summer while in high school was on a construction site. I was an unskilled assistant, a "hod carrier," delivering concrete in wheelbarrows to masons building brick walls. The men I worked for were Mexicans.

I'm looking forward to our Mexican dinner party and start thinking about preparations. The food is gone, stolen from my locker, which I never lock. No one knows who took the cans and cheese. I suspect it's our mamma-san that cleans the BOQ.

As mad as I am, I would honestly like to know what her family thinks of refried beans. Maybe this startling new flavor will begin to corrupt the cuisine of Vietnam. I laugh as I imagine a flourishing black market driven by the demand for tamales.

Chapter Twenty-two

Black Ponies

I have a day off in Cat Lo, but I feel spent. My web belt is getting longer. I've lost ten pounds from sweat. I don't feel hungry; even Mexican food has lost its appeal. I have no interest in visiting Vung Tau and just lie in my bunk listening to Otis Redding. I share his feeling of loneliness as he sings, "watchin' the ships roll in, and watching 'em roll away again." And he sings, "Change Gonna Come" in a soft, pleading voice. I wonder what kind of change might come for me.

It's 1700. Dad said never drink until the sun is below the yardarm. I figure it must be close and walk over the O' Cub.

Steve Hart is sitting at the bar. He says something about Operation Sea Float.

"What's Sea Float?" I ask.

"Bunch of barges tied together," he says, "floating on the Cua Lon. Crazy, a Swift Boat base in the Ca Mau. They're looking for volunteers. Interested?"

"Zumwalt's brainchild," someone adds. "Great duty. They put it on the R&R list."

"Whose list?"

"From what I hear, *Beaucoup* VC!" Steve says with one of his subtle laughs. "Don't have to do board and search—they come to you."

"No shit? VC?"

I finish my gin and tonic dinner, leave the O' Club and start thinking about my next patrol as I crawl into my bunk. Tim Guard has assigned the Bassac.

It's 0700. My crew looks tired as they climb aboard. Moison and Stancil haven't shaved. Hoffman is quiet, almost despondent. I think our galley must be out of beans with Vienna sausage. Gnau looks like he has a hangover, which is unlikely for a man who doesn't drink much. I don't ask. I wonder if sometimes these guys might have received a letter with bad news—a girl problem, or sometimes maybe no mail. No mail is the worst.

We leave Cat Lo, driving PCF 67 south along the coast in heavy rain, but the seas are smooth and the crew sprawls out in bunks or sleeps on the cabin floor. It's a boring three-hour drive. We reach the Bassac River mouth, hug the right side where the channel is deep and head upstream to our patrol sector. Gnau and Hudson uncover the guns.

The refreshing morning downpour has cooled the air and sampan traffic on this stretch of the Bassac is light. I feel oddly relaxed, almost blasé with our board and search routine. We haven't seen any sampans with slithering sea snakes, but no lobster either.

Hoffman decodes orders from Mother. We're to explore a canal. Gnau and I study the chart. It doesn't look bad, but it doesn't look good. We'll be far from help if we need it. TASS 19, a tactical air support group based at Binh Thuy, has been alerted to our mission. They are forward air controllers, just like Bird Dog.

"Have Sepia repeat the coordinates," I say to Hoffman.

Hoffman spends ten minutes sending my request and decoding the reply. The reply is the same.

"Gnau, set general quarters," I say. "But take your time; we're not in a hurry."

We set General Quarters at noon and Hoffman calls "Tilly," the TASS forward air controller for a radio check. There's no reply.

"Let's wait 'til we have air cover," Gnau says.

"They're not going to waste time flying cover," I say. "They won't come unless we need 'em."

"Well, let's at least wait until we have radio contact."

"Hoffman, keep calling Tilly," I say. "Gnau, we're going in. I want to get this thing over with."

"I don't like this," Gnau mumbles as he heads to the fantail.

We enter a canal that runs west into known VC country. I wonder why Sepia is interested in this canal. Hoffman is driving, Stancil on the bow with his M-60, Hudson in the gun tub. Gnau and Moison are on the fantail, probably grumbling about air support.

The canal is manmade, built by the French. It's narrow, less than fifty-feet wide and as straight as a Texas dirt road. It's not claustrophobic, not like the Ca Mau. I see wheel tracks on top of the canal bank, probably from vicious water buffalo pulling carts. Faded brown grasses stretch out in a broad open field to the right. Tall trees, bamboo and thick bushes are on the left, but not so close to the bank as to offer advantage to the VC.

"Mother picked a bad time to check out this canal," Gnau says over his phone. "Tide is out."

"Four feet," Hoffman says, rapping his knuckles on the fathometer, as if that will make it get deeper.

"Slow down," I say to Hoffman. "Let's don't get stuck."

We troll through the canal at an easy pace and reach a group of shacks, each one built on short stilts above the muddy bank. Seems odd, four flimsy houses, so isolated out here, far from any village.

"Looks deserted," Hudson says from the gun tub.

"Probably hiding," Hoffman adds.

"Yeah, hiding."

"Why don't they just leave this place for good?" Hoffman asks.

"Maybe they have," I say. "Can't imagine trying to be a farmer out here in the middle of VC country."

We keep going, but I feel uncomfortable, wondering who might live here and whose side they're on.

"Punji stakes," Hudson says.

I see them, like splinters jutting out from mud along the right side of the canal. Toi told me about punji stakes. They're sliced bamboo, tips sharpened, hardened by fire and then coated in feces. If troops tried to cross this canal, the punji stakes would rip through the bottom of their boots. They would kill a man if he fell on them. And if he lived, it's not just the pain he'd feel, but the infection that would follow. Punji stakes act as a debilitating deterrent.

"God, look at them," I say. "They're everywhere." I wonder why so many punji stakes are in this particular stretch, in such a desolate area. There are so many—they look like gleaming white porcupine quills.

"Wouldn't see 'em at high tide," Gnau says. "They'd be underwater." Gnau is always thinking about the tides.

They remind me of a courtyard in Naples, broken glass imbedded along the top of a wall, protecting the virtue of a young girl I wanted to visit. It's quiet now; no idle chatter on the phones. Punji stakes makes all of us uneasy.

I see something else, more frightening and lethal. Throughout the field on our right, and as far as I can see, giant pointed stakes, six to eight feet tall are crisscrossed and bundled in threes, the way men would stack rifles with fixed bayonets. There must be over five hundred of these bundles, as if stalks of corn in Kansas. They're hard to see in the chest-high elephant grass.

Their purpose is immediately clear. These pikes would easily disgorge the soft belly of a Huey inserting its troops, and they're high enough to

cause helicopter blades to shatter as they landed. I imagine the surprise
these pikes would give to some covert squad parachuting down in the dark,
the pain of a lance as they were skewered like meat. This passive weapon is
hideous, ingenious.

"Wonder if this is what Mother wanted to know," I say to Hoffman as
I jot down coordinates in the log.

"Think maybe we're in VC country?" Hudson asks with a shaky laugh
from his perch in the gun tub.

"Well," I say, "if you have any doubt, look left." On the left bank, in a
small clearing, surrounded on three sides by trees and dense foliage, a Viet
Cong flag hangs from a pole like an emblem of cancer. The upper half of
the flag is red, the lower is blue and a small yellow star is in the middle.

"Tilly, Elbow Golf Six-seven," Hoffman says, "radio check." Hoffman's voice has a sudden sense of urgency.

"Six-seven, this is Tilly, roger. Give me your coordinates."

It's comforting to hear their voice. While Hoffman talks to Tilly, I scan
the clearing. I have a strong feeling the VC are watching from hidden
bunkers and spider holes just beyond the clearing. In my imagination, there
is a smell like dung from a slaughterhouse for cattle. I'm sure the entire
clearing is booby-trapped with claymores. I expect the VC are waiting, as
if vultures, anticipating a very dumb American to race over and grab a war
trophy from this self-serve souvenir shop. The man would be cut down in a
second. The rest of us would be too, as we try to save him. PCF 4 tried to
take home a flag. They lost four men.

"Hoffman, stop the boat," I say. "Hudson, hose down the trees—
Gnau, pump in some 'willy-pete.'"

Gnau fires a white phosphorous mortar round into the trees as everyone else takes pleasure chewing up the flag. I use the M-79 grenade
launcher, lobbing rounds into the trees like spitballs in their eye. There's
nothing left of the flag and a few trees burn from phosphorous mortars.

I doubt any VC are hurt, hiding down in their tunnels like vermin or
snakes. Seems strange, seeing the flag of our enemy, but it's only their drop-
pings we see, never their faces.

We're alone in a shallow canal and it is a long way to the other end.
Maybe we're lucky they didn't want to fight today. The flood tide is coming in and we've gained an extra foot of muddy water underneath us.

"Let's go," I say and Hoffman floors the throttles. The hull rises up on
step as we race down the canal. I'm anxious to get this assignment over
with, get the hell out of this canal.

I see dirt fly from the top of the canal before I hear the distinctive pop-
pop-crack of AK-47s. Rounds are slamming into the muddy bank and
splashing in the water. Hudson opens fire.

"Where are they!?" I yell.

"Bunker, on the left—up ahead!" Hudson yells.

"Shit, they're blocking our exit! Hoffman, stop, back down, turn around." Stancil opens fire from the bow.

"Can't see 'em," Gnau says.

"Tilly," I scream into the mic, "this is Elbow Golf Six-seven, scramble one, repeat, scramble one." I know "Scramble One" means I can't escape. Maybe I can, but I want help now!

Turning around in this tight canal takes time. We're a sitting duck.

"Six-seven, this is Tilly. Air cover en route."

As Hoffman struggles to maneuver our boat, Gnau opens fire. The stern has come around enough for Gnau on the fantail to see the target. Hudson, Gnau, Moison and Stancil are firing without pause. I can't tell if we're still taking fire from the bunker.

"Come on!" I yell at Hoffman. Hoffman is pushing our bow into the mud, backing down and doing it again, trying to twist our stern around. The canal is too narrow and it's taking too long!

I see two wonderful and poisonous airplanes. "Black Ponies!" I yell. They're screaming down our right side at a thousand feet. "Can't believe they got here so fast."

The lead plane dips his wing and rolls right, coming around behind us. I see the second plane staying on his left wing. They streak past our left side, headed in the direction of our tracer fire. Puffs of gray smoke from the lead plane billows from under his belly. I hear an ear-splitting roar as a 20mm Gatling gun rakes the bunker. The ground is erupting, black-gray debris flying like straw in the wind. I'm mesmerized by the firepower from these twin-engine aircraft. The second plane fires two rockets. The explosion rips my eardrums. They're pulling up and banking to the right.

"They're coming around again," Hudson yells in a high-pitched voice.

I don't know what radio frequency the Black Ponies are using.

"Tilly, Six-seven," I call, "relay to Black Ponies, we're turning around, heading out." I can't hear any response. Hudson's fifties are killing my ears.

Hoffman has turned us around. He guns our engines as the Ponies make another strafing run. We're up on step, racing back the way we came—I feel like we're on skis. I feel a weird sensation, as if I'm invincible, like nothing can touch us.

Moison and Gnau on the fantail are still shooting, blasting the VC bunker.

"Keep going!" I say to Hoffman as we pass the smoldering VC flag. That was a dumb thing to say. Hell, I know he's not going to slow down; it's just my adrenalin talking. I watch the Ponies fly past a third time, wagging their wings. I give them a wave, a thank you for saving our butt. They continue to circle until we reach the river. I call Tilly to say we're okay. I thank them profusely.

We pull back into the Bassac and slow down for the first time. I feel a little tired. I walk to the fantail as Gnau pulls off his helmet and earphones, and Moison peels off his flak jacket. They look exhausted, shoulders slumped, tee shirts soaked. Their faces have a vacant stare, like they don't know where they are.

"We were lucky to have air support," I say to Gnau, "but I made a mistake. It was dumb to stop in the canal. Should've kept going, should've kept up our speed." It's our routine to talk about an op, but my comment comes out like a confession. I suppose it is. I ran from a fight.

"Yeah, maybe," Moison says. "But if they had B-40 rockets, would've been point-blank."

"Next time," Gnau says, "let's get air cover *before* we go in." He looks me straight in the eyes. It's a reminder he said that before. I know he's pissed.

"Next time," I say. "Yeah, next time. There's always a next time."

We're all tired, hot, and everyone strips down to shorts. Gnau mentions he felt a sting on the back of his leg while we were taking fire. There's a red streak across his calf.

"Just a scratch," Gnau says. "Not as if we were in the Duong Keo."

Moison and I take turns driving, everyone else resting on the cabin top or stretched out on the fantail. It's a bitch being shot at, wipes out the brain. Feels good to be alive, but the rush of adrenalin saps every ounce of energy.

I'm in a trance as I steer a course through the middle of the river, thinking about that strange sense of invincibility when we have air cover. I know it is naïve and dangerous to feel confident.

Mother calls, says to stand by for a message. I wake Hoffman to take the message while I continue to drive. Mother directs us to exit the Bassac and enter the Co Chin, the next river north. Gnau gets up and plots a course through shallow sandbars that extend miles beyond the Bassac River mouth.

"Hug the left bank," I say. "Go out five miles before you turn left." Our course is simple and straightforward. We'll go another ten miles north, turn left again and enter the Co Chin.

"Piece of cake," Gnau says. "Okay, I got the watch."

I leave Gnau and Hoffman to navigate our course. We're beyond the threat of B-40 rockets and I crawl into a bunk in the main cabin. I'm exhausted and asleep in seconds.

Hard jolting bumps wake me, as if we've bounced over railroad tracks. I race into the pilothouse and scan the horizon, but all I see is water in every direction. We're at full stop.

"What happened?" I ask Gnau. We're miles from the closest land and the fathometer shows we have only two feet of water under our keel. I can tell we are far from our intended course.

"Hit a couple of sandbars," Gnau says.

"How in the hell did we get so far south?"

"Might've dozed off."

I'm tired, impatient and take over the helm. "Steering's jammed!" I yell, staring at Gnau with irritation that is completely born of fatigue.

"Rudder coupling's broken," Gnau says, but it is exhaustion more than remorse that I hear in his voice.

"Fuck!" I yell. I use our throttles, moving us forward and backward, bumping into underwater sandbars in every direction. Gnau jumps into waist-deep, crystal-clear water and explores our surroundings on foot, wading in a complete circle around our boat, only finding deep water fifty feet away. We are trapped in a small tidal pool in the middle of the Bassac delta, miles from land.

I think about consequences. I'm pissed at Gnau and have a morbid wish a shark would swim by as he wades through the water. I realize too, none of us ever gets enough sleep. It's my fault; I should have been in the pilothouse with him.

The Bassac channel is beyond our reach and the Co Chin is still hours away. Gnau climbs back aboard and calculates the tides.

"High tide in three hours," he says.

"Great. And then—how do we steer?" I'm acting like an asshole, not a skipper. Gnau walks away. I don't blame him.

I send Mother Sepia a coded message: "Due to tidal circumstances, cannot reach Co Chin River assignment for five hours." I don't tell them about the rudder. Maybe we can fix it.

Sepia responds in her motherly code: "Are you aground?" I'm sure they can't wait to tell Captain Hoffmann.

Steve Hart and Mike Hudson cruise by en route to their patrol areas in the Bassac and offer to help. Mike has been transferred to Cat Lo from Cam Ranh Bay, and it's good to see him. He has a great tan. His call sign is Ichabod Crane. I think it must be for his tall gangly posture and his deer-in-the-headlights expression.

Moison wades through the waist-deep water to the edge of the sandbar with two towing lines. Steve and Mike attach the lines to their sterns and both Swift Boats pull with all the horsepower they have while I gun our engines full bore—all six V12 diesels—almost three-thousand horse-power—putting their heart into rescuing PCF 67.

It's to no avail. Steve leaves, waving with a friendly laugh as if think-ing, "You poor son-of-a-bitch." But I can sense from Ichabod's face that he's truly sorry for me, for the reception that will be waiting for me in Cat Lo and maybe in Cam Ranh Bay. I think an ambush is better. No waiting, no time to think. I wave goodbye to both guys and wait for the tide.

I pass the time listening to a Booker T tape, "Green Onions," while I write my report describing the ambush and the field of bayonets.

"Hope this intel will soften the trouble I'm in," I say to Hoffman as he begins to code the message. Everyone else aboard is asleep. I wonder if this is where the Ops Boss, Jim Barrett, "High 'n Dry," went aground. I'd like to ask him, but he packed his box and went home months ago.

The flood tide arrives and we're free of our prison. I send Mother a message that our rudder is damaged and she says to return to Cat Lo. Stan-cil and Moison rig the emergency tiller into the rudder coupling on our fan-tail. Our tiller is an eight-foot horizontal steel pipe, connected like an elbow to another pipe that is inserted into a hole on the stern. The eight-foot arm swings left and right, moving the rudders.

The trip to Cat Lo is interesting. Holding a straight course is a learn-ing experience for anyone who has never steered a boat with a tiller. It's counter-intuitive. When steering with the wheel in the pilothouse, we turn the wheel left and our boat turns left, just like a car. With a tiller, we push the tiller left and we turn right. Adding to this new learning experience, we do it blindfolded—the tiller-man can't see the compass.

Gnau goes first, standing on the fantail, wearing earphones and hold-ing the shaft of the tiller with both hands. Moving the tiller is hard.

"Rudder is really screwed up," he says. Moison is in the pilothouse, manning the throttles, watching the compass and speaking into his phone, telling Gnau which way to steer.

"We're off course," Moison says over the phone. "Come left a bit." Gnau, using his hip to add to the effort, pushes the tiller left. As he pushes left, we start turning right.

"No, *left*," Moison says. Gnau pushes the tiller harder to the left. We make a complete circle to the right.

Gnau finally gets the hang of it, pushing the tiller to the right to come left, but now he's tired; it's been an hour. Manning the tiller is hard, physi-cal work. Moison is tired too, watching the compass and giving directions every minute. We rotate both positions: tiller and compass. The learning process begins anew—we make a complete circle with each new crew shift.

It is a long ride from the Bassac to Cat Lo, but that's fortunate. Learning to steer by tiller needs time; maneuvering through the narrow canal to dock at Cat Lo needs precision.

A crowd gathers at the Cat Lo Pier. Most of these guys haven't seen a Swift Boat maneuvered with a tiller since Coronado. They offer cheers and hoots as Gnau stands at the aft throttles and I use the tiller to bring us alongside a nest of Swift Boats.

It's not an elegant way to come home. Doug Martin, a young ensign who was rescued by Irma La Douche, stands with his hands on his hips.

"Hey lieutenant, need any help?" It's hard for me, a full lieutenant, to take a comment like that from a smart-ass ensign. I think about giving him the finger, but instead, I invite Doug to the O' Club, buy him a drink, and we exchange some great stories about going aground.

Our stories are interrupted by Commander Streuli. He hands me a message from Commander, Coastal Squadron One Headquarters.

"Lieutenant Erwin," the message reads, "I am pleased to note your continued propensity to confirm charted obstructions to safe navigation Regards, 'Latch,' Captain Roy Hoffmann."

Commander Streuli laughs. "I've never served a skipper that paid more attention to minute details than Captain Hoffmann. Oh, forgot to tell you, I've recommended you for Destroyer School. It's your obvious next step. After that, you'll get your Department Head slot on a destroyer. But for Christ's sake, try not to go aground again."

"Thank you sir," I say sincerely. "I'll stay in deeper water if you keep me out of the rivers."

We both laugh, but I'm beginning to have doubts about whether to augment to the regular navy and make this life my career. I wonder if I have what it takes to be trusted with command of a destroyer. I'm tired all the time, tired of war and yet, being skipper of a Swift Boat still fills me with the greatest pride I've ever felt.

I remember when I finished Swift Boat training in Coronado. I stood on the upper deck of a ferryboat as she pulled away from the Orange Avenue landing. I remember smiling. I would soon have command of a Swift Boat. I had walked toward the interim bow of the ferryboat *Coronado* as she crossed the bay to San Diego, feeling the warm October breeze on my face. The bay was a smooth navy blue with only the ripple of cat's paws scratching the surface.

I love ships and boats of all kinds; perhaps that's why I joined the navy. But I wouldn't want to be skipper of a ferryboat, endlessly trudging back and forth as if vacillating about what direction to point my impermanent bow. I remember feeling the need for a singular destination beyond the horizon, one that would lead me to the command of a destroyer, a Grey-hound-of-the-Sea.

I think about Commander Streuli's recommendation for destroyer school. To stay up with my peers and get command of a destroyer, I'll need another sixteen years, at least ten of those at sea. And then there'll be three more years at sea as skipper. I wonder if Chantal could be happy if I'm forever at sea.

In my mind, I'm vacillating like a ferryboat.

Swift Boat patrolling a canal at low tide

Chapter Twenty-three

Binh Thuy and Spies

Cat Lo Maintenance personnel are miracle workers with ingenious skills and they repair PCF 67 in a single day. Bob Emory, "Baby Fats," is the maintenance officer.

"I think they could have completed the job in half a day," Baby Fats says, "if my men weren't laughing so much of the time. You know, based on maintenance reports, you might have set a record: most frequent self-inflected damage. Some of my guys are thinking about gettin' autographs. You okay with that? You know, photograph of your boat in the skids. You just sign—'Bent Screw.' "

"It's Preparation H," I say, "and stop using it as toothpaste."

Tim Guard, as if a reprimand, assigns our next patrol back to the Bassac. Steve Hart gives me a chart with a course marked in red ink. He's added red circles designating known sandbars and a little note scribbled next to one. "Great fishing hole," it says.

My orders are to proceed to an LST anchored in the river. It has taken six hours of transit to reach the LST and Moison brings us alongside, bow first, as we grab a line hanging from the LST's boom.

I sit at a table in the wardroom of the LST with a lieutenant who's dressed in serious-looking jungle fatigues. I listen as he describes his operation and what he wants me to do. He talks slow, as if he suspects I'm a slow learner. I discover he's a SEAL officer. He shows me black and white photographs taken from an airplane and we compare it to his chart of a canal off the Bassac. He gives me a piece of paper with hand scribble notes of radio codes and another paper with his rough sketch of a canal.

"Here's our insertion point," the lieutenant says, pointing to his sketch. "And here's our objective," pointing to a small village. Our plan is to get in and get out without anyone knowing we've been there. Understood?"

"Understood," I say. I'm a fast learner. Jesus, this guy is so intense, so serious. He stares at me with a look that shakes my own marginal confidence.

I return to my boat and huddle the crew in the main cabin.

"Here's where we're going," I say, showing them the chart, the sketch of the canal and the village. "If we get into a firefight after we insert the SEALs, do not fire in the direction of the village."

Gnau studies the sketch. I can imagine what he's thinking, perhaps remembering two Vietnamese Marines accidently hit by covering fire.

It is just past midnight as six men climb down a net onto PCF 67. Moison stands back to give the SEALs room on the fantail, as if these guys would pull out a knife if someone accidentally bumped into them. Their faces and hands are smeared with black and green body paint. They look like they've been in a mud fight.

We get underway and the lieutenant stands next to me in the pilot-house, watching Hoffman steer us farther upstream in the Bassac. The Decca radar paints a picture of a small island, each sweep in bright amber-yellow. The main channel is on the right and a small channel to the left.

"Stay left," the lieutenant says. We come to an even smaller canal on the left bank. "That's our canal," he says.

"Hoffman," I say, "turn off the radar, instruments, everything—make it dark."

Hoffman idles the engines as we coast into the canal. It is so dark and the canal so narrow that I stand on the gunnels outside the pilothouse door to give Hoffman direction. There's a mere five feet of water on each side. We go deeper into the canal and slip past branches that make a scratching sound on the hull. The canal continues to narrow. Branches are now scraping the cabin. There is absolutely no way to turn around. When we leave, we'll have to back out almost all the way to the river.

Hoffman is only using one engine, and never more than 500 rpm. He frequently idles the engine to go even slower. It's alarming to hear our metal flappers clink on the cooling-exhaust outlets. I wish I had thought to use tape to hold them upright, to keep them from making that dinner-bell sound.

"Can't believe we are doing this," I say to no one. I didn't mean to say the words out loud.

"Okay, that's far enough," the lieutenant says. I'm relieved—I don't think we can go any farther. The fathometer indicates our keel is touching bottom.

It's pitch black. I can't see the starboard side of the pilothouse six feet away. I stick my head out of the port side of the pilothouse.

"Where are the SEALs?" I whisper.

"Gone," Hudson whispers back. I haven't heard a sound.

I keep looking at the radium dial of my watch and worry it's giving off too much light. I cup it with my left hand. Two hours have gone by and I need to pee. I'd like to pee on a bush and leave my scent, like marking territory, but I don't. I'm afraid the noise of my piss hitting the water below will be too loud. I lean up against the cabin, letting my piss trickle in a warm quiet stream that puddles at my feet.

Menacing scenarios flash through my brain as we wait. If we come under fire, we risk hitting the SEALs if we shoot back. Waiting is agony.

A soft rustle of bushes ignites a jolt of electricity to every nerve in my body. The SEALs have returned and climb aboard as quietly as they left.

"Okay, let's go," the lieutenant says. He says it with a sense of impatience, like I'm a taxi cab and the meter is running.

Hoffman lights off our engines and I stand at the aft helm, backing us out. The sound of our engines makes me nervous. I'm confused which way to turn the wheel and bump into the bank. I step to the side of the wheel, face our stern and it's easier to steer.

I hadn't notice before, but now I see a body in black pajamas lying face down on the starboard engine hatch. One of the SEALs is crouched next to him, a knee pressed into his back. The body's eyes are covered with black cloth, elbows and hands bound behind him. I don't ask any questions. My only job is to get us out of this canal—the meter is running.

It is 0500 when we return to the LST. One of the men on the SEAL team stands the black pajama body upright. For the first time I know he's alive. One of the SEALs ties a line around the man's chest and he's hoisted up to the deck of the LST. He's the first Viet Cong I've seen up close. He doesn't look so menacing, being bound and blindfolded.

Before the lieutenant leaves, he hands me a gun belt with a .45 in the holster.

"Here's a present for you," he says. "Gift from our guest—he doesn't need it."

Stancil takes his turn in the galley fixing breakfast while we stay alongside the LST, waiting for orders from Mother. I caress my gift, sleek blued steel of a .45.

"Hey," I say, "it's made by Remington Rand. Thought they made typewriters. I thought .45s were manufactured by Colt."

I can tell Hudson is jealous, the way he offers to show me how to remove the magazine from the butt of the handle and his careful instructions about a small lever he says is the safety. I think he must know I'm a klutz with guns.

The black leather holster and belt are worn from the elements and could use a good coat of saddle wax. There are twenty-six loops on the belt, half of them filled with bullets. A small pocket on the holster is for an extra magazine, but the pocket is empty.

I undo my .38 and strap on the new holster and belt. I feel so cool with this new gun and can't wait for an opportunity to try it out. I do a "quick-draw" and everyone laughs—*at* me I think.

As I eat powdered scrambled eggs that Stancil has overcooked, men are probably waking up in a village. Some guy might be wondering where his VC buddy has disappeared to. He probably figures it out after a minute or two, and now he's wondering: *Am I next?*

Mother sends a message to come home. On our way back to Cat Lo, Hudson gives me instructions for my new .45. We stand on the fantail as we drive through calm seas.

"Target practice," I announce.

Gnau finds an empty C-Rats box and tosses it over the side. I take aim and empty the .45 magazine at the box. The recoil snaps my whole arm up into the air with each shot. Hudson laughs as I miss the box by more than three feet with each shot. More boxes are searched for and each man takes his turn. Stancil is the only one to get a hit before we use up all the .45 rounds. Hudson helps me clean the gun and I try to memorize how all the parts fit back together again.

We pull back into Cat Lo, this time using our steering wheel.

"Hey Hemorrhoids," Big Daddy Doug Armstrong yells, "Streuli's lookin' for you! Go aground again?"

"No, just blew a tire." I'm beginning to fear my reputation is becoming so notorious that my headstone will be engraved with a broken screw and bent rudder.

Commander Streuli is sitting behind his desk, scribbling notes amid a clutter of papers and stacks of personnel files. I'd rather be in a firefight than buried in administrative bullshit. Filing gives me the hives. I almost laugh watching his yeoman, his head bent just inches from the typewriter, hunting for keys with two fingers.

"Virg, I have an assignment for you," Streuli says, almost smiling. His glasses have slipped down his nose and he pauses to push them back. "I'm giving you some collateral duty."

"Is this a reprimand, sir?"

"Hell no." He laughs. "It's part of Operation Double Shift. You'll be in charge of four boats and I want you to take care of them." I'm sure he means the men, not the boats. "You'll be Operations Officer for a tempo-rary detachment."

I hold my breath—I fear what will come next. "Where are we going, sir?"

"You'll take the boats to Binh Thuy. Can you handle that?"

Binh Thuy, what a relief! I feared he would say Sea Float in the Ca Mau.

"Yes Sir, I can do that."

"Good. You'll depart tomorrow morning." Commander Streuli hands me a list of the three officers. "Good luck," he says. One of the officers is Michael Hudson, "Ichabod Crane." He's a good guy. I'll tease about losing his duffle bag on our flight to Cam Ranh Bay.

Being given this responsibility makes me feel trusted, maybe even respected. Well, respect is a stretch. But it seems all my mishaps have not put me on the "black list," at least not in the eyes of my skipper.

It's 0800 and our little flotilla is underway from Cat Lo. I wonder what it will be like operating out of Binh Thuy. I'm excited to be a part of something new, eager, and as always, a little naïve. I draft a letter in my mind to Dad. I embellish it a bit; imply I have command of a detachment, not just temporary Ops Officer.

It's going to take at least six hours to reach Binh Thuy. I sit in the main cabin and draw up patrol schedules and make an outline of things I need to check: Fuel, ammo, intel reports. I think about how Hal, Matt and Tim have managed our patrols. I want to follow their example, their attention to detail. I hope there's no paperwork.

I like being in the lead boat and look back at our column of Swift Boats, all running at full throttles, a bone in their teeth, white spray obscuring half their hulls, all looking proud and dangerous—a simple picture of good men on fast boats. I can't suppress a smile as I watch our single file spread out, each skipper trying to take the lead, each trying to prove his boat is the fastest. I urge PCF 67 to go faster. Swift Boat crews are competitive about everything: dice cups, volleyball, fastest boat, bragging rights, surviving. I love my sweetheart, PCF 67.

We pull into the PBR piers at Binh Thuy. We are now officially part of Game Warden. I find the Operations Center and report our arrival. The commander is short, gruff looking, big shoulders, broad stomach and almost bald with his military haircut. His khaki's are clean, starched, and his shoes look like they have been recently shined—a stark contrast to my green fatigues, scruffy boots and baseball cap. The commander frowns as he studies my .45 with twenty-six bullets lining the belt.

The commander begins to tell me what he expects while I and the Swift Boats report to him. The way he talks, as if we are still wet behind the ears, makes me wish I was still reporting to Commander Streuli.

"*My* PBRs" he says, "have been moved farther up river. Your Swifts are here to take over their old patrol areas. That's why we're calling this Operation Double Shift." PBRs are being shifted farther upriver; Swifts shifted farther from the ocean. Double Shift. Okay, I get it; I'm a fast learner. I don't envy the PBRs; they always take heavy casualties. But we take our share, especially in the Ca Mau. "I expect aggressive patrols and a report each morning on the previous day," he says.

God, I hate writing reports. I wonder if the commander will appreciate how aggressive we are, trading steak for lobster.

Everything is falling into place quickly. We have almost everything we need. It helps that we use the same fuel and ammunition as the PBRs, all except 81mm mortars. We'll get those from the LSTs bringing in supplies.

This is great duty. We no longer have two and three hour transits from Cat Lo to our patrol areas. And with my new responsibilities, I have an office and desk and a room in the BOQ when not on patrol. Nice. A yeoman gives me mimeographed reports each morning on enemy activity, suspected VC staging areas and other operations we should know about—to avoid stepping into "friendly fire." I know about friendly fire.

For me, this is a new view of the war. Most of this intelligence seems "after the fact" rather than advance information. There isn't much "Intel" to plan aggressive patrols. I know what it's like to patrol rivers and canals. We react to requests for support or we react to ambushes. We seldom have an opportunity to surprise the VC. We just show the flag and act like a target in a carnival game.

I read what appears to be "Hot Intel," a VC camp near the mouth of the Bassac—a suspected POW camp. Maybe this time we'll find one. This is an opportunity to show the commander some aggressive action. I spend three hours drafting a plan. We'll use three Swift Boats, carry troops, Seawolves orbiting out of sight, and Black Ponies manned and ready to scramble if needed. I calculate the transit time to hit the camp at 0500 while it's still dark.

I write my plan in long hand with last minute thoughts scribbled in the margins. I brief the commander.

"Okay!" he says, "This is what I want! Get copies to HAL-3, VAL-4. You coordinate the boats; I'll take care of the troops. We go tomorrow morning! You'll be OTC."

He tells his yeoman to type my op plan and copy the Seawolf and Black Pony detachments, the HAL and VAL guys. I race over to the Officer's Quarters and find Ichabod.

"Wake-up," I say, "we got an op." I begin telling Ichabod about the extravagant plan.

"Shit. You needed to tell this now?" He suggests in very strong language I could have waited a few more hours before briefing him. I should have waited. This is my first operation and I'm excited. I've forgotten how tired patrols make me feel. I walk over to the hangers and find duty officers for the Black Pony and the Seawolf guys. I give them each a short briefing on the schedule, radio frequencies and call signs.

"A yeoman will bring over the typed op plan in an hour," I say. I return to my office and review my check list. I calculate the tides for the third time. Everything looks perfect.

The commander screams for me to come into his office.

"It's sixteen-hundred hours! Where in the hell is that op plan? I got people gearing up and no schedule. I got Vietnamese troops and a Green Beret advisor. What the fuck have you been doing all day? Have you got your shit together, Mister!?"

I'm totally unprepared for this verbal dressing down. I'm sure everyone in the office can hear him. I feel my face burning. The yeoman joins us. He remembers my plan, my notes and instructions. He says it disappeared from his "in basket."

"I thought you took it back to make corrections," the yeoman says.

I sit next to the yeoman, recreating my plan while he types. I see the commander pacing. The last page is done. The commander reviews and approves the plan and the yeoman races out the door to deliver copies. I hand deliver a mimeograph copy to Ichabod and to another Swift Boat skipper just returned from patrol.

"This better be worth it," the skipper says. "My crew's tired." The skipper and Ichabod leave to brief their crews.

It's 1800 and everyone now has a copy. What a cluster-fuck. I hope this is worth it. I don't enjoy robbing men of sleep. I think of all the aborted missions I've been on. Now I know why—dumb asses like me planning operations.

My wake up comes at 0130 and I'm on the dock in thirty minutes. Red flashlights are reflecting off decks, crews checking guns, and there's a subtle glow inside each pilothouse. Vietnamese troops are boarding, filling up the fantail of each boat. I hear the Green Beret advisor say, "Check safeties." I assume he means "Safety's on, but I don't ask.

I board my boat with the advisor and we cast off. We're at full throttle, three Swifts heading downriver in the dark. The excitement of launching an operation loaded with troops is an adrenaline rush. As we drive through the dark, my enthusiasm is displaced by anxiety—fear I've forgotten something.

The pilothouse is busy. The advisor and I are huddled on the left, marking progress on the chart. Hoffman is watching his compass and checking the radar, a rubber boot covering the scope. As OTC I feel nervous, like other OTC's I've known.

"We're only making fifteen knots," I say. "Shit, I planned for twenty." I can see the throttles are pushed to their stops.

The Green Beret advisor gives me a look and taps his watch without saying a word. It's 0500. We haven't reached the insertion point and we should be there now. The Seawolves report in.

"Orbiting, on station," a pilot says.

"Six miles to go," I tell the advisor. Shit, another twenty-five minutes. I call the Seawolves with an update.

"We're aborting," the pilot says. "We'll be too low on fuel by the time you arrive. Scramble the Ponies if you need 'em."

We approach the VC camp. Morning light is illuminating the beach. It should be dark. I've miscalculated our speed; it's the weight of the troops. We're too heavy, too slow and now too visible.

All three Swift Boats hit the beach together and troops scramble off the bows. I want to go too. I don't know why. Maybe I hope I'll get shot for fucking up this operation.

"Can I go with you?" I ask the advisor as he jumps on the beach.

"Follow me, stay behind and stay on my right."

I'm not in my element; I know nothing about ground fighting. I don't even know how to handle my .45. Should a round be in the chamber, should the hammer be cocked, should I have the safety off? Questions come to my mind as I jog in a crouch, following the advisor.

We search six structures, racing from one to the next. I see pots of rice half full and others with water. The fire pits are almost cold.

"They left hours ago," the advisor says. He yells to a Vietnamese soldier, "Check out those spider holes."

I follow this man like a little puppy, afraid the VC haven't left, afraid we'll suddenly be in a firefight. It occurs to me, coming ashore is one of the dumbest things I've ever done. Why didn't I learn the first time in that village with all those screaming kids?

I watch the advisor explore a thatched lean-to. He lifts a straw mat, exposing a tunnel. He drops in a hand grenade and yells, "Fire in the hole!" He casually walks away, as if it were a soda can dropped in the trash. I duck down, just as I had in the Bo De. The explosion is muffled and un-dramatic, just a puff of smoke and a deep thudding echo.

The advisor points to a Vietnamese soldier and then points to the hole. I watch the soldier crawl into the tunnel and disappear. There's no way I

would do that. At best there are dead bodies down there and worse, someone waiting for me in the dark. God, what a way to make a living.

I can't see the Swift Boats beyond the bushes. I remember the day one
of the Swifts provided covering fire with fifties, hitting two marines next to
red smoke. I hope we won't need covering fire. I wish I'd stayed on my boat.

The VC have escaped, no one captured and no POWs liberated. But
they were here, this faceless enemy I've only seen with a blindfold.

"They knew we were coming," the advisor says.

How does he know that? I feel rebuked; I think he's blaming my poor
planning and poor timing. I feel like shit.

As we head back to Binh Thuy, I can't look anyone in the eye. I sit on
the fantail of my boat, thinking about the failed mission. What if those
POWs were Americans? I wanted to find those men.

The advisor sits down next to me and says, "They had intel."

I'm not sure who he's talking about, but then I think about his earlier
comment, "They knew we were coming."

"The VC knew we were coming?" I ask and he nods. It sparks a
thought, "my missing plan." I mention the episode, how I had to rewrite it.
He stares at my eyes as if I have said something stupid.

"There's someone in that office," he says. "You tell your commander.
You need to find out who." I think maybe he's right. Someone could have
taken my notes and passed them on. If true, the VC have an incredible net-
work.

I give a full report to the commander. He's livid.

"Men, helicopters, boats—wasted—because you were thirty minutes
late!"

"Sir, I think my notes were stolen, passed on."

"Spy!?" he says and then laughs. "Trying to cover your ass." He gives
no merit to the Green Beret's suspicion.

I step outside for some air. A Vietnamese mamma-san is dumping a
sack into a trashcan. I don't trust her. I don't trust anyone anymore, not even
with cans of Mexican food. Do these people really care who wins?

I sit in the BOQ writing a letter to Chantal. I'll be home in six weeks.
I ask her if she will come to Colorado Springs at the end of September to
meet my parents. I think about Destroyer School in Newport, Rhode Island:
Six months in a classroom, home each night. Not a bad way to start a marriage. She'd like Newport. I know just the house she would love, if it's available. It has wood floors and a stone fireplace big enough to walk into
standing up. My friend, Lieutenant Con Kepple, rented it back in the
summer of '66. I remember coming in through the kitchen door without

knocking. He was entertaining guests and I felt embarrassed. His guests were Joan Baez and Bob Dylan. Con and Bob had grown up together. These singers were in Newport for the folk festival. I was wearing my uniform and his haughty guests gave me an arrogant stare. I left quickly and without regret. I doubt Con told them what he did for a living—a crypto officer attached to naval intelligence. Well, I didn't care what those entertainers thought. But still, that was a nice house and a great fireplace.

I write a letter to Dad, but I don't mention Chantal or the operation I screwed up. I tell Dad that Commander Streuli has recommended me for Destroyer School—one more step toward command at sea. I don't feel enthusiastic. Maybe I'm just tired, or maybe I'm too incompetent to have command of a capital ship.

Chapter Twenty-four

Target Fixation

My crew and I go on patrol every other day. On my day off, I read daily intelligence reports and draft a short summary from notes each boat skipper gives me. The Game Warden commander ignores me and days drag by.

Tonight I sit at the bar in the Binh Thuy Officer's Club wondering who is the spy, and thinking about this damn war. I feel confused about my future. Alcohol increases my confusion.

"Are you any good at shuffleboard?" a guy asks. "I need a partner." He has a Seawolf patch on his green flight suit. The invitation is a rescue from my self-absorbed depression.

The Seawolf pilot teaches me a new way to play shuffleboard. My partner and I stand at one end of a thirty-foot table and we take turns sliding our steel pucks toward the other end. We try to keep all of them on the board and as close to the other end as possible—the closer to the end, the higher our score.

Our opponents at the far end count which pucks have passed over which lines and tell us our score. They're pilots too, wearing Black Pony patches. My partner thinks maybe they lied about our score. Maybe it's just general distrust; these fixed-wing pilots can't hover like a helicopter pilot. The pucks are so far away it's hard to tell if they lied.

"We're walking," my Seawolf partner says. "We challenge." We both walk to the other end of the shuffleboard and inspect the results. "You pecker-heads," he says to the Black Ponies. "Rules are," he says to me, "they lied, so we get double points plus a round of drinks."

"What if they hadn't lied?" I ask.

"We lose our points and *you* buy them a drink."

It's a great game. The more we drink, the more we challenge. But I think most of the challenges are related to the competitive spirit between fixed-wing aviators and helicopter pilots. Nonetheless, it's a downward spiral for all of us, an unrecoverable spin.

I compliment the pilots for their air support: Seawolves on the Duong Keo, Black Ponies off the Bassac a month ago. I don't tell them I planned the VC-POW raid. We all start saying how one has better duty than the other. They want a ride on a Swift Boat. I want a ride in a Huey and a Bronco, an OV-10.

After another twenty-four-hour patrol, I sit in the office feeling an uncomfortable stare from the Game Warden Commander when I get my first wish. I'm invited to go on a "hop" with the HAL-3 guys, in a Seawolf helicopter gunship. The commander gives me the day off. I'm sure he's happy to be rid of me for a day.

The Seawolf Huey is parked between rows of sandbags about three feet high and there's a ten-foot slatted barrier in front. I strap in between two door gunners. The pilot and co-pilot go through their well practiced routine of flipping switches and turning dials.

My brother has taken me up in all manner of flying machines. He would go through his preflight, checking the magnetos and playing with switches. He said if he was trying to impress a backseat novice, he would go through the routine twice, just to amplify the mystique of aviation. Today, no amplification is needed.

"Comin' Hot!" the Seawolf pilot on the right yells out his side window. I hear the turbines begin to spool up, a high-pitched whine that continues to build into a deep-throated roar. The sound reminds me of the turbine engine on the drone helicopter from my destroyer days, the quarter million dollar, remote-controlled helicopters I crashed into the sea.

The pilot-in-command is sitting in the right seat. I watch him pull up and twist a handle called his "collective." It looks like a fancy parking brake in a sports car. He toggles a small red conical button on the end of the parking brake with his thumb.

"Coolie hat," he says. I have no idea what that does, maybe just more mystique. The Huey slowly lifts up off the ground. An airman, about ten feet on our right, is giving hand signals as we gently back out of the parking space. I wonder why we don't just lift straight up and fly away.

We taxi about three feet off the ground to some designated spot and then the nose pitches down and the Huey accelerates, gaining altitude and speed at an incredible rate. I can't tell if we are about to crash or to fly. In minutes we are cruising at 120 miles an hour and I start to relax. My helmet has earphones and I hear someone say something too cryptic to understand. I glance at the door gunner on my right. He gives me a thumbs-up and grins. I wonder why he is grinning. The Huey suddenly banks to the right and dives straight down. My pucker-factor jumps to ten—I am sure we are going to die.

Just before impacting mother earth, we roll hard left and pull up at the same time. "G" forces are trying to pull my head out through my ass. I'm transfixed on trees about to enter the right door. The door gunner motions for me to look forward. It takes enormous effort to lift and turn my head. I focus on the view between the two pilots, looking through their windshield. It is an incredible scene. We are racing just fifty feet over the river, rolling left and right through a canyon of trees. My nausea and vertigo eases.

Our mission is to look for VC bunkers and ambush sites along the river bank, information I can use to plan aggressive Swift Boat operations and impress the commander. But at this speed, so close to the water and trees, I just see a blur, trying my best to anticipate the pilot's next roll, using my body language to help him miss trees and my telepathy to tell him to slow down and climb higher. As an observer, I'm useless.

I begin to relax, feeling more confident as the pilots dance their Huey over the river with the grace of a ballerina. It is a thrill of a lifetime, but only appreciated after we land.

I return to my office and go through a practiced routine, not switches and dials, but reporting yesterday's Swift Boat activity, checking on how the crews are doing and reading intelligence reports. I feel like a slacker, not earning my keep. I remember how I used to think that patrolling the coast was useless. We moved our operations into the rivers and those patrols became dull and mundane. And then we started canal operations—definitely an adrenalin rush. But Dad was right about war being ninety percent boredom. This tedious monotony is made worse by paperwork.

I look forward to my next twenty-four-hour patrol, anything to get away from the Game Warden commander. It'll be a cold day in hell before he lets me plan another operation. The commander says he wants at least one hour of PsyOps on each patrol. I hate PsyOps.

We cruise down the river playing a god-awful audio tape. The sound blasts out over loudspeakers mounted just aft of the gun tub. We're playing a tape called "Wandering Soul." The title sounds like it comes from an evangelist's prayer meeting. The Vietnamese mono-syllable language drives me crazy, especially when it's this loud and so monotonous. I have no idea what the tape is saying except that it is supposed to encourage the VC to give up and join the South Vietnamese resistance to Communism.

I hate PsyOp missions for another reason: They are *guaranteed* to draw sniper fire. I think that's why most skippers ignore the commander's order and don't play the tape.

We beach our boat at a small village in an area considered friendly. Women are squatting by fires, stirring rice in small pots. Children are trying to climb on our boat. Moison pulls in the bow net, fending off the kids, and Gnau diverts their attention by tossing packages of gum ten feet away. "Wandering Soul" is still playing and I wonder if anyone is listening.

A clink-clink rings just above my head and I turn to look. Two bullets have just pierced the speakers. I see the sniper across the canal with an AK-47, aiming at me from a thicket of bamboo. It's the first time I've actually seen a Viet Cong that is shooting at me.

Hudson returns fire with a couple of short bursts from his twin-fifties. A disposable rocket launcher is lying on top of the cabin behind me. I immediately grab this green tube, lift it to my shoulder and fire the rocket at the sniper. The rocket explodes over twenty feet from the VC, but that's okay. I really just wanted to try out this new weapon.

I hear Hoffman behind me scream, "Goddamn it Mr. Erwin, watch what you're doing!" I turn around and see our American Flag burning. The rocket blast from the back of the rocket lit off our flag; it could have easily fried one of my crew to a crisp. I apologize and help put out the fire. I hope the VC sniper hasn't seen this little episode. I imagine him telling this story to his VC buddies, all of them laughing until it hurts.

The PsyOp program is a pain in the ass.

After another day in the office, I eat dinner alone and then go to the O' Club and sit at the bar. I buy a round for the Seawolf pilots, thanking them again for my ride, telling them how good it feels to still be alive. I promise reciprocity on a Swift Boat whenever they want.

"I know just how to find some action—Psy Ops," I say. But compared to the speed and agility of their Huey, a Swift Boat might be a little too tranquil.

One of the Black Pony pilots comes into the bar. I think he wants to upstage the Seawolf pilots. He offers me a ride, "In a real airplane," he says.

The Seawolf and Black Pony pilots start exchanging humorous insults.

"To hover is divine," a Seawolf pilot says.

"Skids are for kids," the Black Pony pilot replies. I think his retort refers to the fact that Huey's don't have wheels. I enjoy their bravado, each pilot saying their skills are more refined, that their flying machine is more unforgiving; that they fly lower to the ground or their machine has higher performance.

The Black Pony pilot is sucking back drinks pretty fast and I sense he's depressed.

"Problem is," the Pony pilot says in a somber tone and slurring his words, "target fixation. Too focused on the target. Followed his tracers right into the ground."

It is suddenly quiet, no jokes, no retorts, no one saying anything, no one looking at each other. I realize the Black Ponys have lost two pilots today—pilot error, buried in the ground.

I think about the year before my brother was born. It was 1949. Dad was a gunnery instructor in Pensacola, teaching aerial combat. He came home from the air station and I heard him tell Mom he lost another pilot—a crash and burn story. He didn't cry.

"Men don't cry," he told me. Dad said he lived just for today. I didn't know what he meant back then.

I lay in my bunk in the BOQ, the booze making it easier to relax. I think about tomorrow's patrol, and the promised ride in a Black Pony.

Our Swift Boats are ordered to practice medical evacuation with a US Air Force helicopter based at Binh Thuy. The helicopter is weird looking with two sets of rotor blades mounted next to each other, synchronized as they spin to avoid destroying each other. It's obvious why the pilots call this an "eggbeater." Their call sign is "Padre," appropriate for their humanitarian mission.

We set the speed of our Swift Boat at fifteen knots, heading down the middle of the Bassac River. Padre is following us as they lower a wire basket. They creep forward, then match our speed as they try to position the basket over our stern. In theory, we would place a wounded man in the basket and Padre would hoist it up to their door and pull it into the helicopter.

Stancil tries to grab the basket as it swings in the blast of rotor wash. Moison and Gnau manhandle a fifty-pound sandbag, trying to drop it into the basket. The basket keeps getting fouled in our lifeline stanchions and almost becomes permanently attached to our fifty-caliber barrel. We give up trying and Padre returns to their base. I hope we never have to do this for real.

The evening is calm as we cruise through the river, watching for any sampans violating curfew, watching for the VC. The sky is black, an overcast blotting out stars. Suddenly, flares appear several miles away, floating below the unseen cloud layer. A brilliant streak flashes from the sky, flowing down as if a tongue of blood-red lava is licking the ground. I hear a faint hum, like someone softly caressing the base cord on a violin, as if to accompany the artist of these graceful curving pulses of red light.

"Puff the Magic Dragon," Moison says as we all stare at this specter. It is mesmerizing. I can't take my eyes off this scene and begin to see the faint outline of an aircraft. I hear Stancil join Moison as they quietly sing Peter, Paul and Mary's "Puff the Magic Dragon."

"Call sign is 'Spooky'," Hoffman says. "It's an Air Force DC-3 with Gatling guns. Six-thousand rounds per minute. You're just seeing the tracers, one every twenty rounds."

"I'd hate to be anywhere near that target," Gnau says.

It seems strange to think of such breathtaking violence as beautiful.

The rest of our patrol goes by as if on some kind of automatic control and we return to Binh Thuy as a morning rain shower passes. I check in with my commander and he gives me the okay for my Black Pony hop.

I show up for my preflight briefing: what buttons and switches to keep my hands off.

"We're going to Vung Tau, pick up some parts and return," the pilot says. There's no pretense of aerial reconnaissance; for me it's a pure joy ride. I caress the fuselage of this twin turbo-prop fighter, anticipating my ride as if it were sex. I stare with envy at the 20mm Gatling gun nestled under the Pony's belly, wondering how I can get one of these for a Swift Boat. This 20mm cannon would be awesome. We could replace the fifty-caliber and 81mm mortar on our aft deck. I wonder why no one has thought of this.

The pilot is going through the briefing, pointing out that OV-10s have ejection seats.

"If we need to eject," he says, "the canopy will blow and you'll get punched out first. That's so you don't get fried to a crisp from the blast of my ejection seat." His comment reminds me of the back blast from my rocket launcher. "Now, on the other hand," he continues, "you can eject and leave me sitting up front—fat, dumb and happy. No problem with the blast.

"Last week the front-seat pilot got hit, slumped over, not talking. The backseat didn't know if he was still alive. Now, I don't know too many guys to land a Bronco from the backseat. Not easy, kind of hard to see. He could've punched out and saved his own ass, but he stayed with his buddy and landed—little rough, but he landed. Pilot was dead; took a single round through the cockpit."

A klaxon horn blasts three times, a scramble alert, Scramble Code One (under fire, men hurt, can't escape). My joy ride is cancelled. The damn Viet Cong have ambushed some PBRs and priorities have changed.

This war is starting to piss me off. I return to the operations office and sit, shuffling through intel reports. Ichabod Crane walks through the door. He looks exhausted, sweaty, in need of a shave.

"Last night a Spooky shot up a village," Ichabod says. "I found eight wounded Vietnamese in a sampan early this morning, men, women and children, trying to get to a hospital. I brought them here. Army doctors said they couldn't treat them, couldn't help them. Why?"

"I don't know. I've seen lots of Vietnamese in that hospital. What did you do?"

"One of women was crying. Her kid was a mess, unconscious. She kept saying '*bac si*;' she was asking for a doctor and pointing downriver. We found a Red Cross sign on the riverbank at Can Tho. It's a Vietnamese hospital. We dropped them there."

"Had to be an accident. The kid going to be okay?"

"I don't think so."

Seawolf "comin' hot"

Lt Michael Hudson, "Ichabod Crane"

Chapter Twenty-five

A Jeep is Missing

It doesn't feel like this war is going to end soon. For the older Vietnamese, I suppose it's become a way of life. For the children, it's the only life they've known. The Paris Peace Talks seem to be dragging without a sign of concession from any side, so I doubt their lives will improve anytime soon.

Here in Binh Thuy, as operations officer for this detachment, I feel useless and bored. I'm climbing the walls as if I have cabin fever.

Another day is over—designing new and innovative ways to get my notes typed in time for the VC messenger-spy. I head to the club, skipping dinner and fully intending to muddle my brain with a few drinks. A lieutenant is sitting at the bar. He seems engaged in the same singular purpose. He's skipper of an LST that's unloading supplies at our base.

We share a few stories and drinks, getting to know each other.

"If you can get some wheels," the lieutenant says, "I know a great place to eat." He says Binh Thuy is his regular supply run and he talks like he knows the area. I'm hungry for something besides boiled chicken and powdered mash potatoes.

"Wait here," I say.

I walk to the operations office. It's 1800 and the office is nearly deserted. The commander has a jeep and I find the keys on his desk. I feel like a teenager stealing car keys.

Now we have wheels. There's no canvas top on the jeep and the windshield is folded down. The skipper invites two of his junior officers from the LST to join us and they climb in the back of the jeep. I'm driving, the lieutenant giving directions.

The skipper has a weathered face and looks older than any lieutenant I've ever seen. He might be a "Mustang," promoted up through the ranks like Commander Streuli or possibly passed over for lieutenant commander, or maybe both. His khaki uniform looks like it has never been washed. The lieutenant bars on his collar are green from corrosion, but I don't think he needed to soak them in saltwater. Despite his appearance, I like him immediately.

We follow a dirt road through mostly open terrain, rice fields on each side. There are occasional trees lining the road and I wonder which one might hide a sniper. I wish we had some weapons, but the lieutenant seems confident of our safety and sure of our destination.

"How much farther?" I ask.

"Just keep going," he says.

I'm starting to worry. How can I be so dumb as to go on a dinner junket with a man who has no idea about jungle warfare? I am once again out of my element, like stepping off my boat with a Green Beret advisor.

"Pull off here," the lieutenant says. It's a small compound, a couple of watchtowers and a tall wire fence. "Just want to say 'Hi' to some friends." It looks like an outpost for some US military advisors, out in the middle of nowhere.

We get out of the jeep and walk over to where several men are playing with a monkey. The monkey has a collar around its neck and a leash tied to a post. One of the men hands the monkey a piece of banana and the monkey immediately grabs the man's hand, pulling fingers into its mouth. The monkey has huge canine teeth looking all the more lethal with his lips curled back. But then he relaxes and gently mouths the skin between the man's thumb and index finger. The monkey's eyes remain focused on the man's face.

Everyone laughs, but one of the men warns me, "If that monkey gets hold of you like that, don't try to pull away. If you pull back, he'll bite worse than a dog and he won't let go. You'll be lucky not to lose a finger. Just relax and after a minute or two, he'll release you." I keep my distance.

We climb back into the jeep and drive to a small village, parking in front of a restaurant with an open-air front, just a corrugated metal roof and three walls. There are no doors and the louvered window shutters on each wall are propped up with long slender poles. We sit at a table at the front of the restaurant with our backs to the side wall.

"It's a good idea," the lieutenant says, "always have your back covered and be able to see the jeep." I learn it isn't fear of having our jeep stolen, but to make sure no one attaches something harmful underneath, something that goes boom. It doesn't take much imagination to understand why we need our back covered, but I wonder why it makes any difference; we don't have any weapons. I wish I'd brought my .45. Wonderful neighborhood, I think.

My dinner is steaming hot, a soup packed with chicken and noodles, and spices of nutmeg and ginger, and the beer's good too. I consume a lot of beer and I'm a little inebriated. For some absolutely ridiculous reason, I insist on driving as we head back to the base. Maybe if arrested for drunk driving, they'll send me home. This is a perfect time for the VC to ambush us: we're *all* drunk. It's fortunate we don't have guns; we'd probably shoot off our toes before hitting the enemy.

The sentries have a startled look as they wave us through the gate. I think they know we've had too much to drink. As we approach the LST, the lieutenant says in a laughing challenge, "Bet you can't drive this jeep aboard my ship!"

The ground slopes down toward the river and it is covered in mud with deep wheel tracks. I think the LST skipper is just trying to avoid walking through that muck. The LST's bow doors are swung open like the maw of a gigantic whale, her oral cavity now empty of trucks and supplies.

Alcohol has an interesting effect on my judgment. It makes me think every challenge is directed at my manhood. I put the jeep into four-wheel drive and down we go toward the gaping bow doors of the LST. Floodlights shining down from the bow make it harder to see where I am going. We slide sideways as if on a ski slope, but we make it to the ramp. The jeep skids into the cavernous hold of the LST and I slam on the brakes just in time to avoid smashing into a bulkhead.

"How's that?" I ask.

The lieutenant laughs and says, "For that, young man, you need a reward." We climb several ladders and end up in the wardroom. The lieutenant pulls out a bottle of scotch and we start to drink, telling sea stories until late in the evening. I know booze isn't allowed aboard ship, but *C'est la guerre.*

I talk about boredom, but admit to this lieutenant that I have been afraid, referring to times in the Ca Mau. I start to ask his opinion about making the navy a career, but it's late and I'm tired. I realize I'm knee-walking drunk, too shit-faced to drive the jeep or even crawl back to my room in the BOQ. The lieutenant offers me an empty bunk in the officer's quarters.

A speaker on the bulkhead blasts me awake with the shrill sound of a boatswain's mate whistle. I bump my head on the ceiling. I wonder how I managed to get into the top bunk last night. I vaguely hear, "Set special sea and anchor detail." The message has a familiar ring, but it doesn't register in my brain. It is early morning; I need coffee and I have a patrol in two hours. I have an enormous hangover and stagger back to my area of the base.

As I enter the Operations Office, the commander is screaming at all the enlisted men, "Where's my jeep? Who stole my jeep!?" Oh shit, I forgot about the jeep. I pretend not to notice, not to act guilty. I'm hoping he'll think the VC messenger stole it.

I return to pick up the jeep and see the LST as she backs into the channel. She's heading to the Philippines. I am sure they still have the jeep.

Swift Boat operations continue with unending repetition. Another troop insertion is planned, this time by the commander himself. He assigns me as OTC. I think he wants me out of his sight. I think he suspects I had something to do with his missing jeep.

The commander is meticulous in his planning—we arrive at exactly low tide. I have the last laugh as we dump Vietnamese troops into waist-deep mud. The troops assemble on the bank and then head off into the jungle, and we sit waiting for the troops to return. I tell Stancil about my episode with the jeep and he laughs.

"I met a girl who is working at the Base Exchange," Stancil says. "I rode with her on a bus to her home, met her parents and they invited me to stay for dinner. Mr. Erwin, she is out-of-this-world beautiful. I've seen my share of bar girls in Vung Tau. She's no bar girl; she's different."

"How was the dinner?"

"Good, but after dinner, I realized I had no idea where I was or how I was going to get back to the base. I was worried. Fortunately, she helped me find the right bus."

"Are you going to see her again?"

"I don't know. I have the feeling her parents are looking for a way to move to the US. Maybe they're pushing her to find an American husband."

We load up the troops with their muddy boots and return to Binh Thuy. I remember Carr always made everyone wipe their feet before coming aboard. He'd cry if he could see our decks now.

I have a message from Commander Streuli; my orders to destroyer school have arrived. I feel enormous pressure to decide if I am going to stay in the navy, but I'm tired—it's hard to think clearly. I've always felt the need to work hard, to put in extra effort at everything I do, just to stay up with my peers. I know I'm not the brightest lieutenant in the navy. Maybe the dream of commanding a destroyer is beyond my reach.

I wonder if Chantal could be committed to me and to this way of life, and put up with the loneliness while I'm at sea. We hardly know each other. I wish I could see her, have a couple of weeks to talk. I wish I could to talk to Dad before making this decision.

I remember my grandfather saying to my dad, "Why don't you get an honest job, get out of the navy, stop living off our taxes." How could he say that to his son? I hate my grandfather for saying that.

I crawl into my bunk in the BOQ. My .45 holster is draped over a chair. It's too far away if I need it. I slip the .45 under my pillow. It feels good there; it makes me feel safe. I wonder who is a spy.

Operation Double Shift ends and we're ordered to return to Cat Lo. The Game Warden Commander walks down to the piers to see us off. He has to walk; he doesn't have a jeep.

"Give this envelope to Commander Streuli," he says. He isn't smiling. I imagine what is said in the envelope. I'm sure it's about my performance and I imagine how it might get caught in the wind and fall overboard. But I don't really care. I have less than three weeks before leaving Vietnam. I am feeling very "short," just like Duck McFarland felt those last few weeks. I feel that same anxiety, almost there, counting the days.

Our detachment of four boats, returning from Binh Thuy, enters the canal to Cat Lo. I notice a Swift Boat at anchor in the Vung Tau harbor, flying the South Vietnamese flag. It's a Mark II, a new boat, with lots of upgrades. The pilothouse looks larger and the foredeck is definitely bigger.

The Vietnamese Swift Boat is loaded with plywood, lumber and building materials piled on top of the cabin. I've never seen a South Vietnamese Swift Boat on patrol. I wonder what they are doing. Obviously, they are not going on patrol with all that lumber. The image of a Swift Boat being used like a cargo vessel angers me. But why should I care; I'm going home.

I report to Commander Streuli and give him the envelope. He takes a minute to read the typed pages.

"The commander in Binh Thuy gave you and the crews high marks for the operation," Commander Streuli says.

"That's hard to believe," I say. "What'd he really say?"

Commander Streuli laughs. "You did good, honest. Virg, you got two weeks to go. I'm taking you off patrols."

"God, I thought I'd never hear those words. Thank you. What about my crew?"

"Bill Alexander will take your boat with a new crew. We're sending the Sixty-seven to Qui Nhon. Your crew will get on other boats."

I think about giving up my boat. She's a sweetheart. She's been good luck from the very beginning, no one killed. I'm relieved my patrols are over, but I don't want anyone else to have my boat. And I don't like being separated from my crew. We're family. I depend on them. But getting off patrol is a godsend.

I break the news to my crew. They already know. The scuttlebutt net-work is faster than a yeoman's typing. I can't tell if they're disappointed, but I hope so. Taylor is already home, Moison and Hoffman will be soon. Gnau, Stancil and Hudson will move to another boat. It's clear this is goodbye, maybe *adieu,* maybe we'll never see each other again. I'll miss these guys; I would serve with them anywhere, anytime.

I've little to do after turning over PCF 67 to Lieutenant Alexander. I hang around the Operations hut, looking at weekly reports. My boat is now in Qui Nhon with Coastal Division 15. I still think of her as my boat. One of the reports says Division 15 initiated operation START, Swift Training And Rapid Turnover. It won't be long before the Vietnamese Navy takes over all the Swift Boats; we'll be out of a job. Division 15 is training the Vietnamese sailors on boat systems, color coding the engine room piping with stenciled arrows for the direction of flow for fuel, hydraulics and salt-water.

I have to laugh. I remember when Suggs was trying to teach some Vietnamese sailors about a diesel filter. Toi, my Vietnamese liaison, said there's no word in Vietnamese for diesel filter. Suggs was frustrated, trying to convey the filter's purpose and why it needs to be changed periodically.

"I explained to these sailors," Toi had said, "the filter removes evil spirits from our fuel."

I knew we were being had. The Vietnamese and the Viet Cong know how to rig underwater mines, set off Claymores in trees, and hit Swift Boats with B-40 rockets. This evil-spirit crap had to be an inside joke between the Vietnamese sailors, their way of having a little fun with the Americans. What a laugh, but I still wonder who can be trusted and who really gives a shit.

I miss my boat and I miss my crew, but I don't miss the fatigue. As skipper of PCF 67 I had a purpose, adding my part to winning this war. Now, with nothing to do, my anxiety is growing and I begin to have dreams that scare me. I'm spending too much time thinking about what can go wrong before I get on that divine freedom bird taking me home.

I wonder if the Binh Thuy spy will ever get caught.

Chapter Twenty-six

Last Patrol

It's not dreams I'm afraid of—it's missing my plane. I have six days and a "wakeup" before leaving Vietnam. I need to get out of this country. I'm no longer invincible—my once hard shell has been ground into sand.

Dreams come more often as I tick off each day: the base being over-run by the Viet Cong, dark gargoyle faces searching for me, men wearing black pajamas, straw coolie hats, brandishing AK-47s. They're everywhere, overpowering the sentries, crawling through the base like ants. I shoot them and they fall like paper targets in an arcade, but more keep coming. I'm running, stumbling and can't get away, not sure where to hide.

It's a relief to be awake. I hate these dreams.

A noise jolts me—it takes seconds to grasp: it's a knock on the door. I sit up too quickly. I feel faint, my vision blurry, my head spinning and wish whoever it is would go away. It's almost noon. I never get enough sleep, even in this cocoon, my room in the officer's quarters—the only sanctuary I've known from endless patrols on brown muddy rivers and dirty canals.

My sheets are soaked and the butt of my gun has slipped from under the pillow. I remember a year ago, arriving late at night in this vile Vietnam, obsessed with the need for a gun. I'm insane to sleep with a gun. I'm a klutz—I could accidentally shoot myself. I eject the round from my .45 and shove the gun into my locker. I know other guys sleep with guns, guys like me with just days left before our one-year tour is up.

I'm irritated by another knock and I jerk open the door. Two sailors in the hallway are holding a wooden box—a crude, inelegant suitcase for ship-ping my gear home. I'm no longer annoyed; they have my going-home box, which is different from another kind of going-home box, one draped with a flag.

My wet tee-shirt stinks like old tennis shoes, and I peel it off as the sailors depart. It's at least ninety degrees and my fan only knows how to blow hot air. I'm anxious to start packing. I feel sorry for the guys who just arrived—they still have too many patrols to dream about. And I feel pity for the South Vietnamese. They're not leaving, not now, not after a year, not ever.

Another knock at the door. Maybe another box.

I swing open the door, ready to say, "Put it anywhere," but it's just a young kid, a yeoman, awkwardly shuffling his feet.

"Excuse me lieutenant, Commander Streuli would like to see you. He's waiting at the Officer's Club."

"Very well," I say. I'm disappointed; I could use another box. I wonder what the commander wants. It can't be another reprimand. I haven't damaged a boat since June and he can't possibly know about the missing jeep, but it doesn't matter if he does. Maybe it's about my orders to Destroyer School, an important step if I am going to make the navy a career. Dad would be so proud if I had command of a destroyer.

Commander Streuli is at the bar and offers a drink. He's having a Coke.

"Thank you sir, a Coke sounds good." I like Commander Streuli, his easy-going style, his calm voice and the way he shows empathy for the risks we take, driving our boats into narrow canals, day after day, exposing our thin aluminum hulls and sweat-covered bodies to Viet Cong ambushes and B-40 rockets. I admire his efforts, trying to pull men off patrol their last month in-country, inventing odd jobs on the base as an excuse. We call him "Snaky Jake" behind his back for his illicit scavenging of parts to keep our Swift Boats running. He's a "Mustang," a former enlisted man, coming up through the ranks before becoming an officer. My dad is a Mustang. Mustangs make outstanding officers. Commander Streuli is the best skipper I've ever served.

"Hope I didn't disturb your day off," Commander Streuli says, pushing his glasses back with a finger the way I've seen him do a hundred times when he pauses to think. "I need a favor."

"Yes sir?"

"I need you to take a Swift Boat down to Sea Float and bring one back that's been shot up pretty bad."

I feel air has been sucked from my lungs. I'm speechless. *Please, no, not me*, I want to say, but I can't put the words in order.

"Commander, I have a plane home in a week."

"I know. Don't worry, you'll be down and back in two days, three at most. You have plenty of time. I need you to leave tomorrow morning."

"Sir, I don't have a crew."

"I've pulled one together. They're all on stand-by, waiting for boat assignments."

I realize I have no choice; I can't say no to an order, and especially not to this man. "Aye-aye sir," comes out of my mouth as if someone else has control of my mind. But now, the full impact of what he's asked me to do sinks in: Ferry a boat to Sea Float, a ramshackle fortress made from barges and shacks with corrugated rooftops floating in the middle of a river—in the Ca Mau jungle, the heart and soul of the Viet Cong. I'll have to go through the Bo De River to get there. My first firefight was on the Bo De.

And Christ! Take a crew just arrived. They're cherries, kids—they won't know shit! I can't admit it out loud, but I'm scared, scared of dying, scared of being wounded and maimed, even more—scared of missing my plane home.

I've had incredible luck for almost a year. How absurd it will be: killed in the last week of my tour. It would be more humane to be killed in the first week—skip this year of adrenalin rushes, the constant uncertainty and the wasted dreams—different dreams, dreams of a future.

God! I just realized: Chantal already has her ticket, coming from France—a surprise visit to meet my parents. We're secretly engaged. There's no one to tell her not to come if I'm dead.

It's not fair. Why me? Why not someone else? I look at Commander Streuli. He's studying my face—maybe waiting for me to say more, but still no words come that will change this moment.

"Thank you," Commander Streuli says, "you'll be okay. Have another minute?"

"Yes sir." I feel my stomach tighten, as if I'm about to receive a reprimand from a man I respect.

"Admiral Zumwalt is looking for an aide. He wants someone who has skippered a Swift Boat. And he specifically wants an officer who did *not* go to the Naval Academy. Are you interested?"

"What does an aide do?"

"Just about anything the admiral wants, but mostly keeping track of his appointments, scheduling transportation, handling correspondence, stuff like that. You'd be on duty twenty-four hours a day."

"Sir, I haven't decided to augment to the regular navy. I have my orders to Destroyer School, but I'm not sure what to do. Doubt he'd want someone like me."

"Virg, I'd like to see you follow your original plan, make the navy a career. Aide to an admiral, especially *this* admiral, is your brass ring, your ticket to command a destroyer some day, assuming you don't screw up."

Commander Streuli laughs. I'm sure he's chuckling about how many times I've gone aground or disobeyed orders. It's amazing he still has faith in me. "And you can't know what the admiral is looking for until you talk to him." He puts his hand on my shoulder. "Doesn't hurt to talk."

"May I think on this, sir?"

"You got time, sleep on it."

He wouldn't say that if knew about my sleep, about my dreams. And talk does hurt. The admiral could ask me to take the job. How in hell could I say no? Zumwalt is a god. His aggressive strategy is winning this war. Because of Zumwalt, we have penetrated the Ca Mau and threatened the Viet Cong in their own sanctuary. We have the Viet Cong on the run. Admiral Zumwalt could steer my career to rewards beyond my reach.

If I ask for an interview, I have to first want the job. But why would the admiral, who graduated fifth in his class at the Academy, make a provision to select someone *not* from there? This admiral is so radical in his ideas. He's a man who gets results.

I wish I could talk to my dad. Like me, he didn't go to the academy. I know Admiral Holloway helped my dad's career. I know what dad would say: "Aide to Zumwalt? Hell yes, go for it!"

"Oh, by the way," Commander Streuli says, "if you become his aide, it will mean another year in Vietnam. Let me know your answer when you get back from Sea Float."

At least he didn't say, *If you get back.*

Another year in Vietnam. How could anyone in his right mind stay here another minute? This war is confusing. I'm so tired I can't think. I don't know who is Viet Cong and who is not. I wonder why the South Vietnamese don't fight harder—I wonder if they care who wins.

This chance scenario is bizarre: being sent to Sea Float and invited to then interview with its architect, all just a week before returning to the "World" —and to a girl. I feel numb, dizzy, like something is spinning away.

I assemble my green, untested crew who are all waiting for boat assignments. We check out the refurbished Swift Boat, running the engines, checking head-spacing on the fifties, loading mortar rounds in the ready-service locker and reviewing charts of the Bo De.

"Fuel's topped off," the quartermaster says.

"What's in those sacks?" I ask.

"Mail. And we got a ton of spare parts," he says, nodding at boxes filling the forepeak and cabin.

"Feel like a delivery truck."

There are welded aluminum patches in the pilothouse, cabin and hull, all freshly painted. The damage is almost invisible from a B-40 rocket. Men working for Cat Lo Maintenance are magicians, repairing boats and washing off red stains, as if they are plastic surgeons, trying to patch up a man who's been mauled by a dog.

We work until midnight getting the boat loaded and ready. I don't know why, but I feel resentment for these men. I keep correcting them and feel they're starting to resent me too. I wish Gnau, Taylor, Stancil, Moison, Suggs and Hoffman were with me now. I feel so alone, naked and vulnerable without them.

"We'll get underway in an hour," I say to the quartermaster as I crawl into the lower bunk in the main cabin. I can't sleep and just stare at the bunk above me.

It's 0100 and we light off the engines, take in our lines and head out of Cat Lo at a slow ten knots. As we pass fisherman shacks next to the base, I smell a pungent seaweed perfume. The South Vietnamese Swift Boat is still anchored in the Vung Tau harbor.

"Don't see anyone on watch," the quartermaster says.

"Guess it'd be too much to ask them to make this delivery," I say.

We clear the harbor and floor the throttles, following a southerly course to the Ca Mau. The seas are calm and we have a slice of moon. I keep busy, checking the radar and plotting our course, not asking the quartermaster for help. I give the sandbars of the Bassac a wide berth. Going aground would not be good.

I find myself thinking about Commander Streuli's comments: "Admiral Zumwalt is looking for an aide. He wants a Swift Boat Skipper. Are you interested? It would mean another year in Vietnam." I know Commander Streuli wants me to say yes.

I remember that day in January when Zumwalt ordered Division 11 and 13 to stand down for twenty-four hours and come to Saigon. He wanted to meet us and just talk. We were taking a lot of casualties in the rivers back then; we're taking a lot more now. He said we were doing an important job. He wanted to boost our morale. General Abrams was there, too. I remember the contrast between how these two senior officers talked. The admiral stood out; he really cared about us. Zumwalt was not aloof. I could tell he has the strength of his convictions. This is a man I would feel admiration to follow.

"Watch your helm," I say to the quartermaster. "You're ten degrees off course. Are you tired?"

"A little," he says. I call the engineman to take his turn at the helm.

I stand at the chart table, watching the radar and checking our progress. I've been on watch for seven hours. I'm tired, too.

"Set General Quarters," I say as we near the Bo De River. Each man dons flak jackets, helmets and plugs in their phones. "Load a 'beehive'," I tell the engineman. It's a new type of mortar round, a flachette, an explosive packed with hundreds of sharp black nails with tiny fins. "It's like a giant shotgun shell—spike a man to a tree."

"Yeah, we heard," the quartermaster says in a tone that suggests he's getting pissed at being treated like a newbie.

"Test fire your guns," I say. Each man cuts loose with a short burst as we enter the Bo De.

The contrast from last October is startling. Thick ground foliage is gone and the trees are denuded—dead branches without leaves. The riverbanks are exposed, naked and ugly.

"Agent Orange," I tell the quartermaster. "First time I've seen this defoliation. A year ago, before Operation Sea Lords, you couldn't see the riverbank."

"What speed do you want?" the quartermaster asks.

"Balls to the walls." We drive the boat at full bore, making over twenty-five knots on the calm water. I remember how our slow speed in October had made PCF 67 such an easy target. "Keep to the middle of the river. VC have B-41 rockets now. Longer range than the old B-40s."

As we cruise on this caramel brown water, I look with continual amazement at the devastated forest, as if it were from some eerie storybook tale describing the home of the wicked witch of the north. Even though the defoliation has made it safer for me, I feel some regret. Sometimes while patrolling the Ham Luong, the Co Chin or Bassac, I thought about how beautiful this country is. I wondered what it would be like to cruise these rivers in a private yacht, visiting local villages and exploring the Mekong all the way to its source near Tibet. But now that thought is repugnant. I'm full of hatred for the Viet Cong and the communist north, and I'm disillusioned by the apparent indifference of the South Vietnamese. I can't wait to leave this country and never come back.

I don't need to remind myself we are alone. I keep calling on the Prick 25, hoping to contact another Swift Boat, but no one answers.

"The Bo De is connected to the Cua Lon," I tell the quartermaster. "Same river, just different names at each end." I point to the chart, to where we are now.

"How come we didn't just go around the Ca Mau? Could've entered the Cua Lon from the Gulf of Thailand." He looks at me as if I hadn't thought of that.

"This way's faster," I say. "Taking the long way around would add another three hours. I want to get to Sea Float and then get the hell out of here."

We pass the remains of one village, long ago burned and raked by heavy machine guns or mortars.

"Must have been a hell of a firefight," the quartermaster says. I see debris from sampans chewed to a pulp and remnants of what were once thatched-roof huts.

"Well, those villagers are either dead, moved to safer areas or looking for revenge."

Maybe it's the sight of this village, a reminder that we are in VC country, that my gunner on the twin-fifties' requests permission to unload a few bursts into the leafless trees.

"Permission denied," I say. "Might be friendly troops in the area. And I don't want to advertise our presence." I can tell he's not pleased, kicking his boot against the gun tub. This temporary crew is eager. I know they need to break the tension, it's their first trip on the Bo De. "As long as we are not being fired at," I add, "this trip will remain a simple boat delivery." I'm burned out. I just want to go home. Let the new guys, the 'cherries' carry on as I have for Duck McFarland.

PCF 31 responds to my radio call, but I can't figure out where it is. The skipper says he's busy—no time to chat.

"Sir, are we now on the Cua Lon?" the quartermaster asks as we follow a hard left turn in the river.

"Does it matter?" I reply. I'm acting like an asshole. We track our progress on a worn faded chart, so we can quickly identify our location if we're ambushed. "Not as if we can get lost; just follow this river as if it were the 'Yellow Brick Road.' "

"Aye-aye—*sir*," he says in a sharp tone.

"Sea Float," I say, pointing to the chart, and trying to soften the air between us, "is anchored in the middle of the Cua Lon, next to this Nam Can village. The village was overrun by the Viet Cong during Tet of '68."

As we near Old Nam Can, I spot a Swift Boat. It brings a feeling of relief—we're no longer alone. The Swift Boat is heading toward us. We both slow and pull close to each other. The skipper tells me where to berth just ahead. He looks tired. I'm tired, too. I haven't slept since Commander Streuli gave me this assignment yesterday.

It's almost noon as we tie up to another Swift Boat alongside one of the Sea Float barges. Sea Float looks like a rusted junk pile lined with sandbags and flimsy structures for berthing. We remove the beehive round from the mortar, storing it in the ready-service locker. It's dangerous removing a live explosive from the mortar.

"Should have fired it into the trees," the gunner's mate says. It's a reproach and I know he's right. I remember a year ago, arriving in Cam Ranh Bay and my first briefing about PCF 98. A crewman tried to remove a mortar round that misfired. He was decapitated as the round exploded in his hands.

My crew begins refueling and getting the latest news from other crews as I report our arrival.

"We've been expecting you," Commander Emery says. "We have an op for tonight. We need another boat, so you'll be joining the patrol."

I can't believe what I am hearing.

"Sir," I say, "this is not supposed to happen; this is not part of my orders from Commander Streuli." Begging is not becoming of a naval officer, but I'm close to getting on my knees. "I'm supposed to deliver this boat and take one back to Cat Lo. That's all."

"Lieutenant, I've checked with Commander Streuli. He knows."

"Commander, I've got a flight home in five days. Will you release me in time for that?"

"Lieutenant, you'll make it. You look like shit—get some sleep."

I brief my crew on our new unexpected orders; they're ecstatic. I just shake my head in disbelief. I feel panic, fear I'm never going to get out of Vietnam. I'm exhausted, crawl into the lower bunk and fall hard asleep.

It's dark as I wake in a puddle of water on the vinyl mattress, sweat collected in the depression from my hip, enough to fill a cup. I should have put a towel over the mattress, but we don't have one. I'm embarrassed and look around the cabin to see if any of the crew has noticed. I'm wearing nothing more than a pair of saturated green skivvies. I grab a dry pair from my bag and start getting ready for the operation.

My crew seems nervous, their earlier enthusiasm less evident. They're busy checking weapons.

"Three boats got shot up this afternoon while you were asleep," the gunner's mate says.

"Who?"

"The five, thirty-one and the forty boat," he says.

"Shit, I was talking to the thirty-one this morning." After eleven months of war, it's hard to keep track of who's been hit, like trying to remember what I did the morning after a hard drunk. Back in my destroyer days, I seldom drank alcohol. That's changed.

The OTC briefs me for the operation. His eyelids are red and he hasn't shaved. He stinks. I don't think he's had a shower for days.

"We'll be probing this canal," he says, pointing to the chart. "Been ambushed twice. Anyone there is VC."

I pull my crew together in the main cabin.

"We'll be the last of three boats, single file," I say, looking at each man, pausing to make sure they're listening. "No one shoots unless we receive fire—or if I tell you to. Understood?" Each man nods, almost as if I were scolding them. I look at the engineman. "Load a 'willy-pete' in the mortar, not the beehive."

"Okay."

"Try to mark the target with your first shot."

"Okay, okay, I got it."

"For the helm," I say to the quartermaster, "you can't go faster than the boat in front, so keep some distance." I hear myself talking to them like they're children getting ready to go outside and play. I wish I had my old crew.

It's 0200 as we finally pull into the Cua Lon current with two other Swift Boats. We're tail-end-Charlie, moving at fifteen knots, the pace of the lead boat. We enter a narrow canal, just wide enough to turn around. Darkness makes it hard to judge distance. The lead boat has slowed and we all bunch up, a better target for the VC and worse, the boat in the middle is trapped, unable to maneuver.

"Watch your distance," I remind the helmsman, "keep back fifty yards. Turn off your compass and instrument lights—you can see better."

There's still a small slice of moon and it's low tide. I see muddy banks of the canal next to me lined with punji stakes. Not a good sign.

Fifty-caliber fire erupts without warning.

"Lead boat's firing!" the gunner's mate yells. Suddenly, flares are bursting in the air. More gunfire is coming from ahead. I can't tell what's happening. The boat in front of me isn't speeding up. Shit! He's slowed down. I can't tell if we're taking fire.

I launch two handheld flares. Flares are drifting down all around us, little parachutes with brilliant stars. The flares illuminate a VC bunker on the port side. It looks like a haystack. Machine gun fire is contagious. Without command, my men are shooting at the bunker, fifty-caliber guns raking the mound, tracers screaming into the dirt.

My aft gunner just fired his white phosphorous mortar round, hitting the base of the bunker. Pieces of phosphorous are leaping and twisting, leaving spiraling corkscrews of illuminated smoke trailing in the air.

Shooting stops.

Searchlights are sweeping the banks. The boat in front of me has turned on their boarding lights. Our boats continue to creep forward, now less than five knots. My bow almost touches the boat ahead. All three of us are now nose to tail close to the left bank.

My helmsman idles the engines, but we continue to drift forward. Now I see them, three sampans alongside the muddy bank. My boat's hull rubs against the wood frame of one sampan as we come to a stop. In the center of the sampan is an enormous bundle of bamboo punji stakes. Inert bodies in black pajamas are slumped next to Kalashnikov AK-47s and B-40 rockets. An old man with a weathered face is crumpled at the bow. His mouth hangs open, a grisly picture illuminated by a flare.

A Viet Cong body at the rear of the sampan is laying face up. Her straw hat is cocked to one side, her head reclined against stacks of bamboo. Her silky black hair frames a smooth and delicate face. Her face is beautiful, serene, not the callous image of the Viet Cong. Her eyes are closed as if she is sleeping and one arm is resting alongside the bulge of her pregnant belly. Her black shirt is ripped across her breast where a fifty-caliber bullet entered.

The sampan is beginning to sink, water seeping in through holes that mix with dark pools of blood. Brilliant lights swing beneath tiny parachutes. The lights cast multiple shadows of a crewman on the boat in front of me. His eerie shadows overlap each other—they seem to dance like mystic sorcerers that flicker across the old man and girl's swollen womb. My vision whirls as if I'm spinning. I try to convince myself that it is the shadows that are moving and not me. Vertigo overtakes my sense of balance; I feel nauseous and wobbly. I grab the rail outside the pilothouse to keep from falling and kneel down to steady myself. I shake my head hard, trying to rid my brain of confusing shadowy images.

I stare at the bodies of the fierce and dreaded VC. I've been hunting them for almost a year. The old man and girl were planting punji stakes, as if it were springtime. I could have told them they were planting the wrong crop. Punji stakes won't grow in this vile fucking mud, mixed with weapons and entrails.

Their faces are not what I expected. I regret I can't ask the old man if this young girl is his daughter. I'd like to know if they are both victims of coercion, like the threatened fourteen-year-old boy who would do anything to save the life of his father.

I stare at the girl, thinking about the life that was alive inside her a few minutes ago, a fetus that will never know the glory of war. The old man in the bow is too old to be a warrior. I wonder again if he is the girl's father. I wonder if he thought he could protect her.

We return to our base floating on the Cua Lon. No one boasts about tonight's operation, about how many sampans we destroyed or the body count or the bunker we tried to pulverize. Night ambushes drain the body, numb the brain—everyone just wants to sleep.

"The Viet Cong are losing this war," I say to my quartermaster.

"How do you know?"

"They're forcing old men and young girls to do their work. The VC are defeated, they just don't know it yet."

Chapter Twenty-seven

Going Home

It's Thursday morning, September 11th. My flight home is on Sunday. Commander Emery releases me and my crew to return to Cat Lo. We board the damaged Swift Boat that's to be repaired in Cat Lo. It is a floating disaster, filthy and in need of some serious TLC. All the cabin windows are covered with plywood and one of the pilothouse windows is splinted with bullet holes. The cabin smells like a high school locker full of athletic gear.

"Engines can make fifteen knots, but not more," someone says. The starboard engine rpm is surging, as if it's ready to die. I pray the engines will hold on until we reach Cat Lo.

"Onan's dead," my engineman says. His comment makes me laugh; I don't know why.

As we prepare to cast off our dock lines, Commander Emery says, "The *Gallup* is having transmission problems. They can't make more than five knots." He orders me to "escort" her to Vung Tau. For the first time, I notice the huge gunboat in the middle of the Cua Lon. I've never seen one of these before.

"It's 200 miles to Vung Tau," I say. "At five knots, that's almost two days!" I wonder if I'm ever going to make it home.

"Cast off lieutenant, and good luck."

The *Gallup* is huge—a hundred and sixty-feet long! She has twin diesels and a J79 jet-turbine engine, the same engine on F-4 Phantom jets. But the *Gallup's* combining-transmission gearbox is broken, bless its little heart. I can't believe my orders. A little fifty-foot Swift Boat is going to escort this huge gunboat.

The *Gallup* has a three-inch rapid fire gun on the bow, a 40mm gun aft, twin-fifty-caliber machine guns on each side of the bridge and an assortment of other firepower. I once thought the Black Pony's 20mm cannon was cool. The *Gallup* has more firepower than two Swift Boats, a Seawolf and a Black Pony all put together.

The two of us set off for our trip north, crawling at five knots through the Bo De. The *Gallup* is leading, perhaps to save face.

The *Gallup* calls me on the Prick 25 to say they are going to do some harassment and interdiction fire; not to worry. I can't believe the destructive power of their forward mount. The rapid gunfire is earsplitting, humbling. The three-inch-diameter projectile weighs thirteen pounds. I watch leafless trees, easily five inches in diameter, splitting in half and dropping to the ground as if some giant buzz saw is clearing a hayfield.

"Can we shoot, too?" my gunner asks. It would be hard to say no.

"Go ahead," I say, "burn up your barrels, get your kicks." What the hell, our little twin-fifties won't even be noticed.

We exit the Bo De without being fired at, which is not surprising. I imagine one of the VC somewhere along the riverbank. He turns to his buddy and says, "Hey, let's shoot a B-40 rocket at that big gun boat." And the other VC says, "Yeah, go ahead. I'll hold your wallet." My morbid humor is just a release of emotion. I'm so tired.

I know on earlier occasions the VC weren't afraid to take a shot or two at these big PGs and their B-40 rockets were on target. There were serious casualties. But today, we're all lucky.

We leave the Bo De and enter the clean blue ocean. The seas are rough. The salt spray feels refreshing as the *Gallup* and my boat turn north, but at this slow speed, we're like a piece of cork going nowhere. My Swift Boat is rolling hard and it's strenuous just to stand. It's just like the day I was officer-of-the-deck on a destroyer, rolling in seas off Cape Canaveral when my ship collided with a British nuclear submarine, the *HMS Resolution*.

"Request permission to increase speed to ten knots," I ask over the radio. "We need maneuvering speed."

"Permission granted," the captain of the *Gallup* says. "But remain within visual range." The fading light and our slowly increasing distance from the *Gallup* makes visual contact more difficult, but I can still see her on our Decca radar. I call the *Gallup* every hour, saying nothing more than "Radio check."

As we wallow north, I am fighting fatigue. My flight home is in two-and-a-half days and I try to focus on the decisions I need to make.

I remember my father was not yet forty-five when he retired from the navy. It was a glorious ceremony. Governor Love, navy admirals, air force generals, Air Marshall Simmons from Canada and the mayor of Colorado Springs were there. On cue, a formation of jet fighters passed overhead, a band played and men spoke of my father's distinguished career. But I wasn't there. I was at sea on the *USS Berry*, headed for the Mediterranean. I had requested destroyer duty. It was my father's advice.

It's hard to let go of a dream. My whole life has been the navy. I'd dreamed of becoming a naval officer since I was fourteen. Each year as I grew older the dream grew larger.

I wonder what my father will think of me if I leave the navy. I will never forget the day he administered the oath as I received my commission.

"I'm proud of you," my father had said. Oh God, how I had longed to hear those words, his praise, his recognition that I had achieved something. I felt the heat of his hand through my white glove, a firm masculine grip. He was looking straight into my eyes, his face ridged, stern, serious. He meant that; he did—he was proud; he was finally proud. My chest could not have swelled more, a wave of emotional adrenalin rushing through my body, so intense I could barely contain my need to scream, to jump, to sprint across the parade ground, to dissipate my sudden burst of exuberant energy. I could smell his Old Spice, a scent I had known since childhood. I used it too, to be just like him. I wanted to hug him, to wrap my arms around him—but I couldn't. It wasn't the place to show such affection.

I remember the tight starched collar of my dress whites chafing my neck raw. But I reveled in my image, the immaculate uniform with white shoes, gold buttons down my chest and the emblem of my reward standing proud: black shoulder boards with a gold star and the single gold-braided stripe. I was now an ensign, a commissioned naval officer. I was going to follow my father's career.

"Thank you, sir," I had said as I saluted my father. He was in his dress whites too, standing tall, a chest full of ribbons, four stripes on his shoulder, and he returned my salute. I was in awe of him, this senior naval officer. At that moment he was not just my father, but Commander, Naval Forces, North American Air Defense Command. He was a navy captain, but he was filling the shoes of an admiral's billet. And he said he was proud of me! I had worked hard to gain his respect. What a day to remember, to treasure forever.

Back then I thought a life at sea would be romantic, the only downside being away from a family. We moved every three years, each new assignment enhancing Dad's career. I know that part. It was a tough life for Mom. I keep thinking about Chantal. She has no idea what it would like, a life as a navy wife. I remember Col. MacVey's advice: "It's hard being a navy wife; it's the hardest job in the world. You'll be at sea; Chantal will need to be strong. Think it through."

I think I could do a good job as aide to Admiral Zumwalt. I'd work hard to prove myself. If Zumwalt selects me, I'll be committed to this course, another year in Vietnam, and then after that, a life at sea, fighting wars or preparing to fight wars. The military is all about war. God, I love the navy, but I'm tired of war.

I pound my fist on the chart table so hard it makes my helmsman jump in his seat. My decision is made. I can't do this any longer. I make some notes on a sheet of paper for my crew with the course and speed to maintain, my "Night Steaming Orders."

"Wake me if there is nuclear war," I say to the quartermaster. "Otherwise, let me sleep." In my mind, I am now headed home.

It is early morning. The sky is like mother of pearl and the seas have softened. There's no sight of the *Gallup* on radar. We've been heading north for eight hours, five knots faster than the *Gallup*.

"They're forty miles behind us," the quartermaster says. "They are not responding to calls on the Prick 25."

"Send her this message on HF," I say to the radioman. "Unless otherwise directed, we are preceding to Cat Lo at best speed."

The radioman codes the message and sends it out.

"No response," the radioman says.

"Okay, send it again and leave the radio on. They're big boys; they can make it to Vung Tau without me. Increase speed to fifteen knots, more if she'll do it."

It's Friday as we pull into Cat Lo. There aren't many boats, not even Swift Boats with South Vietnamese flags. The pier is almost deserted. The pace of operations is stretching the limits of available boats. I see sailors cleaning guns. It seems the fabric of fatigue is draped over the shoulders of every sailor I see on the pier. But they still look elite.

I shake hands with each of my crew and wish them good luck, but I don't look back as I walk up the pier.

I call on my skipper and give him my decision.

"I'm leaving the navy," I say to Commander Streuli. He smiles and takes my hand in a firm grip.

"Good luck, son." It sounds nice to hear him say son. He'd be a good father.

I go to my room in the BOQ and find my box still waiting and empty. I start packing with an overpowering sense of urgency. I'm not sure what to do with my .45 pistol. I can't take it with me.

Saturday morning a sailor sticks his head through my open door and says, "Commander Streuli wants to see you down at the piers."

I am sure the *Gallup* has sent a message, reporting my dereliction of duty, leaving her to flounder at five knots in a war zone. I wonder if this is a hanging offense or just a firing squad. With serious apprehension, I walk to the pier. There are six men gathered with Commander Streuli. None of them have guns.

"Fall in," Commander Streuli says. What the hell is this all about? We all stand at attention facing our skipper. It feels like I am back in officer candidate school for a uniform inspection. My worn jungle greens are frayed. I have more than enough "Irish Pennants" for everyone.

"Erwin," Commander Streuli says, "front and center." I stand in front of this line of men, looking my skipper in the eye. He begins reading something. I don't understand what this is about; he's reading a script about an operation I was on. Commander Streuli stops reading and presents me with the Bronze Star. I'm too embarrassed to say anything. I haven't done anything remarkable, nothing to deserve such a medal.

Men standing with me each receive recognition in turn, two receiving the Navy Commendation and three receiving promotions. But they all still have patrols ahead—I am going home. Every man serving on these boats risks their lives every day. I don't know why Commander Streuli submitted me for this award. But he did that for many others, too.

Of all the skippers I have served, Commander Streuli is the best. He's a Mustang, like Commander Dermody, my destroyer skipper. But this man is somehow different. Commander Streuli's dignity penetrates the confusion of war. He has unshakable values, values I respect, like showing reverence for people who are different. And he cares for the men he sends into harm's way. I just shake his hand and say thank you. I hold back a show of emotion. I've been taught to do that.

I stop into the O' Club for a drink and spot the SEAL who gave me the .45 pistol.

"I cleaned it," I say as I unbuckle the holster and return the .45. "She's been a good sleeping companion, but I can't take it home."

"Maybe I can get it to you after my tour," he says. We exchange addresses, finish our drinks and I return once more to my room in the BOQ. I call a yeoman to have someone pick up my box to be shipped home. My flight is tomorrow; just a "wakeup" left of my tour.

A few of the officers that have already completed their tours booked flights to circle the world, going to Singapore and then Paris or London before heading home. I just want to go straight home and see Chantal. One officer received permission to marry a Vietnamese girl and they have moved to Hue. I cannot imagine a love so strong that it would give me the courage to remain in Vietnam, and to move north, so close to the DMZ.

Lieutenant Jim Will interviewed with Admiral Zumwalt. He's now the new aide, but he's headed home for a thirty day leave before he returns to Saigon. I have no regrets. I'm leaving. This once beautiful country is in ruins.

It is Sunday afternoon. I stare out the window from a seat in the Continental Airlines jet as we sit on the Ton Son Nhut tarmac. I hear the door being closed. I see a jeep pulling a string of baggage carts. They are loaded with going-home boxes, the kind parents and wives have dreaded. I hope they are not putting them on this plane.

Chapter Twenty-eight

Chantal

I arrive in Colorado Springs and the Rocky Mountains are ablaze in an Indian Summer. Aspen trees are flecked with leaves of gold, but the autumn air feels cold. I can't stop shivering. Mom and Dad give me a hug. There's no welcome home banner at the airport. I'm a pariah, a baby killer, something to be hidden from society's eyes. I'm exhausted and just want to sleep—I feel I could sleep for a year. We arrive home and Mom gives me another tight squeeze.

"I know you're tired," she says. "Get some sleep. We'll talk in morning." I crawl into my old bed from high school days, wrap myself in warm blankets and I am out in seconds.

I wake to the sound of fifty-caliber machine guns and roll onto the floor. My fingers are clasped behind my neck. I'm trying to squeeze underneath my bed, staying as low as possible. I'm crawling, as if cowering under a chart table on a boat in the Bo De or running from a dream in Cat Lo, hiding from people shooting at me.

Dad laughs, standing in the doorway of my bedroom. "Relax," he says and laughs again. "It's a jackhammer—on the street in front of our house."

I feel confused, disoriented, embarrassed. Dad has seen something no one should see, not my crew, not Mom and especially not him.

My trip was forty-two hours of flights and refueling and taxis, and more flights. My mind has not caught up with my body. Mom is fixing breakfast and she wraps her arms around me as I enter the kitchen. She doesn't know about the bedroom scene. I hope Dad won't say anything. The smell of pancakes, sausage and maple syrup envelops me; I am safe—I am home.

"Mom, I'm freezing."

"It's seventy-five degrees," she says.

I light a fire and stand in front of the fireplace, piling on more wood. Mom turns off the air conditioning. I can see perspiration beading on her forehead. She gives me a quizzical look. I guess she thinks I'm acting strange, but she digs out one of my old sweaters and offers it to me.

"You're home," she says. "Stay by the fire as long as you want."

I tell Dad about my decision to leave the navy. He doesn't seem disappointed or surprised. I thought he'd be mad, thought he'd try to change my mind. I can't believe how much time I wasted worrying about what he would say or how he would feel.

"I have some contacts here in Colorado Springs," Dad says. "I'll help you get interviews."

We're not talking about Vietnam or the navy, or my decision. Mom must sense that I'm still feeling uncomfortable about memories that are just a few days old.

"Don't talk about it; it'll go away," she says. It would help to talk. Dad should know, but it's a long time ago since he's lost friends. Maybe he has somehow buried his memories of World War II and the Korean War, carrier flight ops and losing pilots.

My romantic dream of the sea has died. My active duty in the navy is over.

"For the first time since I was a junior in high school," I say to Dad as we sit by the fire, "I don't have a goal."

"You'll begin a new life." He puts his hands on my shoulders. "You'll find a new direction, a new goal. Don't worry."

"But I don't know what I want."

"Whatever it is, you can get it. You've had far more responsibility than most young men your age. You've learned to lead. You can do anything."

It feels good to have his advice, to know I have his love and respect, even though I will never reach that one dream, command of a destroyer.

"I've invited my girlfriend to come for a visit," I tell Mom. "I've asked her to marry me."

My mother's eyes open wide. "When does she arrive?" she asks. Before I can respond, she asks, "What's her name, where did you meet her, how long have you been engaged?" She only hears half my answers as she races upstairs and starts cleaning the guest room, putting on the best sheets, taking fresh towels from the bathroom and replacing them with towels that have never been used.

I tell Dad my news. "She's from France." He smiles, shakes my hand and slaps my shoulder, which almost knocks me down.

Chantal steps from the door of the plane and I see her pause, scanning the waiting crowd at the edge of the tarmac. I'd forgotten how beautiful she is. She looks frightened. I wave with both arms and she smiles.

Mom and Dad fall in love with Chantal at first sight. We sit by the fireplace chatting. Mom is asking so many questions, but she's gentle and she listens as Chantal talks about her home and her mother. Chantal's voice and her accent are honey to my ears. I want to lick the words from her mouth. Her English is hesitant. She frequently pauses, searching for the right word. I jump in too often to help her.

"Virg, me, we marry," she says, looking first at my mother, then my father. "*D'accord*? Okay?"

"Yes, yes it's okay," Mom says, jumping up and hugging Chantal. "Of course it's okay, it's very okay."

Chantal makes me laugh. In a private moment she gives me a kiss and says, "*Mon petite chou.*"

"I'm a little cabbage?" I ask. "I'm not so little. How 'bout something more masculine."

"*D'accord.*" She laughs. "*Mon grand* cabbage." She caresses my neck. "Your Apple's Adam feels hard."

"Adam's Apple," I say and she laughs again. It feels good to hold her in my arms. It feels safe.

Preparations for an engagement party take on a frenzied pace, more thorough than planning a river incursion. If needed, even the tides will be calculated. A photographer is hired. Chantal and I pose in the backyard and the photographer takes a complete roll of film of Chantal by herself.

"I'd like to add Chantal to my portfolio," the photographer says. "I have clients who create advertisements for jewelry, perfume and swim-suits."

"No swimsuits," I say before Chantal can respond. I don't trust this slick photographer, the way he is ogling Chantal.

Mom recruits my cousin, Barbara, to help with the engagement cele-bration. Barbara is like a big sister. She is the only confidant I've ever had. I hear Mom and Barbara whispering and giggling with Chantal in the kitchen. Mom is acting like a giddy teenager. Invitations for an engagement party have been mailed and Randall has been given liberty from the Naval Academy to attend.

It's been two weeks of preparation and guests are now arriving. Pre-sents, wrapped in bright paper with silver bows, are being stacked on a table. I watch Randall using his finger to reach a strawberry at the bottom of his champagne glass, manners he's obviously learned at the academy.

"Chantal looks so beautiful," someone says. "She should be on the cover of *Harper's* or *Vogue*. Where did he meet such a beautiful girl?"

I have no idea what *Vogue* is. I'm sitting in the corner of the living room staring at the floor.

"Hey honey," Barbara says, "what's wrong?"

"Everything's so trivial," I say.

"Oh sweetie, tell me, what's wrong?"

"I don't understand my feelings."

I should be ecstatic, full of beaming pride to find this dazzling and precious girl who wants to share a life together. But I feel lost in this throng of people who are laughing and rejoicing. Don't they know men are still dying in Vietnam? I feel nerves vibrating in my arms and legs, but they have nothing to do. I'd like to find some place to hide.

I learn Jim Will met a girl on leave and they are getting married. He told Admiral Zumwalt he's leaving the navy and not coming back to Saigon. I wonder who will be Zumwalt's aide. I suspect some academy "ring-knocker" has been selected.

A package arrives at my parent's home. There's no note inside and no return address. It's my .45 with its holster and belt. I guess SEALs have special privileges about what they can bring home. I store it in the top of a closet where it will remain hidden. I don't need to sleep with it anymore and I don't want to look at it.

My friend and shipmate, Joe Watson, from destroyer days, arranges an interview for me with Dow Corning. On Joe's recommendation, I'm hired and Chantal and I move to Midland, Michigan. We haven't set a date to be married. I feel empty of emotion. I can't quite seem to acclimate to this normal life. My coworkers are talking about marketing strategies and sales quotas. I think about guys still patrolling the Bo De. The evening news has scenes of huge crowds protesting the war.

"You do Nam?" a guy asks as we wait to be seated for lunch in a restaurant. Maybe it's the way I look, short hair, clean clothes. I stand out from long-haired hippies wearing dirty shorts, tie-dyed tee shirts, beads and sandals.

"Yeah," I say. "You?" He just nods. And that's it. An unsaid rule: Don't talk about it. I don't know who made the rule. It's just like Mom said, "Don't think about; it'll go away."

"What do you do?" I ask.

"Work for Mattel. Engineering, plastic molding, Barbie Dolls, stuff like that." He's a nice looking guy, blue button-down shirt, tie, tan slacks, black loafers. Says he went to West Point. "And you?" he asks.

"Sales. Dow Corning, plastic tits." The guy laughs and I laugh, too. "Actually," I add, "they're silicone implants."

"Kind of funny," he says, "fighting a war for a plastic society."

We share another secret. We both live with someone—out of wedlock.

"Management's family oriented," I say. "If they knew, I wouldn't have gotten this job."

"Mattel's the same, maybe even more. They'd probably fire me."

I return to our apartment and Chantal is fixing dinner. I can tell she's been crying.

"I don't have a car," she says. "I can't walk to the market, it's too far."

"What did you need? I could have gotten it for you."

"Doesn't matter, dinner is ruined. I hope you're not hungry."

"Please, stop crying. It's okay." We've only been in Midland two weeks and I feel our relationship is in a tailspin. I don't know what to do about it.

"I waited for you," Chantal says, "a year. Now you're home, but you're *not* here. *Merde*! Where are you?"

"Please, stop crying. I have to work. Tell me what you want, what to do."

"I don't know you! Do you still love me? Why don't you share your feelings?"

"Give me time. I just need to figure out what's wrong. Something's eating at me."

"I don't understand what you're saying. What does that mean—eating?"

"I have dreams."

"Tell me."

"I can't. Not yet."

"Do you still want to marry me?"

"I don't know; I think I do. Wait, don't walk away. I do. Can we talk about that later? Please, don't make demands now. Just give me time." My comments are too spontaneous—words without thinking.

It is Friday afternoon. I return from work and Chantal is gone. She left a note: "I love you, *Adieu.*" I know *Adieu* means goodbye forever. I race to the airport, risking an accident. I wish I would have one.

An agent at the ticket counter remembers Chantal, but she is reluctant to tell me anything.

"Please, this is important," I say. "She's a stranger here in America. She might not know where she's going."

"She was crying," the agent says. She looks around me, as if hoping someone will interrupt us.

"Please, tell me," I plead with tears of my own.

"She boarded a plane for Detroit, connection to New York, then to Paris. Please, I have passengers to check in."

I return to our apartment and sit on my bed. I cry, but I don't know who I am crying for—I just know something hurts. I feel like a bullet is ricocheting inside me and there's nothing inside to stop it. While in Vietnam, the image of Chantal kept me going, anticipating a life together, planning a future—and now she is gone. I've pushed her away and I don't know why.

I go to work and try to focus on learning my job, learning medical technology, about silicone implants that I'll sell to plastic surgeons to make people feel beautiful, people searching for self-worth in all the wrong places.

A Western Union telegram arrives from a minister in Detroit. Incredible, it was *mailed*. I thought telegrams were hand delivered. I call the minister.

"I found Chantal wandering the streets," the minister says. "She was lost and crying, and I brought her to my home. My wife and I have been caring for her."

"I thought she returned to France."

"She was confused, upset. She didn't take her connecting flight. She's been crying for a week."

"Can I talk to her?" I ask.

"She's been waiting all these days for you to call. She gave up and left yesterday."

"I just received your fucking telegram today! Jesus, it took a week to get here!"

The minister hangs up and I'm left with a dial tone of shock. I call back, but there's no answer.

Chantal is delicate and sensitive. I can't believe I've hurt her. I feel sterile and empty. I *hate* myself. I don't have love to give anyone. I feel emotionally dead. I'm afraid to call her in France, afraid her tears will tear me apart.

My dreams of Chantal are now ashes. Now I only dream of a young girl with burns, a man with no arms and no legs, a dying marine with a hole in his chest and a pregnant Viet Cong. In my dreams the VC girl is sleeping, but she never wakes up.

I think about Gnau, Stancil, Hoffman, Moison and Taylor. I remember them giving coloring books and crayons to children standing on the bank of a muddy canal. The memory makes me cry. It's a stupid memory. I don't know why it affects me.

I can't share these memories with Chantal or anyone. War is not heroic or romantic like Don Quixote fighting windmills. It's not glamorous. War is not pretty.

Shoeless in Colorado

Chapter Twenty-nine

Rebirth

Work is my sweet elixir, filling my day, no time for guilt, no time to think of how I've hurt Chantal. I apply myself with intense dedication—meeting little goals, one at a time. Dow Corning promotes me and I move to Los Angles. I have the premier territory, selling breast implants to the wealthiest plastic surgeons in Hollywood. But I wonder if this is the career I want—wonder where it is leading me.

Men are still coming home in a box draped with a flag or coming home shattered by claymore mines. I am catering to a society of beautiful women who want to attract men who are still whole.

On weekends I walk the docks of King Harbor at Redondo Beach, wistfully gazing at beautiful, sleek curving lines: sloops, schooners, ketches and yawls, measuring their seaworthiness with a nautical eye. I undressed them without embarrassment, layer by layer, imagining what they look like below the water line. I enjoy reading names painted on their sterns and think of what I would name my boat—if I had one.

An elderly couple is sitting in the cockpit of their sailboat, a "For Sale" sign hanging from the bow.

"We're retired," the man says. "We have our savings, dreams of a cruise, but we've waited too long; we're too old to stand watches and manage sails without a crew."

"And we don't want a crew!" his wife adds with a pitiful laugh. She's sipping a cocktail, her eyelids saying it's not her first this afternoon.

"I'd love to have a boat," I say, "maybe sail to the South Pacific someday. But I don't have any savings."

"If you want my advice," the old man says, "find a way, follow your dream—do it now while you're young and strong." His wife nods; she seems sad to agree. Their regret reminds me of George Bernard Shaw who wrote, "Why is youth wasted on the young?"

I wonder: Why is youth wasted on war?

This brief encounter ignites a powerful wanderlust I didn't know existed. Or perhaps it's a need to escape, but escape what I don't know. I begin saving every dime, every month calculating a plan to borrow part of my future retirement and spend it now while I'm still young enough to enjoy it. Surviving Vietnam, and maybe the philosophy of my dad, instilled a need to live for today, not wait thirty years to fulfill a dream that may never come.

I meet a pretty girl. Her name is Pam and her voice has an Oklahoma twang. She has a Master's in social work and helps children whose parents are strung out on drugs. Pam embraces my dream of cruising to the South Pacific. She trusts me; I don't know why. We marry and I'm transferred to San Francisco. Every weekend Pam and I search for a boat we can afford.

By pure coincidence while walking the docks, I meet Bill Ruth. He was the first skipper of PCF 43. We don't talk about other skippers who came after him, who commanded that same boat.

Bill has a beautiful sailboat and we chat about sailing in rough seas.

"The 'Potato-patch' outside the Golden Gate Bridge can be bad," Bill says. "It's rough when the tide is going out and the wind is pushing in. Huge choppy seas, but nothing compared to Vietnam."

"I remember the Ham Luong was a bitch."

"A Swift Boat got pitch-polled while trying to get into a river," Bill says. "I was the investigating officer. Waves at the mouth of that river were monsters. It was just a freak accident—boat flipped over, upside-down. No way the skipper could see it coming, and no way to avoid it. Not everyone survived."

"I like your sailboat," I say. It's more comfortable to talk about sailboats.

"There's another one just like it," Bill says, "and it's for sale."

I inspect the boat for sale and it's love at first sight. Pam and I approach a sympathetic banker. I show him our earnings and savings.

"I was a navy lieutenant too," the banker says, "aboard a destroyer." He looks at me, straight in eyes, and then he smiles. "Okay," he says. We have our loan and we have the boat of our dreams.

"I christen you *Renaissance*," Pam says, "for a rebirth of wonder." She doesn't break a bottle of champagne over the bow—we drink it. Pam is now my first mate, legally and nautically.

Renaissance is a thirty-two foot, double-ended cutter. She's beautiful—a lady without weakness of structure, just like another lady I have known. She weighs 22,000 pounds, has a majestic bowsprit, teak decks and a warm mahogany cabin. We find a berth in Sausalito, just north of the Golden Gate Bridge, move aboard to save money and prepare for a trip to the South Pacific.

Christopher is born and we bring him home to his floating cradle.

"You are not taking my grandson with you," Pam's mother says, almost threatening to take legal action. "Not on such a small boat!"

My mother feels the same way. I don't tell these grandmothers that I nearly flunked out of officer candidate school because of poor grades in navigation. And I don't tell them it's 3,300 miles to the Marquesas with only stars to guide us.

"Here's a chronometer," Dad says, giving us a very precise timepiece for celestial navigation. "Take good care of this young sailor," he says, giving Christopher a tight hug.

Just weeks after Christopher's first birthday, we quit our jobs, cast off our dock lines and sail to the Marquesas, to Tahiti, Bora Bora, to Hawaii and then home again—ten thousand miles—a year and half living life to its fullest, like Irma La Douce, feeling passion for everything that makes life worth living. I'm pleased to see that Christopher has developed a pronounced salty-swagger.

Along the way, I buried memories at sea. An enormous weight has been lifted and now I am eager to find a job. Actually, I'm a little desperate—we're broke.

"What's your worst fault?" Wynn Hoag asks. It's my third interview with Millipore Corporation.

"Impatience," I answer. "I tend to make decisions too fast, sometimes before I have all the facts."

"And your strength?"

"Impatience."

I'm hired by Millipore. The management is bright, dedicated, intense, and they love what they are doing. They compare well to Swift Boat sailors.

Year after year they give me opportunities to succeed and I'm promoted to manager. As I learned aboard a Swift Boat, I listen to my team— to their advice, their caution and their career aspirations. We coach each other, develop skills and I reward their success. Their success pushes me up the corporate ladder.

I thoroughly enjoy working for Millipore, and most especially for Gerald Walle, a Frenchman with the vision of an oracle. But there is something I miss. I miss the extreme camaraderie that only exists when life itself is at stake. I learned so much in Vietnam, about compassion, conviction, prejudice. I gained a sense of confidence—that I can do almost anything or at least not be afraid to try. In that one incredible year I was given a precious gift—a respect for life.

And all along this journey, Dad is my hero. I want to be just like him.

I feel content. I have two wonderful sons. I have had command of a Swift Boat, sailed to the South Pacific and now work for a great company. But there is one thing more I need to do in my life.

I take flying lessons. I earn my pilot's license and begin new lessons— aerobatics, performing elegant loops and rolls in a glider, soaring silently above clouds as if I were an eagle.

I'm going to take Dad up with me, surprise him—impress him—show him that I, too, can fly.

Christopher, manning the rail and Pam on watch. Diapers added two knots to our speed.

Celestial navigation has never been my best skill

Renaissance moored in Bora Bora

Survivor's Guilt

My retirement dinner is in Glasgow, Scotland, thirty-six years after Vietnam. I've enjoyed a successful career, becoming vice president of worldwide sales. But retirement leaves a void. I feel adrift without deadlines, demanding schedules, flights to Europe and Asia and conference calls at 4:00 a.m. I return to my home in San Diego and someone asks, "What do you do?" I feel embarrassed to say I'm retired. I have nothing to do. I have lost my identity.

Something begins to creep into my body, filling the void of retirement. A brief memory of a Vietnamese Marine brings spontaneous crying without warning. I don't understand why this happens.

Memories of Vietnam begin to emerge more often. I feel something on my neck, as if a cold wind has chilled me. But there's no one to talk to about my feelings, no one who can understand. Even after all these years, I am still a pariah who must keep all my memories secret.

I begin to have dreams that wake me at night, dreams of the Viet Cong crawling through the base at Cat Lo. It's an event that never happened, just my brain recreating the sense of fear I once had. But real events, memories I thought were buried at sea, emerge with frightening clarity. I struggle with a demon called alcohol to soften the memories. I feel depressed and I begin to cry too often. I hide my tears from friends—hide in my cloak of weakness with a bottle.

Alcohol makes crying and depression worse, and I check into a clinic. It is hard asking for help—to admit there is something I cannot control. I'm given a label: an alcoholic with PTSD: "post traumatic stress," the therapist says. It seems odd to have this happen to me after so many years. I know my experience does not compare to those who were wounded. I had it so much easier than most.

Dan is my sponsor at AA. He flew helicopters as a navy pilot in Vietnam, flying search and rescue missions. Dan has been sober for two years. He is encouraging me to accept help from a higher power. So is Barbara, my cousin, my confidant.

"Someone has been looking after you for a very long time," Barbara says. Maybe she's right.

I receive a note from Commander Streuli. His words epitomize the memory I have of this naval officer: "I got orders to the best duty a man could ever dream of, Commander, Coastal Division 13. The officers and men of that division are the absolutely finest men in the entire navy, proof of which is what most of them did and became after their tour in Vietnam. I have never ceased to be amazed at what was asked of them and what they did. To this day I am proud to brag about each and every one."

I will forever honor the memory of Commander Streuli and his leadership of the "Black Cats," the men of Coastal Division 13. He was the best.

Bob Shirley contacts me through the Internet. I don't know how he found me. He skippered a Swift Boat, PCF 45. Bob invites me to attend the dedication of a Vietnam Memorial on the Naval Amphibious Base in Coronado. It's where we trained on Swift Boats. We drive over a bridge to Coronado.

"Ferryboats are gone," he says.

"Swift Boats, too," I say.

"Not all of 'em. You'll see."

A magnificent memorial honors navy and coast guard sailors who made the ultimate sacrifice. Their names are engraved on steel plaques that grace a beautiful wall. Don Droz's name is there, skipper of PCF 43, lost on the Duong Keo River. Bob Anders and Bruce McFadyen are on the wall, too. There are 2,564 names of navy and coast guard sailors, pilots, corpsmen and SEALs.

Patrol Craft Fast 104 stands between a PBR and a Mobile Riverine Command vessel, their fifty-caliber machine guns pointed west, standing watch, guarding the wall, perhaps watching for the "Green Flash" each evening as the sun sinks below the Pacific horizon.

Jim Will attends the ceremony. We laugh, wondering who became Admiral Zumwalt's aide. Zumwalt became Chief of Naval Operations nine months after I left Vietnam, the exalted position of leading the entire US Navy. He was the youngest CNO in history. Being aide to this god, holding onto his coattails, would have been a smart move for anyone wanting to make the navy a career. My dad's friend, Admiral Holloway, followed Zumwalt as the next CNO.

There are South Vietnamese sailors attending the ceremony, standing in uniforms they once wore. They all served on Swift Boats. Their demeanor is somber and I sense memories they must have. Somehow these men escaped the re-education camps and the debacle of communist rule.

"We left them to fight alone," I say to Bob Shirley.

"I know," Bob says. "My wife is Vietnamese."

"They fought with more courage than I gave them credit for," I confess. I regret the feelings I had in 1969, doubting their bravery and commitment. But I don't say more—it's too hard to put into spoken words—respect for the Vietnamese and what they endured.

My body jolts as if hit by an electric shock as a volley is fired by a Marine Honor Guard—a twenty-one-gun salute for men on the wall. A navy bugler sounds taps. Bob Shirley helps me understand that it's okay for grown men to cry. My tears flow hard. Bob cries too. I begin to understand my tears are not just of sorrow for so many men, but also of pride, for what we did, for our commitment.

My youngest son, Bret, a marine corporal with the 3rd Battalion, 5th Regiment, has just returned from Iraq. He looks magnificent and proud in his dress blues, standing with me at the memorial, his shoulder pressed up against mine. I could not be more proud of his character and courage.

"I love you, I'm proud of you," I say. I hope he will remember I said that.

I think of Dad and Bret. Three generations—each one of us going to war. Bret is so much like me. I wanted Dad's respect. Maybe Bret was trying to gain mine, not knowing he already had it. Bret will never know how much I worried, checking causality reports on the Internet each day.

Bret volunteered to become a "Personal Security Force," his job to protect a marine major in Fallujah. Bret's training in urban warfare and his love for fast driving matched his assignment, and he didn't have to worry about tickets for speeding.

"When I drove the major in a Humvee," Bret says, "I watched for ambushes, avoided getting boxed in—no route for escape." Bret said he rehearsed in his mind the "what ifs." His conversation about Iraq reminds me of how I had worried about having enough room to turn around in shallow canals and not going aground in a firefight.

Bret tells me of patrols and of nights watching for the enemy. I encourage him to talk about it, to tell me how he feels. He talks in a cavalier fashion, as if describing a walk through a shopping mall. I think Bret is guarding his memories and feelings, hiding them as I have. I hope he can let his memories fade in a gentle way, to talk about them anytime he feels the need. I'll always listen.

"Why did you join the marines?" I ask.

"Because you told me they were elite—the best. Why did you volunteer for Vietnam?"

"Thought I was invincible."

Bret, home from Iraq, with Jacqueline and a proud father

This memoir has helped me understand my life as if writing an epitaph. It has refreshed the pride and honor I felt, having served on a Swift Boat with a crew I trusted with my life—a crew that became family.

Perhaps if still alive, my father would read this memoir and say, "I'm proud of you." Or he might say, "I love you."

Acknowledgments

I am indebted to men who contributed so much to this memoir:

Hal Amerau, "Kentucky Colonel"	Skipper, PCF 96 & XO, CosDiv 13
Michael Bernique, "Creek"	Skipper, PCF 3
Jim Barrett, "High 'n Dry"	PCF 23 & Operations Officer, CosDiv 13
Steve Carroll	Skipper, PCF 23
Jack Chenoweth	Skipper, PCF 93
Allen Cott	Radarman, PCF 32
Jim Deal	Quartermaster 2nd Class, PCF 78
Donovan Current, "Short Circuit"	Skipper, PCF 28
Matt D'Amico, "Swarthy Buccaneer"	Skipper, PCF 37 & XO, CosDiv 13
Keith Evans, "Ancient Mariner"	Skipper, PCF 51
Ked Fairbank, "Harvard Yard"	Skipper, PCF 95
Robert Gnau	Quartermaster 2nd Class, PCF 67
Mike Haecker	Yeoman 3rd Class, Nha Be Naval Base
Arthur Hill	Master Chief Photographer's Mate
Jim Hoffman	Radarman 3rd Class, PCF 67
Roy Hoffmann, "Latch"	Admiral, Commander of CTF 115
Michael Hudson, "Ichabod Crane"	Skipper, PCF 17
Chuck Rabel	Skipper, PCF 35
Russell Puppe	Skipper, PCF 51
Rex Retanus	Vice Admiral, Staff Intelligence to Adm. Zumwalt
William Rockhill	Radarman, PCF 40
Bill Ruth	Skipper, PCF 43
Bob Shirley, "Axelrod"	Skipper, PCF 45
Bill Shumadine	Skipper, PCF 5
Michael Stancil	Engineman 3rd Class, PCF 67

Joseph Streuli, "Snaky Jake"	Commander, Coastal Division 13
Wey Symmes	Radarman, 2nd Class, PCF 56
Ronald Suggs	Engineman 2nd Class, PCF 67
Larry Wasikowski	Radarman 2nd Class, PCF 58
Jim Will	Skipper, PCF 102

Websites:
US Naval Archives: www.history.navy.mil/branches/org
Robert Shirley's Patrol Craft Fast: www.pcf45.com
Swift Boat Sailors Association: www.swiftboats.org/index.html
Larry Wasikowski's Swift Boat Crew Directory: www.swiftboats.net
Jim Deal's: www.MyFamily.com

I am proud to acknowledge those who gave me advice and direction, each one with a spoon, feeding me the enormously difficult skills for a craft called literary memoir. I still have so much to learn.

Thomas Larson is a gifted author and my mentor. His book *The Memoir and the Memoirist* offered inspiration. In critique sessions, Thomas taught me to write with integrity while dredging up memories deep from the gut, memories that still make me cry.

Sue Diaz, another brilliant writer and Pulitzer Prize nominee, encouraged me to find my own voice. Her critiques offered gentle, patient corrections with the compassion and understanding of a mother with a son in Iraq.

Writing professors, all published authors at the University of California San Diego, added their special touch to my pen, such as Judy Reeves, Nicole Vollrath, Peggy Lang and Marni Freedman.

Wey Symmes, who wrote the Foreword, is a Swift Boat sailor and board member of the Hoffmann Foundation. He and his wife, Terry, reviewed my draft and gave me the courage to publish this memoir.

Scott Collins, a graphic artist, created charts for this book.

And last, I wish to thank retired Senior Chief Photographer's Mate, Arthur R. Hill, US Navy, for permission to use his photography. He rode our boats armed with nothing more than a camera.

LaVergne, TN USA
08 October 2009

160327LV00001B/1/P